The Transformation of Sin

The Transformation of Sin

Studies in Donne, Herbert, Vaughan, and
Traherne by Patrick Grant

1974
McGill-Queen's University Press Montreal & London
University of Massachusetts Press Amherst

This book has been published with the help of a grant
from the Humanities Research Council of Canada,
using funds provided by the Canada Council.

FOR GLORIA

Hoc et documentis morum eius et

fide non ficta rationibusque certis tenebamus

Contents

Contents

Preface

This book is mainly a study of four Anglican devotional poets: John Donne, George Herbert, Henry Vaughan, and Thomas Traherne. That they belong together is clear enough, but I have been unable, after trying as well as I know how, to isolate stylistic affinities which would adequately account for the bonds uniting these "metaphysicals," so intense and brilliant in the early and middle years of the seventeenth century (beginning with Donne), yet so abrupt in demise after the Restoration (ending with Traherne). Increasingly I have sought for enabling causes of the poems in the cultural background, and particularly the background of ideas. My line of inquiry has been directed, with growing interest and concern, at what kinds of transformation in the intellectual and spiritual life of the period have found expression in Donne and his devotional followers.

In chapter 1, my key terms *guilt* and *enlightenment* suggest an approach to these issues that attempts to cut across the familiar distinctions of Middle Ages, Renaissance, and Reformation. In one sense the changes to which our poets bear witness represent, obviously enough, a movement away from the spirituality and values of a medieval world and toward those of a post-Renaissance and modern dynamic society. But the allegiances drawn by the proponents of both revolution and tradition remain equivocal, especially in the midst of change. Like Pasternak's doctor, the poets especially live out the full if paradoxical realities, keeping a cultural lifeblood flowing until the men of surgical intellect have made their necessary modifications. In this context the "guilt culture" and "enlightenment" hypothesis of chapter 1 presents a reintegration of familiar particulars and, I hope, illuminates the equivocal status of the poets faced with problems of responsibility living through an unpredictably shifting firmament of values.

By "guilt culture" I indicate, broadly, a spiritual and theological tradition deriving essentially from the influential thought of Saint Augustine of Hippo, remaining most vital during the Middle Ages, and vigorously revived during the Reformation. The function of the Franciscans in mediating and developing the heritage of Saint Augustine into seventeenth-century England is also crucial to the continuity I wish to describe. In one sense, my study becomes a kind of history of the progressive hybridization of the Augustinian tradition in poetry of early and mid-seventeenth-century devotion and religious meditation.

On the other, and "enlightenment," side of the polarity, directed mainly at the modern as distinct from medieval world, are the hybridizing energies themselves, characterized essentially by an emergent rationalism and powered by the development of a new science, a new religious toleration, and a new parliamentary procedure. The means by which such challenges and temptations were met by the spiritual men of the period are represented in our four poets by a shift of focus from the basically Augustinian Donne and Herbert to a more speculative Vaughan and Traherne who seek new spiritual models to meet contingencies consequent on profound cultural change.

Within this general argument the individual chapters provide scholarly suggestions and interpretations which I hope are innovative and of some interest and value in themselves. Indeed, such particular arguments are the building blocks which suggested an overall structure for the book only when they had been gathered together and reflected upon. They are, in one sense, the real core of the study. First, in this respect, Donne's *Holy Sonnets* are dealt with in context of his study of Augustine in the Franciscan tradition. The ways in which Donne's spirituality is medieval have not been fully described, and the Donne chapter suggests that a tradition both Catholic and peculiarly English informs the *Holy Sonnets*. Yet in Donne we detect the conflict of two types of inspiration—that of a traditional Augustinian piety as against the "enlightened" ideals of the latitudinarians.

For Herbert, who, like Donne, is influenced by the Franciscan

Augustine, a medieval equanimity is upset by Puritan views of individualism and election and by a growing lack of commitment to the organized church. The first of two Herbert chapters concentrates on the continuity of medieval, and specifically Franciscan, traditions in *The Temple* and, as one means of doing so, establishes the genesis of the hitherto anonymous but influential Renaissance book the *Biblia Pauperum*. The second Herbert chapter, concentrating on the Carolingian context of *The Temple,* examines at some length the influence of the important if neglected thought of the Spanish Reformer Juan de Valdés on the Little Gidding community, a significant spiritual influence on Herbert.

With Henry Vaughan the balance shifts. Although still shaped in the mold of Augustinian devotion and carrying its language and insights directly into *Silex Scintillans,* Vaughan's sensibility draws from an enlightenment, more specifically Hermetic, view of man. An examination of Vaughan's prose in relation to his interest in Hermetism helps to reveal the extent to which his poetry is transitional.

Last is Thomas Traherne. The foundations of his unique and peculiar thought have consistently eluded satisfactory critical formulation. My suggestion here is that Traherne's admiration of the Fathers of the Pre-Nicene tradition led him to the thought of Saint Irenaeus, and we find in Traherne an Irenaean type of theodicy which best explains the intellectual structure of his thought. Traherne's use of a source in Pre-Augustinian tradition links directly to Vaughan's Hermetic interest: both poets belong in the traditions of Augustinian devotion, but both seek new models to enable expression of spiritual experiences in fresh contexts of social and cultural change.

A provocative issue latent in all this, namely, how much the poetry actually enabled such change, or vice versa, must remain, in the end, a moot point. The book implies merely that the complexity of a man's commitment to his own largely tacit presuppositions within the intense coinherence which any vital culture manifests renders dogmatism on this question foolish. The good poets, the good philosophers, and the good scientists do what they can, but not without each other. Suffice it to say that the artistry and beauty of the four poets considered in this study have caused me to feel that the subsequent labor of attempting to understand them in terms of their culture was worthwhile. In their own day I would hope that something of the same reaction obtained.

So much for the study as it is. In my own mind it has developed in three stages, each with a tutelary spirit to be acknowledged. The first stage was as a doctoral thesis at the University of Sussex, supervised by Laurence Lerner. Both as an undergraduate at Belfast and as a graduate student, I have learned most about literary criticism from Laurence Lerner. In the present study, the chapter on Vaughan in particular, and especially the first section, I still feel is rather his than mine. It derives from a paper delivered at the University of Sussex in 1966. But his influence, less specifically, is throughout.

The thesis stage was without the Franciscan materials, and, as a second stage, my discovery of these I owe to David Jeffrey of the University of Victoria. David Jeffrey's profound knowledge of medieval Franciscan spirituality provided the insight, and much of the language, which enabled me finally to see Donne and Herbert in satisfactory relation to Vaughan and Traherne. I also acknowledge David Jeffrey's unfailing generosity and, in particular, his assistance with the *Biblia Pauperum* argument of chapter 3.

Thirdly, with the study complete, my debt of gratitude is to David Clark of the University of Massachusetts for having done so much, and with magnanimity, to help the work toward publication.

Many others have also assisted me in many ways. I cannot name all of them, but I would like to acknowledge Tom Cleary, Sandy Hutchison, U. Milo Kaufmann, Terry Sherwood, Henry Summerfield, and research assistants David Munk and Steve Naylor. Thanks are also due to the University of Illinois Press and editors of the *Journal of English and Germanic Philology* for permission to reproduce materials from my article on "Hermetic Philosophy and the Nature of Man in Vaughan's *Silex Scintillans*" (July 1968), pp. 406-22; to the Johns Hopkins University Press and editors of the *Journal of English Literary History* for permission to reproduce materials from my articles on "Augustinian Spirituality and the *Holy Sonnets* of John Donne" (December 1971), pp. 542-61, and "Original Sin and the Fall of Man in Thomas Traherne" (March 1971), pp. 40-61; and to the Corvina Press for permission to reproduce plates from the *Biblia Pauperum* (Budapest: Corvina Press, 1967). I am also grateful to the Humanities Research Council of Canada for a grant to assist publication. Finally, the dedication of this book acknowledges a deepest and most personal indebtedness.

Chapter One Guilt Culture to Enlightenment

Introduction

The seventeenth century, especially in England, is a crucial period for the emergence and establishment of attitudes and institutions basic to modern European civilization. As Douglas Bush's near aphorism has it, "In 1600 the educated Englishman's mind and world were more than half medieval; by 1660 they were more than half modern." [1] There is also, assuredly, an effective argument stating that the innovations were for the most part long in preparation, and revolution was often nurtured within the matrices of older and medieval ways of thought. But there were also events that cannot be interpreted as other than revolutionary. In England, perhaps the most significant of these is the execution of Charles I. There, in a single violent stroke, the medieval divine right of God's anointed, with all its assorted panoply of hierarchy and sanctified order, abdicates to the secular and democratic procedures of Cromwell's middle-class saints. Yet the execution, though in a sense straightforward, is fraught also with bewildering complications, as the history of the ensuing fifty years demonstrates. The momentous import, the paradoxes and ambiguities are a measure of the period within which it occurred.

The trauma and disorder of civil war and regicide in the seventeenth century are more happily offset, however, by positive achievements no less significant, even if no less complex. A new energy accompanying the breakdown of a feudal and predominantly agrarian economy is felt everywhere as people flock to the cities bent on making a fortune and bettering their social rank. A rash of courtesy books offers endless advice on behavior to new gentlemen; and, among others, James I (though without much appreciating the underlying causes) is whimsically rueful about "those swarms of gentry, who through the instigation of their wives . . . did neglect their country hospitality and cumber the city." [2]

The precipitous development of commerce and mercantilism throughout the period is accompanied by an equally prodigious and energetic rise of modern science, which begins at last assuredly to establish its own foundations and methodology. Philosophy likewise talks in modern tones—skeptical, critical, materialist—and as one consequence, religious toleration, by the end of the century, is also well advanced. In view of such achievements, the secularization of a state which had so long endured as theocracy was soon inevitable, as was the secularization of literature. Milton's *Paradise Lost,* the last great religious poem of the period, remains something of a monument already half out of date in its own day and hardly able to achieve its promise of a Dantesque assurance of God in a world with sights set on *The Rape of the Lock,* Voltaire, and David Hume.

With all this, man's interpretation of his place in history also explores new dimensions. While there were those (as always) who feared the imminence of last days and claimed the long decay of nature was clearly at an end,[3] there were others who looked in a different mood to the new siren Progress which, perhaps, tempted a fall more catastrophic than Eve's, though its consequences in history are not yet clear because they are not yet lived out. However, even in the dissent of the sixteenth century, people still believed with either an Erasmus or a Luther that man is fallen, and Voltaire's vision of an eighteenth-century Paris more delectable and better to live in than Eden is still at the far side of the seventeenth-century divide.[4]

The gain and loss between a Luther and a Voltaire represent, in brief, the burden of the rulers and statesmen, the scientists, philosophers, poets, and theologians who occupy the interim, and although this book will deal mainly with the poets and theologians, it will attempt not to ignore the more complicated and wider context of which they form a part. Certainly, our chief figures, Donne, Herbert, Vaughan, and Traherne, share the obvious broad problem of sustaining traditional modes of medieval devotion while encountering the challenge of Reformation and the new world of commercial enterprise, of secularism, of science, of religious toleration and enlightenment. But the transition was not calm, nor were its terms always so obvious. Although the poets sometimes thought of themselves as comfortably maintaining a sane and moderate *via media* between Catholicism and Protestantism, their actual predicament was not at all so simple. As Helen Gardner says, men like Donne were in the process of forging a middle way rather than acquiescing in it,[5] and "the Anglican firmament" was, as M. M. Ross explains, "a whirling jumble of every conceivable dogmatic stress." [6] The problems of religious toleration, of emerging science and commerce, of political reform that involves regicide, are not simply either Protestant or Catholic, and the paths of their consistent interpretation in terms of a middle way reconciling old and new, medieval and modern, are devious.

Hypothesis

One way to approach the "whirling jumble" which Ross describes, is by the adaptation of some terms first given currency by anthropologists. In distinguishing what are known as shame cultures from guilt cultures, Ruth Benedict writes that "True shame cultures rely on external sanctions for good behaviour, not, as true guilt cultures do, on an internalized conviction of sin." [7] This description puts in a nutshell the concepts on which classical scholar E. R. Dodds bases his brilliant discussion of Greek religion and art. Dodds sees the Homeric Age as a shame culture:

> Homeric man's highest good is not the enjoyment of a quiet conscience, but the enjoyment of *tímé*, public esteem: "Why should I fight," asks Achilles, "if the good fighter receives no more τιμή than the bad?" And the strongest moral force which Homeric man knows is not the fear of god, but respect for public opinion, *aidós:* αἰδέομαι τρῶας, says Hector at the crisis of his fate, and goes with open eyes to his death.[8]

In *The Iliad* loss of face is unbearable, and this explains, says Dodds, why "cases of moral failure, like Agamemnon's loss of self-control" are projected onto a divine agency whereby the dreaded feelings of shame can be transferred to an external source.[9] Moreover, the gods of *The Iliad,* like the men, are "primarily concerned with their own honour," [10] so that to neglect them or to maltreat their cult is to make them angry. Nowhere in the poem does Dodds find that Zeus, for example, is ever "concerned with justice as such." [11] The formulation of abstract norms against which feelings of guilt are experienced as distinct from shame has not yet emerged.

In *The Odyssey,* however, a developing guilt culture is evident. "The Zeus of the *Odyssey* is . . . becoming sensitive to moral criticism." [12] He complains near the beginning of the poem that men are always finding fault with the gods, and the whole poem can be read as a vindication of divine justice. "The suitors by their own wicked acts incur destruction; while Odysseus, heedful of divine monitions, triumphs against the odds." [13] The moral education of Zeus which is already beginning in *The Odyssey* can be followed, according to Dodds, through Hesiod, Solon, and Aeschylus,[14] and it basically involves the discovery of moral standards which are transferred to the gods who then come to represent the ideals to which men should aspire. Before such ideals men now measure their own worth, and there is a consequent internalizing of conscience. The "external sanctions for good behaviour" of the shame culture are no longer relied upon to enforce morality, and they are replaced by "an internalized conviction of sin," the hallmark of guilt culture.

In such a context, the problem of sin and evil in the world soon becomes acute. As an obvious fact of life, people who seemingly do not deserve it are afflicted with misfortune and suffering, and the Greeks "were not so unrealistic as to hide from themselves the plain fact that the wicked flourished like a green bay-tree." [15] Yet the guilt-culture Zeus represents, increasingly, an ideal of justice, and the problem of explaining the obvious evil of the world in terms of this just god quite naturally becomes critical. "Hesiod, Solon, Pindar, are deeply troubled" by the problem, Dodds tells us, "and Theognis finds it necessary to give Zeus a straight talk on the subject." [16]

Briefly, the most widely received solution to the problem of evil in the archaic age (the characteristically guilt-culture phase of Greek religion) lay in the belief that a successful sinner should be punished in his descendants.[17] His guilt would be inherited and his family would suffer. The effectiveness of such a belief of course depended in turn on a strong conviction of family solidarity, a condition which prevailed in archaic Greece and other early societies:

The family was the keystone of the archaic social structure, the first organised unit, the first domain of law. Its organisation, as in all Indo-European societies, was patriarchal; its law was *patria potestas*. The head of a household is its king, ὅίϰοιο ἄναξ; and his position is still described by Aristotle as analogous to that of a king. Over his children his authority is in early times unlimited: he is free to expose them in infancy, and in manhood to expel an erring or rebellious son from the community, as Theseus expelled Hippolytus, as Oeneus expelled Tydeus, as Strophios expelled Pylades, as Zeus himself cast out Hephaestos from Olympus for siding with his mother. In relation to his father, the son had duties but no rights; while his father lived, he was a perpetual minor.[18]

In such a situation, sins against the father or the family group are especially horrifying, and, for instance, a typically guilt-culture mentality is responsible for the Sophoclean Oedipus, inheritor of a family curse and a wretched outcast because of sins against his parents.

As we might expect, guilt culture remained dominant in Greece only as long as the family unit itself remained strong, and it is well established that one major effect of the rationalism of the fifth-century Greek philosophers was precisely to loosen the individual from the bonds of family and clan. This is fully described in Glotz's *La solidarité de la famille dans le droit criminel en Grèce,*[19] and Dodds is in accord with the major conclusions of Glotz's study.[20] "With the rise of the Sophistic Movement," Dodds writes, "the conflict became in many households a fully conscious one: young men began to claim that they had a 'natural right' to disobey their fathers." [21] The young men who listened to Socrates were no doubt stimulated to new ideals of human responsibility, but in espousing their mentor's equation of virtue to knowledge, his insistence on individual responsibility in ethical matters, they found themselves also inevitably opposed to the established mores of the guilt culture of their fathers. It is no accident that the trials of Socrates, Anaxagoras, and others were essentially heresy trials.[22] The charges laid against Socrates were that he corrupted the young and defamed the gods.[23] In a guilt culture so emphasizing the unit of the family in theological contexts, these charges are one and the same.

An archaic-age guilt culture was challenged, then, by the fifth-century enlightenment, inspired by noble ideals of *logos,* ethical self-sufficiency, and the rule of reason. But the situation was no simple confrontation of mutually exclusive viewpoints. For even long after the liberation of the individual from the bonds of family and clan was complete in law, "religious minds were still haunted by the ghost of the old solidarity." [24] The greatness of Plato, for instance, lies in the honesty with which he encounters the morality of an enlightenment and the ideals of Socrates, even though his mind is still infused with the old guilt-culture explanation of evil. In the *Republic,* Plato's wholehearted trust in the desirability of an ethically responsible reason is everywhere threatened by a conviction of the human propensity for irrational behavior. The facts of human fallenness and guilt, somehow absurdly an inheritance of human nature, present a constant and living rebuke to Plato's dream of rational man. Despite the Socratic dictum equating knowledge to virtue and vice to ignorance, the burden of the mystery of guilt remains, and in the progress of the work we are moved from psychology to metaphysics and finally to eschatology and the myth of an afterlife as Plato attempts to resolve it.

The *Republic* is, in consequence, a chiaroscuro of aspirations to reason, the sun, the philosopher king, and how these are threatened by the irrational, the cave, the tyrannical Thrasymachus. In the end, Plato's myth of sanctions in the afterlife and his projections about reincarnation (both borrowed from the foreign soil of the Pythagoreans) provide an alternative to the traditional theory of inherited guilt, but the ghosts of the old order stalk through all of Plato's works, and although he is no lover of the family he cannot rid himself of it. However reluctantly, he gives it a place in his legislation.[25] A key description of his tyrannic man in the *Republic* demonstrates briefly how real was the entire guilt-culture consciousness to Plato's mind. The tyrant, unlike the philosopher ruler, is subject to his irrational passions, to those "pleasures and desires" we are all born with but which, in the philosopher, are disciplined by law and reason. These passions, Socrates explains, are the sort that emerge in our dreams, when the reasonable and humane part of us is asleep and its control relaxed, and our bestial nature, full of food and drink, wakes and has its fling and tries to secure its own kind of satisfaction. As you know, there's nothing too bad for it and it's completely lost to all sense and shame. It doesn't shrink at the thought of intercourse with a mother or anyone else, man, beast or god, or from murder or sacrilege. There is, in fact, no folly or shamelessness it will not commit.[26]

To the tyrant, Socrates continues,

when he was still democratically-minded and under the influence of the laws and his father, they only appeared in his dreams; but under the tyranny of the master-passion he becomes in reality what he was once only occasionally in his dreams, and there's nothing, no taboo, no murder, however terrible, from which he will shrink.[27]

In the total plan of the *Republic*, the tyrant is the most absolute threat to the philosopher king and his enlightened rule of reason, and the most horrifying sins of the tyrannic man as Socrates describes them are precisely the crucial sins of the guilt culture—rebellion against the father and incest, the sins also of Oedipus.

The great drama of the age, as we might expect, also expresses the cultural upheaval we are describing, and Sophocles' *Oedipus Tyrannus* is a good example, for it reduplicates the main problems of Plato's *Republic*. The hero, afflicted with a family curse of inherited guilt, attempts to be rational man, to solve riddles, answer the sphinx, discover the pollution of Thebes. But the deepest riddle of himself he cannot answer—the miasma of his fallenness, the grip and irrationality of his guilt. Paradoxically, Oedipus's dedication to logos drives him irrationally to murder his father Laius and incestuously marry his mother Jocasta. Again, the most awesome sins of the guilt culture are the price of his enlightenment, and he is hopelessly torn between an old mythology of guilt and a new promise of reason. As in the *Republic*, both compel a separate allegiance: Oedipus is a sinning and guilty tyrant, and he is a hero.

There are of course important differences between such a description of religion and philosophy in ancient Greece and the religion and thought of the Middle Ages and Renaissance. But we find in Dodds some useful criteria for describing a characteristic guilt-culture sensibility in relation to literature and philosophy, and these criteria help to illuminate particular spiritual problems of the Renaissance, for which, significantly, the rediscovery of the literature of Greece was of singular importance. From Dodds's argument we may suggest that guilt cultures tend primarily (a) to solve the problem of evil through a theory of inherited human guilt; (b) to operate within a patriarchal system in which the idea of family is of first importance; (c) to dictate that sins against the father (or his equivalent, the king, the Lord) are the worst sins; (d) to deny that man is ethically self-sufficient and to reject salvation by reason alone.

Guilt Culture in Europe: Saint Augustine

Western culture has had two great periods of tragic drama, one in fifth-century Greece and the other in sixteenth- and seventeenth-century Europe. In each case, we suggest, the drama develops from a similar encounter between a guilt culture and an enlightenment: Europe before and, to a considerable extent, during the Renaissance has all the marks of a guilt culture. The use of this term to describe the Middle Ages does not deny, however, that the most characteristic medieval literature and art have their own form of humanism. Indeed, the task of this essay is really to distinguish a humanism of guilt culture from a humanism of enlightenment, without suggesting at all that the Middle Ages are some period of superstition or repression liberated by an enlightened reason in the seventeenth and eighteenth centuries.

For the Middle Ages, which we are, then, describing as a guilt culture but without using that term in a pejorative sense, the basic theological formulations derive from the enormously influential theology of Augustine. Basically, Augustine's doctrines of the fall of man and original sin establish a theory of inherited guilt which remains ascendent in the West until challenged, especially in the Renaissance, by a series of more optimistic assessments of human nature, one aspect of which is a revival of interest in Pelagianism during the sixteenth and seventeeth centuries. Reform creeds such as the Augsburg Confession and the Thirty-nine Articles specifically rebuke Pelagianism because it repudiates the traditional Augustinian teaching of inherited guilt by claiming that man is not prevented by the fall from doing good works.[28] Cardinal Carnesecchi, an early martyr to the Inquisition, confesses his fears that the Catholic church "returns furtively to the ideas of Pelagius," [29] and Ernst Cassirer sums up the prevailing mood when he talks of Nicholas of Cusa:

> Although Cusanus never doubted the doctrine of original sin, it seems to have lost for him the power that it had exerted on the whole of medieval thought and on its sense of life. The Pelagian spirit is reawakening now, that spirit so bitterly fought by Augustine, whose polemics became the basis of medieval religious doctrine.[30]

The Pelagian phenomenon described by Cassirer was just as clearly a reaction against Augustinian theology at the end of the Middle Ages as it had been in the fifth century. And in the original confrontation, Augustine was quick to understand that Pelagius was a real threat to a guilt-culture expression of the Christian faith.

The influential teaching on original sin which Augustine formulated against Pelagius is well enough known in its general outlines. Basically, it combines the fall story of Genesis, chapter 3, with an enthusiasm for certain aspects of Plato. What results is a transformation of the biblical Garden of Eden into a perfect world of forms occupied by a mature and perfect Adam, archetype of humanity.[31] Adam, in such a state of perfection, was tempted by Eve. He fell, and the reward of his sin was the curse of death, of suffering, of broken will and decayed intellect.[32] Adam's sons inherit his sin and they do so by two means: first, through a Platonist and mystical identity with the archetypal father "in whom" (in quo) we all participate;[33] and second, by the inherited taint of the original sin passed through the generations by human reproduction.[34] In the family of man, the sins of the father Adam are therefore visited on the sons who inherit his guilt and are culpable. Human reason is distinctly and vigorously repudiated as a sole means of salvation,[35] which can be won only through the miraculous intervention of God himself in history.[36]

Throughout the Middle Ages, naturally enough, opinions as to the efficacy of reason and works to nurture and promote the grace of God vary widely, but orthodox Christians agree fundamentally with Augustine that salvation requires grace won by atonement. The mystery of guilt and the mystery of salvation are in Augustinian Christianity one and the same. The first Adam is redeemed by the second Adam, and the sons who inherit their human father's guilt are redeemed only by the guiltless son of their heavenly father.

In Augustine's theory not only is sin inherited from the transgression of the father Adam, but the church through which salvation from guilt is communicated is modeled after a hierarchical family. This view of the church is present from earliest Christian times. Saint Irenaeus, for instance, describes the church as a mother who provides the milk of spiritual nourishment.[37] A favorite figure of Cyprian represents the church as a mother who joins all her children in a single family.[38] It is impossible, claims Cyprian, to have God as father unless we also accept the church as mother: "habere non potest deum patrem qui ecclesiam non habet matrem." [39] If we, as children, sever ourselves from the family unit, from the womb of our mother and the jurisdiction of our father, we condemn ourselves to banishment and death. The man who does so "is a stranger, he is unholy, he is an enemy" [40]—an outcast much as was Oedipus in his sins against an earlier and not dissimilar family solidarity.

In Tertullian the same themes recur. In his interpretation of the Lord's Prayer for catechumens, Tertullian makes clear that in the opening words "Our Father" we are to understand also the Son and our Mother the Church. "Not even the Mother, the Church, is passed by, that is, if in the Son and Father is recognized the mother, by whom the names of both father and son exist." [41] In the closing sentences of *On Baptism* the complete family constellation and its connection with the inherited guilt of original sin is made plain:

> Therefore . . . when you come up from the most sacred bath of new birth, and in the house of your Mother [*apud matrem*] for the first time open your hands [to pray] with your brethren, ask the Father, ask the Lord that to the grace [of baptism] a very special gift may be added, the distribution of charismata.[42]

By the grace of baptism original sin is washed clean, and the outcasts and strangers become brethren, sons of the same father and lord and of the same mother. The language of sin and its remission is expressly related to the imagery of family reunion.

The figure of *mater ecclesia* occurs in such other early Fathers as Clement of Alexandria and Origen,[43] and Augustine himself adopts the Cyprianic formula wholeheartedly: "Nec habebit Deum patrem qui Ecclesiam noluerit habere matrem." [44] The church as family reappears in various forms throughout Augustine's writings, as, for instance, a mother nourishing her children,[45] or as a mother bearing us in her womb.[46] From here the idea readily extends into the mainstream of Christian tradition and merges easily with that important institution of the medieval church which is obviously relevant here, namely, the papacy. Theoretically, the authority of the Heavenly Father is invested in the pope as his earthly representative, and consequently the pope has power to rule within his family, to excommunicate, to bless or to damn his children. Excommunication is, however, an extreme measure, and reducing a man to the outcast status described by Cyprian is not incurred with frightening impartiality as in, for instance, the archaic Greece described by Dodds. The church's function as mediator of the sacraments and celebrator of the real and living sacrifice of Jesus in the Mass helps to mitigate horrors such as those incurred by the seemingly blind transgression of an Oedipus or an Orestes. The balance and harmony of medieval culture at its best consequently do not yield extreme experiences of the type described in Greek tragedy. At the same time, the unyielding opposition to Pelagianism, the thorough acceptance of some form of Augustinian anthropology, and the predominantly hierarchical and paternalistic structure within the medieval church confirm its guilt-culture foundations.

Augustine's critically important theory on the fall of Adam is further made amenable by analogy to immensely varied application throughout many fundamental institutions of medieval culture. For instance, the structure of delegated paternal authority first invested in Adam is analogically invested, by God's grace, in the pope and, on the same principle, permeates all ranks of Christian society—the communities of monasteries, universities, kingdoms, and families.

Even in individual men, as Augustine makes clear, a proper hierarchy of the faculties, described in terms of the Garden of Eden, must be maintained.

Just as in the fall the three main participants were Adam, Eve, and the serpent, so in everyman, according to Augustine, there is also an Adam, an Eve, and a serpent. Continuing to combine Platonism with Genesis, Augustine equates the highest of man's faculties, wisdom (*sapientia*), with Adam, the father of the first human family and the ruling principle of each individual mind. Knowledge (*scientia*) he equates with Eve, Adam's wife, over whom Adam must exercise control, while the senses (*sensualis animae motus*) are compared with the serpent.[47] In *De Trinitate* Augustine points out the differences between sapientia and scientia in terms of their different objects, and the first, he says, pertains to knowledge of intelligibles, the second to knowledge of tangible or material things. He goes on to describe the relationship of these two aspects of the mind as a "hidden wedlock," which he parallels to the relationship of Adam and Eve in the Garden of Eden. This relationship can be distorted in just the manner in which the proper relationship between Adam and Eve was distorted in original sin, so that the pattern of that action, the fall of man, is repeated in every individual transgression:

> For as in the case of that visible wedlock of the two human beings who were made first, the serpent did not eat of the forbidden tree, but only persuaded them to eat of it; and the woman did not eat alone, but gave to her husband, and they eat together; although she alone spoke with the serpent, and she alone was led away by him: so also in the case of that hidden and secret kind of wedlock, which is transacted and discerned in a single human being, the carnal, or as I may say, since it is directed to the senses of the body, the sensuous movement of the soul, which is common to us with beasts, is shut off from the reason of wisdom.[48]

We must, therefore, guard against any blindness of sapientia to the "sensuous movement of the soul," which is the third force operating in each man and which corresponds to the serpent. The lower reason (scientia), corresponding to Eve, should refer to the sapientia for judgment those things that impinge upon it from the lower realm of the bodily senses. In this way the bodily senses will not overcome and blind the higher reason, thus usurping the proper internal hierarchy and bringing chaos in place of order. But whenever the carnal sense does introduce to the scientia some inducement to enjoy itself without referral to the highest reason and ultimately the highest good, then "the serpent discourses with the woman. And to consent to this allurement, is to eat of the forbidden tree." [49]

In this psychology which at once describes the transgression through which the whole human race incurred the curse of Adam as well as the sin of each individual, the guilt-culture ascendancy of the father and the importance of a family unit, properly "married" and properly ordered, is again evident. Adam's sons inherit his disordered nature, which is concupiscible, curious, unwise; and, most important, a man's every sin confirms his primary guilt, thus by analogy reenacting the overthrow by Eve and the passions of the father, the reason, and the just marriage of the first creation. So a typically guilt-culture theory of man's original fall is lived out in every man's personal life as fully as it is reflected in his institutions. It is, in a sense, the very ground of his civilization.

To summarize, there are distinct correspondences between the criteria derived from Dodds in the first section of this chapter and the traditional Augustinian theology. First, the problem of evil in the world is, in Augustine, explained basically in terms of inherited guilt. Second, the medieval institution of the church is characteristically paternalistic, and it is commonplace to see the church as mother, the pope as Holy Father whose delegated authority is that of the Heavenly Father uniting the brethren through baptism within a family that retains exclusively to itself the means of salvation. Third, as a consequence of Augustine's psychology it is clear that sin against the head of the family, the father, the reason, Adam, is a sin of capital importance that causes both the fall of the entire race and every individual human sin. It is the archetype of all sinful human action, and with this in mind, Dante, for example, symbolically preserves his central place in hell for betrayers of their lords. Fourth, Augustine is anti-Pelagian. Ethical self-sufficiency that denies the power of Adam's curse upon his sons is totally disavowed in his theology. Salvation may be found, but not by reason alone, and emphatically not by the moral endeavors of man acting by his own light.

Egyptian Gold: Guilt-Culture Humanism

By common consent, one important distinguishing factor of the Renaissance in relation to the culture of the Middle Ages lay somehow in the rediscovery of ancient literature and philosophy, especially the Greek. But it would be foolish to think that Christians of the fifteenth century encountering the new literature were somehow overwhelmed by the truth of Greek rationalism and inspired through some new pagan individualism to a splendid release from shackles which had bound them from a "dark" or "middle" age. It is not true that the Middle Ages were somehow incompetent to handle the enlightenment glories of Greece. On the contrary, Plato's *Timaeus* had exercised a profound influence throughout the Middle Ages,[50] as had much of Aristotle (and not only in Aquinas but from the time of Boethius). Vergil was of course revered,[51] and even Ovid's outrageous advice on love found its due place.[52] The fact itself of pagan literature is less significant in this case than the attitude toward it, and it is once more by extrapolation from Augustine's guilt-culture theory of the fall that the characteristic medieval attitudes to the legacy of the pagan world are best described.

Within the guilt-culture institution of the medieval church, supported by a universally accepted theory of guilt inherited from Adam, salvation from original sin was a uniquely Christian prerogative. Augustine (however regretfully in certain instances) refuses salvation to those outside the church.[53] So do Dante and Thomas Aquinas. Admittedly, Augustine can interpret the church in a spiritual sense and include within it the holy people who lived before Christ but believed that he would come, and Aquinas also admits a "growth of faith according to the succession of the ages." [54] Nevertheless, the supreme power of the corporate institution of the medieval church to administer the means of salvation was not seriously contested, and the matter of excluding some or all of the ancients from the beatific vision was not in the Middle Ages the problem it became in the Renaissance.

Yet there is no question that the pagan gods survived and flourished in medieval culture, and theories had been sought from earliest Christian times to accommodate pagan wisdom to Christian revelation. There were a number of hypotheses. For instance, the pagan myths were said to be derived from Moses and therefore must contain some truth, which a Christian could use, even though it was not so pure as the wholly inspired wisdom of the Bible. Justin Martyr and Clement of Alexandria lent their names to this idea.[55] There was also a popular but harsher theory that the pagan myths were devilish interpolations, cunningly wrought by fiends (who had overheard the prophets) in order to confuse worthy Christians and lead them astray. Tatian espoused this view, and it is strongly reflected in Augustine, whose characteristic bias is to see the pantheon as demonic.[56] Another favorite (though two-edged) theory was euhemerism. A satiric criticism of the religions of his own culture by Euhemerus was used also by Christians to debunk pagan myths. Once the divine stories of the ancients were seen to have purely natural and human origins, they could be adapted in good conscience by Christians to elucidate the superior, revealed, Christian message. Tertullian and Arnobius represent this view.[57] It is retained notably in Isidore of Seville[58] and remains popular throughout the Renaissance.

If the currency of such theories among the early Fathers and their later exegetes opened the door to the riches of the pagan world, these riches were clearly not to be enjoyed by Christians without qualification, and perhaps the most notable consequence in the Middle Ages of the theoretical subordination of paganism to Christianity was the development of allegorical interpretation through which the works of the ancients could be acceptably modified to fit Christian precepts. So in the Middle Ages virtually every available pagan source was inveterately moralized, and the single analogy (tirelessly reiterated) that best describes the rationale of this whole process of subordination-becoming-allegory is Augustine's description of "Egyptian gold" in *On Christian Doctrine*.

Augustine states that Christians should simply appropriate the works of the ancients to explicate the Christian way of salvation, just as the Israelites appropriated the gold of the Egyptians to assist their exodus from captivity. Basically, "every good and true Christian should understand that wherever he may find truth, it is his Lord's," [59] and this truth he may take and use to assist God's purpose. Thus, "If those who are called philosophers, especially the Platonists, have said things which are indeed true and are well accommodated to our faith, they should not be feared." [60] On the other hand, Augustine does not hesitate to advise that we "ought to abominate and avoid" all that does not promote the faith.[61] Despite his own considerable appreciation of the Platonists, Augustine condemns them for the sin of pride: "that *the Word was made flesh and dwelt among us,* I read not there." [62] The philosophers, in the last analysis, worship "the idols of Egypt" and *"changed the truth of God into a lie."* [63] Augustine characteristically views the pagan gods as demonic, but "when the Christian separates himself in spirit from their miserable society," he may take their treasure with him, "for the just use of teaching the gospel." [64]

The basic attitude expressed by the analogy of Egyptian gold remains constant throughout the Middle Ages, even when applied to particular theories as diverse as those expounded by the early Fathers. It is, for instance, the general attitude of Chaucer to the classical stories of lust and metamorphoses in relation to the Christian and Boethian message of *Troilus and Criseyde.* It is the attitude of Dante to Vergil. It occurs in Bernardus Silvestris, in Theodulf of Orleans, is clearly articulated in Boccaccio, and appears later in George Herbert.[65] It is still the attitude of Milton's Christ to the temptations of Satan in *Paradise Regained,* and Coluccio Salutati conducts a Renaissance defense of poetry specifically in terms of Augustine's *On Christian Doctrine.*[66]

In short, despite some attacks by friars and others on the Christian use of pagan poetry (such as the one that gave rise to Salutati's defense), the prevailing tendency of Christian humanism throughout the later Middle Ages, as D. W. Robertson has cogently argued, is to accept the works of the pagans, suitably interpreted, as moral exempla for Christians.[67] The "mediaeval reader expected to find philosophical utility in poetry through allegorical analysis," [68] and true philosophy, as Hugh of Saint Victor makes clear, is the Christian love of God, to which pagan poets and philosophers are necessarily preparatory.[69]

Clearly, from the consistent emphasis on subordination and on the uniqueness of the Christian message, the theory of Egyptian gold does much to preserve the guilt-culture basis of Augustine's influential anthropology, which itself springs directly from a profound conviction that all men's participation in Adam's sin is redeemed only by the Incarnation and Atonement of the second Adam, and exclusively within the family of the Christian and Catholic church. Before such revealed wisdom, the achievements of the ancients must occupy a decidedly second place.

The elements which constitute a medieval guilt culture can now be summarized. First, and most important, is the universal acceptance of an Augustinian anthropology which stresses the fall of Adam and the debilitating results of the guilt inherited by his sons. Second, salvation from sin is found within a church which is consistently represented as a paternalistic family structure. Third, sins against the father, the Lord, the reason, Adam, are the worst sins. Fourth, salvation is by grace, Pelagianism is rejected, and the Christian revelation affords a unique truth, to which the works of the ancients must be subordinated.

Renaissance: Guilt Culture and Enlightenment

The rediscovery of ancient sources in the Renaissance is an event of enormous import; yet, as we have said, it is untrue that Renaissance thinkers recoiled in revulsion from the Middle Ages. Most Renaissance thinkers in fact accepted some version of Augustine's teaching on the fall and the inherited guilt of original sin. Most regarded the church as a family, hierarchically ordered and paternalistic, and most were not overtly Pelagian (despite the growing threat of this heresy) in their beliefs on works and grace. As far as the wisdom of the ancients was concerned, again nothing very much changed. Boccaccio and Erasmus argue for Egyptian gold as readily as Augustine and Bersuire,[70] and theories of pagan inspiration from Moses and of euhemerism grow rather than diminish in popularity.[71]

By and large, Renaissance thinkers did not simply fashion some novel theory of human nature to express a sublime sense of freedom. Rather, they encountered the bewildering complexity of the newly discovered antiquity by gunning the old guilt-culture ideas for all they were worth, until, inevitably, the barrels melted. The favorite theme, for instance, of a single superior revelation from which the pagans had borrowed the best of what they knew could simply no longer contain the sheer volume of new evidence unearthed and paid into it by archaeologists, antiquarians, and historians of all sorts. The old theories broke down quite often despite the worthy scholars who were in good faith about the tolerance of the old and well-tried metal. In the field of mythology, for example, so much new material was made available from remote and exotic sources that it soon became difficult to maintain simply that it had all been borrowed from the Hebrews. Comparative mythology inevitably prompted an awareness that the Hebrew myths themselves may be rooted in the same general human experience as the myths of the pagans and that the Hebrews were not uniquely superior. Especially in the seventeenth century, clear realization began to dawn about such issues, and in men like Lord Herbert of Cherbury, Bayle, Fontenelle, and Spinoza medieval attitudes of subordination to a special revelation yield to theories of natural religion. "Men were becoming increasingly aware that a heathen could have Christian ideas without having any contact with Christianity. Even the Natural Light was beginning to take form as the collective imagination of mankind." [72]

Such a transference of attitudes from guilt-culture subordination and hierarchy to enlightenment equality and toleration is not easy to describe, even though there is no doubt that the enormous energy in virtually every field of human endeavor in the years, say, from 1400 to 1800 accompanies a transvaluation of values in the cultural life of Europe which these terms do, in an abstract manner, represent. Less obviously, the energy comes not from writers and thinkers aligning themselves simply on one side of a question or the other. To those involved, the questions and alternatives were often not plain, and the paradoxes which surround the great figures of the Renaissance, who initiate attitudes which inherently challenge their own theoretical foundations, are part of the great fascination of their work. [73]

The syncretists of the Florentine Academy, for example, under the tutelage of Marsilio Ficino, rejoiced in wholly traditional terms in the superiority of Christianity and in the assurance that Socrates, Plato, and the Pythagoreans "conceal divine mysteries in figures and *involucris*." [74] But Ficino's school "made Plato and the Platonists the heroes of the philosophical Renaissance," [75] and a sheer enthusiasm for the wealth of new material soon extended the traditional and allegorical "Egyptian gold" methods of synthesis to bizarre limits. The "indiscriminate zeal," as Seznec calls it, [76] naturally blurred the primacy of the Mosaic or Christian focus the Florentines theoretically maintained. "Neoplatonic exegesis, which had presented them with hitherto undreamed-of possibilities of reconciliation between the Bible and mythology, had now so obscured the distinction between the two" that "Against this background, it was inevitable that the same idea which declining paganism had evolved should occur to the humanists—namely, that all religions have the same worth, and that under their varied forms, however puerile and monstrous in seeming, is hidden a common truth." [77] Among the Florentines the medieval guilt-culture theory of subordination was clearly weakened, even though theoretically advocated.

As a disciple of Ficino, Agostino Steuco was inspired to compile his elaborate *De perenii philosophia libri X* (1540). Steuco hypothesizes an original revelation imparted to Adam but lost with the fall, though retained in fragments by various cultures such as the Chaldean, the Egyptian, and the Greek. The Hebrews of course preserved the revelation best, and it has been renewed uniquely by Christianity.[78] In Steuco there is clearly a traditional guilt-culture theory of the fall, of the family of man, and of the unique restoration by Christianity, and these emphases lead to a typically guilt-culture "Egyptian gold" theory of paganism: Steuco devotes most of his formidable book to hunting for evidences of Christian truth in a vast number of exotic and pagan sources. His example is followed by Francesco de Vieri, whose *Compendio della dotrina di Platone in quello che ella e conforme con la fede nostra* (1577) is, as the title states, a compilation of passages from the Greek philosophers in which Christian teachings are found. Again the underlying theory is a traditional one, but as in Steuco the eclecticism and sheer zeal for adducing endless parallels reduce rather than confirm differences between pagans and Christians. These Neoplatonist syncretists in consequence move close to the point where they are in fact equating the wisdom of the ancients to the Bible. This is indeed the very method of Francesco de Vieri, and Steuco's search for a perennial philosophy has a similar effect of blurring the lines between Christian and non-Christian revelation.

Luther and Calvin reacted particularly strongly against such latitudinarian tendencies, and, in Italy, Giovanni Crispo clearly pointed out the dangers of the Florentines. He singled out Ficino and Steuco for attack, claiming of Ficino that "he wants Plato to be the basis of everything" [79] and indicating that the primacy of the Christian revelation should be firmly insisted upon or heresy would inevitably ensue. But Crispo could not stop the inevitable, and by the next century men had been led seriously, and naturally, to doubt the unique and inherent priority of the Judaic and Christian revelations. The guilt-culture and subordinationist theory of Egyptian gold suffered a severe decline. Early in the seventeenth century, Lord Herbert of Cherbury had already outlined criteria for natural religion,[80] which placed the essence of salvation in man's naturally inspired praise of God. Benedict Spinoza pointed out that mythology is a natural part of the infancy of all religions,[81] and John Spencer's learned *De legibus Haebraeorum ritualibus* (1685) showed that Christian and Jewish customs and rituals (and therefore truths and philosophies) were often borrowed from the pagans. The priority in these instances is the reverse of what had long been suggested. Egyptian gold gradually ceased to be viable currency, and the "passion for allegory ceased to possess men like a taste for strong drink; myths became myths whether they were Hebrew, Persian, or Greek. The search for an elaborate pattern of a universal theology divinely revealed was ended now that men like Bayle, Fontenelle, and the French rationalists were making themselves heard. The supernatural had begun to lose its prefix." [82]

Although this involved process of transformation can be observed throughout the Renaissance, it is, as we have said, particularly interesting in the seventeenth century. So, as a final example, we will take the work of Theophilus Gale, *The Court of the Gentiles; or, Discourse touching the Original of Human Literature Both Philologie and Philosophie from the Scriptures and Jewish Church* (1669). Gale adopts as his main thesis the well-worn idea that the best philosophy and mythology of the Gentiles (and even their languages) were derived from the superior and central revelation given to Moses. But because available information about ancient religions was fast increasing year by year, Gale's book has something in it of the fantastic and the bizarre. He is forced to contain a simply enormous amount of new and diverse information from Phoenician, Greek, Roman, Egyptian, Syrian, Hebrew, and other sources within an increasingly creaky hypothesis. It is difficult to accept, for instance, that the Phoenicians brought Mosaic culture to Ireland and that Abraham invented astronomy.[83]

It is interesting, but no accident, that Edward Herbert in his *De religione Gentilium errorumque apud eos causis* relies heavily on Gale's favorite source, Vossius,[84] but by a slight readjustment of focus comes up with a thoroughly enlightenment theory of natural religion in place of Gale's old Egyptian-gold hypothesis. Herbert simply claims that similarities in mythologies and religious practices, such as Gale had noted at great length, are not due to many cultures borrowing from a central revelation; rather, all religions are based on similar impulses within human nature to worship God. Herbert, moreover, in making his point, is forced to confront and rebuke one by one the characteristic tenets of the guilt-culture attitudes we have described earlier. For instance, he singles out a traditional guilt-culture paternalism by denouncing priesthood as a seat of corruption.[85] He implicitly attacks the doctrine of inherited guilt redeemed within the family of the church by claiming the church has been too severe in its theory of the fall and wrong to confine salvation to the body of the elect within the corporate institution. "The Principle of *Evil* cannot be deriv'd from *Adam*," he writes, "for all our *Sins* and *Transgressions* are our own meer voluntary Acts." [86] The Augustinian attitude to Egyptian gold is rejected as Herbert ridicules the allegorical indirections of the priests who "did excogitate many incongruous *Rites* and *Ceremonies* to establish a *Worship* of the *Deity*." [87]

On the other hand, Herbert substitutes wholly enlightenment emphases. He enjoins a universal toleration and extends salvation to all men who live good lives according to their natural lights.[88] He thus stresses fraternity rather than paternalism[89] and plays down the Augustinian teaching on the fall. He claims that men would come to the right church by purely natural reasoning and so adopts an essentially Pelagian position which enhances the ethical power of the will.

So Ficino and Steuco and Vossius and Gale, traditionalists all, ironically destroyed their own roots by an overfertilization which produced some rare and exotic blooms indeed, though the plant itself was broken by their very weight. Not until the end of the Renaissance did new enlightenment attitudes begin at last to find definition in distinction from their obscure expression within the Renaissance philosophers and theologians who maintained a guilt-culture framework and prepared the way, though often without clear knowledge of the fact. It should not be surprising in the midst of this that John Donne, for example, a medieval scholastic and Augustinian, should be deeply concerned with problems of the fall, of toleration, and of the salvation of the ancients, or that, in his best poems on the nature of man, the traditionally Augustinian Henry Vaughan should experiment with the Egyptian lore of Hermes Trismegistus.

Hermes the Magus

The mention of Hermes Trismegistus will serve to introduce a brief and general assessment of the enormous contribution of Egyptian studies to the process we are describing. Not only did the hieroglyphics of Horapollo and the discovery of obelisks and other archaeological materials fire the syncretizing spirits of the early Renaissance, but the philosophy of the Egyptians, thought to be contained in the *Corpus Hermeticum*, was more highly revered in some respects than even Plato. Its major influence, moreover, was not only in the encouragement of that "indiscriminate zeal" for synthesis that led eventually to a modern critical approach to the history of religions; it promoted, in a peculiar way, that other major revolutionary achievement of enlightenment, namely, empirical science.

When Ficino was about to undertake the translation of the assembled manuscripts of Plato and Plotinus, a request came from Cosimo de Medici that he lay aside these documents and concentrate instead on the newly acquired manuscripts of the *Corpus Hermeticum*.[90] Although this work is in fact an eclectic body of Neoplatonist and Stoic documents dating from the first or second centuries A.D.,[91] every Renaissance scholar well knew that it had been written by Hermes Trismegistus, an Egyptian sage of extreme antiquity, contemporary with Moses, who even shared with Moses that divine revelation which passed through the Judaic tradition into the New Testament. The genealogy of this Hermetic tradition owes something to the influence of the notable Greek scholar from the East Gemistus Pletho, who maintained there was an ancient tradition of revelation extending from the Egyptian Hermes Trismegistus through Orpheus,

Aglaophemus, Pythagoras, and Philolaus to Plato and Plotinus.[92] This group of *prisci theologi* constituted a tradition which was therefore responsible (because of the shared revelation of Moses and Hermes) for maintaining in the Greek and Roman world the same revelation which through Moses had led directly to Christianity.

In the Christian tradition the myth of a shared revelation from Moses was not new, and belief in the antiquity of Hermes Trismegistus was also long standing, both Lactantius and Augustine having speculated on it.[93] So in the preface to his translation of the *Corpus Hermeticum*, Ficino confidently articulates a full-blown theory of prisci theologi, encouraged no doubt by the interest of Augustine in Hermes as well as by the promise, derived from Pletho, of an enhanced view of the dignity and worth of the ancient philosophy which Ficino was privileged to translate. Of Hermes Trismegistus he writes:

> Therefore he is called the first author of theology: Orpheus, who took second place among the ancient theologians, followed him. Aglaophemus, who was the initiate of the holy Orpheus, was succeeded in theology by Pythagoras, whom Philolaus, the teacher of our divine Plato, followed.[94]

He goes on to argue that Hermes foresaw the coming of Christ, that his works are truly divine, and that we should turn our minds toward them as toward the sun.[95] In his commentary on book I he states further that Hermes deals with the Mosaic mysteries.

Following Ficino, the ardent Pico della Mirandola was even more enthusiastic about the idea of the prisci theologi and an original pure religion than his inspired mentor,[96] and Lazarelli is not atypical when he flatly states to the old king whom he is initiating into the mysteries in the dialogue *Crater Hermetis*: "Christianus ego sum o Rex: et Hermeticum simul esse non pudet." [97] The mystery itself which the old king is to discover, Lazarelli goes on to claim, is only hinted at by Christ, the Cabala, and the *Asclepius*. In a commentary, Lefèvre d'Etaples accuses Lazarelli of indeed equating the inspiration of Christ and that of the *Asclepius*.[98] Again, the zeal for syncretism has the immediate consequence of elevating the philosophy of the ancients above its traditionally subordinate status.

But Hermes Trismegistus was not only a sage, he was also a magician, and Hermes as magus is especially significant because of the interest among magicians in the empirical investigation of nature. In the *Asclepius*, according to Ficino one of the two "divine" works of Hermes,[99] we are told how the wise man, through his own divine reason, can captivate the superior powers of the cosmos—the stars and the planets—to animate statues.[100] Although Augustine had soundly condemned this particular part of the *Asclepius* as idolatrous,[101] Ficino avoids the condemnation and in his own work on magic, the *De vita coelitus comparanda*, discusses the efficacy of the magus in drawing down the influences of the world soul.[102]

The philosophers themselves, Ficino among them, however, distinguished carefully the philosophic or natural magic, associated with the prisci theologi and *Corpus Hermeticum*, from evil or demonic magic which sought the aid of the devil.[103] They were sure that man's God-given reason remained sufficiently godlike for him to guide for his own use the powers of the heavens, manipulated by sympathetic influences through the metals and stones and other elements of nature, as recounted in the *Asclepius*. As can be well imagined, this newborn enthusiasm of the magus for the control of nature was an important impetus to the flourishing scientific endeavors of the period, one of the hallmarks of the triumph of enlightenment. Tommaso Campanella's *Magia e grazia*, for instance, contains a curious passage on "real artificial magic" involving weights and pulleys, vacuums and pneumatic and hydraulic gadgets, which suggest a genuinely scientific side to his occult interests.[104] The Elizabethan John Dee was both a magician and a mathematician of some importance. Indebted to Pico della Mirandola, he claims that by numbers all things can be made known to man. He "is a very clear example," in short, "of how the will to operate, stimulated by Renaissance magic, could pass into, and stimulate, the will to operate in genuine applied science." [105] The same tendency is found in the *De harmonia mundi* of Francesco Giorgio,[106] and even Copernicus's momentous *De revolutionibus orbium caelestium* adduces the authority of the prisci theologi and of Hermes Trismegistus.[107]

Other pioneers of science such as Paracelsus, Agrippa, and Kepler were also fascinated with Hermetic philosophy, with the mysteries of the stars and the influence of the planets on the things of the earth.[108] The influence of the magus extends even to Francis Bacon through Bernardino Telesio,[109] and the single most influential source book for natural magic, the *De vita coelitus comparanda* of Ficino, was part of a textbook of medicine, the *De triplici vita*. Finally, the general conviction of an accomplished scholar of the subject is that the whole scientific revolution of the seventeenth century found a major impetus in the "religious excitement caused by the rediscovery of the *Hermetica,* and their attendant Magia." [110] Extreme as the statement may sound, there is certainly a basis for it in the demonstrably widespread connections between the Hermetists and early scientists.

In the entire theoretical confrontation of guilt culture and enlightenment which the argument has thus far been considering, we can see, in broad terms, that the former is rooted in an Augustinian spirituality, while the latter introduces novel tendencies toward religious toleration (by blurring the lines between Christianity and other religions), ethical self-reliance (by creating an awareness of the natural bases of religious experience), and the inquiry into nature that characterizes modern scientific endeavor (through the *Corpus Hermeticum* and the magus). Such attitudes offer a series of challenges to the traditional theory of inherited guilt absolved exclusively within the family of a church that insists on the unique superiority of the Christian revelation in the economy of salvation. To say, then, that the early seventeenth century is more than half medieval is to attribute to it an avowal of guilt culture and Augustinian spirituality. To say that its latter years are more than half modern is to talk in terms of enlightenment and, as in the opening pages of this argument, in terms of its first fruits—the emergence of science, of ethical rationalism and religious toleration. During the Renaissance itself, however, the alternatives (as in Plato and Sophocles) were not in fact as clear-cut as they appear in theory, and the issues, together with the characteristic paradoxes and confusions that accompany them, can well be exemplified in the figure of Pico della Mirandola.

Pico della Mirandola

The basic contention of Pico's *Oration on the Dignity of Man*, besides the claim that man is a most wonderful piece of work, is the idea that all philosophies and creeds contain some degree of divine truth. Pico openly embraces the optimistic spirit of Ficino's prisci theologi, beginning his oration with the celebrated assertion of Hermes Trismegistus in the *Asclepius*, a "great miracle, Asclepius, is man," [111] and going on throughout the work to conflate ancient and biblical sources in reckless and often startling ways. "Moses and Timaeus bear witness" to God's plan; "Empedocles . . . expound[s] to us the words of Job the theologian"; and "Bacchus the leader of the Muses" experiences the same inspiration as Moses.[112] The doctrines of the Cabalists and Moors are paralleled to David, and by "philosophizing through numbers," a hidden tradition linking Moses, Pythagoras, the Egyptians, Plato, and Jesus Christ can be brought to light.[113] The Mosaic religion is seen by the same method to contain the doctrines of the Trinity, the Incarnation, original sin, the Atonement, and the heavenly Jerusalem, as well as the philosophy of Pythagoras and Plato.[114] Christianity may indeed contain more divine truth more clearly than the Zoroastrians or the Chaldeans, but for Pico the truth it expresses is not essentially different from these.

As with the other Florentine syncretists, Pico does not abandon in his oration the traditional idea that Christianity is a unique and superior revelation. But again, the uncritical optimism and enthusiasm for a "cosmopolitan carnival" [115] of pagan divinities lay the foundation for an important transvaluation of values in terms of the relation of Christianity to the religions of other cultures, and so ultimately to the nature of man himself. All the key enlightenment attitudes are present in the *Oration*. There is a theory of religious toleration, an interest in nature and the empirical control of its forces through knowledge, an almost Pelagian trust in the self-sufficiency of the human will, and a belief that man is essentially free from the hierarchy of creation. The oration itself is a challenge to the "reverend Fathers," [16] symbols of the paternalistic structure of an old order which in fact conducted an inquisition against Pico. The work, in short, has all the hallmarks of enlightenment humanism. Yet, paradoxically, these enlightenment attitudes are expressed from within a traditional framework, and the *Oration*, like all of Pico's writings (and so much else in the Renaissance), maintains a traditional Augustinian and guilt-culture focus. Let us consider the enlightenment side first.

To begin with, it is not surprising that Pico's openness to all creeds and systems of thought should produce an essentially tolerant philosophy. "It is the part of a narrow mind," he writes, "to have confined itself within a single Porch or Academy. . . . There is in each school something distinctive that is not common to the others." [117] It is wrong to hate what you do not understand, and the comparison of "several sects" and "manifold philosophies" brings God's truth more brightly to our attention.[118] Briefly, the essence of Pico's syncretism is that all creeds should be tolerated and indeed admired for the divinely inspired wisdom that is in them.

Secondly, Pico was deeply interested in magic, and his *Oration* is a fervent vindication of the magus. The opening eulogy to man the "great miracle," for instance, is straight from the magician's source book, the *Asclepius*, and the tone of that work is retained as Pico enjoins: "If you see a philosopher determining all this by means of right reason, him you shall reverence: he is a heavenly being and not of this earth." [119] Pico, like the other protoscientists interested in this subject, is also concerned to distinguish demonic magic from natural magic, and he does so in explicit terms:

> I have also proposed theorems dealing with magic, in which I have indicated that magic has two forms, one of which depends entirely on the work and authority of demons, a thing to be abhorred. . . . The other, when it is rightly pursued, is nothing else than the utter perfection of natural philosophy.[120]

Following this, he makes clear the relation of the magus to the man of science. The magus, he tells us, "wed[s] earth to heaven" and "brings forth into the open the miracles concealed in the recesses of the world, in the depths of nature, and in the storehouses and mysteries of God, just as if she herself were their maker." [121]

Finally, Pico's celebrated vision of Adam created free of the hierarchy of creation and able to choose his own place and his own nature attests the optimism about human nature for which Pico is best remembered. "O highest and most marvellous felicity of man," he writes of the creation of Adam, which he goes on to describe in these terms:

> He [God] therefore took man as a creature of indeterminate nature and, assigning him a place in the middle of the world, addressed him thus: "Neither a fixed abode nor a form that is

thine alone nor any function peculiar to thyself have we given thee, Adam, to the end that according to thy longing and according to thy judgment thou mayest have and possess what abode, what form, and what functions thou thyself shalt desire. The nature of all other beings is limited and constrained within the bounds of laws prescribed by Us. Thou, constrained by no limits, in accordance with thine own free will, in whose hand We have placed thee, shalt ordain for thyself the limits of thy nature. We have set thee at the world's center that thou mayest from thence more easily observe whatever is in the world.[122]

Yet such a combination of religious toleration, ethical individualism, and scientific methodology does not make of Pico simply a harbinger of enlightenment. Pico, despite his high estimate of human reason in the *Oration*, still feels, paradoxically, the compelling truth of Augustine's traditional fall theology. This is evident especially in his *Heptaplus*, which describes the depths of man's fall in altogether traditional terms.[123] But even the *Oration*, redolent as it is of trust in human reason and of faith in its divine potentialities, is careful, if only by omission, not to tamper too boldly with traditional teachings of human fallenness and inherited guilt. In the celebrated passage praising the creation of man, a newfound Renaissance glory in humanity is most often acknowledged, and the rhetoric of the passage on the creation of Adam does leave this impression. The critical point, however, is that Pico is describing Adam before the fall, and the only difference between Pico and Augustine is that Augustine never hesitates to show man what he has lost by recounting the present legacy of guilt and sinfulness in relation to prelapsarian perfection. Pico pointedly does neglect to do this and thus leaves a strong impression of the human dignity his *Oration* undertakes to express, while at least implicitly maintaining the orthodoxy of the traditional guilt-culture teaching on the fall, which he also obviously believed. He is, in this doctrine, both for Augustine and seemingly against him too. He embraces the prisci theologi and the magus, has a high regard for man's ethical self-sufficiency, and is suspected by the church;[124] yet he feels deeply the truth of the traditional fall theology, and in fact he ended his life a follower of Savonarola. Cassirer therefore overstates the case when he writes that "man's failure is hence for Pico not merely guilt" and that "when we consider with what vehemence Pelagianism had been fought in the medieval church since the days of Augustine, and how unconditionally it had been rejected as heresy, we must be astonished at the frankness and boldness with which Pico reaffirms the basic Pelagian thesis." [125] Pico, we feel, was more affected by Augustine than this passage allows, and yet Cassirer does clearly anticipate one direction of our argument by seeing Pico as breaking away from an Augustinian culture associated with "guilt" and as moving toward a new Pelagianism. Perhaps the most satisfying judgment is that Pico, like so many of the major figures of the period —and not least the poets with whom we will be concerned in the seventeenth century—is fascinated both by the traditional Augustinian guilt culture and by the spirit of the enlightenment which challenges it. As with Plato and Sophocles, Pico's true complexity is discovered in the struggle to reconcile opposing truths, each of which commands his assent.

Reformation: Enlightenment and Guilt Culture

It is impossible, especially in relation to Anglican poetry of the seventeenth century, to consider the Renaissance without its inevitable adjunct, the Reformation. The relationship between the two movements is highly complex, but the Reformation is so obviously and profoundly influenced by Augustinian anthropology that we may claim a strong guilt-culture orientation to be at once evident. The main Reformers first of all agree on a severe interpretation of Augustine's fall theology. They stress the debilitating nature of the curse inherited by all men from their first father Adam, and they are violently opposed to theories that regard man as ethically self-sufficient: the Reformation is profoundly anti-Pelagian.

Secondly, the Reformers stress the unique revelation of the Bible and severely subordinate, if not reject, the wisdom of the ancients. Luther mocks at the medieval allegorizers, not because he does not believe pagan art is subordinate to Christian revelation, but because he rejects pagan art altogether. Consequently, Renaissance fads such as the prisci theologi and the cult of the magus, with their tendencies to blur distinctions between Christian revelation and pagan wisdom, with their optimistic assessments of human nature, and with their general enlightenment leanings, are universally repudiated by the Reformers.

Thirdly, the movement which began by vindicating freedom of conscience was, tragically, itself not tolerant of dissent for very long. Paradoxically, religious toleration may never have been realized without the Reformation, but the principal Reformed communions hardened almost as soon as they were conceived into small infallible churches no more tolerant than Rome. Despite the fact that the pope and other visible symbols of the paternalistic Roman structure were rejected, Protestant sects were just as insistent as the Roman church, in fact more so, on exclusive family solidarity. Far from rejecting guilt-culture paternalism, they confirmed it—only now the family of the elect was the center of attention, and the unmediated judgments and overwhelming sense of the presence of God the Almighty Father induced in Reformation theology an acute sense of original sin, of human impotency and inherited guilt, with which the guilt-culture father is so closely bound up.

On the other side of the coin, however, the Reformation looked (often inadvertently) to enlightenment. Protestantism stressed, above all, an individualism of religious experience and so opened the door to religious toleration even though the sects themselves did not often enjoin it. Also, the very destruction of the visible hierarchy of the Roman church did much to clear the way for a new secularism in which church and state could be separate. After all, Cromwell's Puritans executed the king, symbol of the visible order of guilt-culture theocracy, and Cromwell's tragic mistake was simply his attempt to impose a theocratic rule of his own.

In general, then, the Reformation is a reactionary movement: in terms of this argument, it reasserts a traditional guilt-culture consciousness in face of a threatening enlightenment. At the same time, by insisting on individualism and by attacking the corporate structure of the church, it prepared the way for the very movement it in other respects resisted. Its paradoxical nature is totally in tune with the times. We will look now in more detail at the guilt-culture component.

First, it is not surprising that a movement so influenced by Augustinian anthropology should be especially concerned to combat Pelagianism. The Augsburg Confession, the Thirty-nine Articles, and the statement of Carnesecchi which we have mentioned make it clear that Reformers, whether in Italy, Germany, or England, felt Pelagianism as a special threat. The same is true of Luther in his famous debate with Erasmus on the freedom of the will. He complains that "Erasmus by far outstrips the Pelagians," and he "will not accept or tolerate that moderate middle way which Erasmus would . . . recommend to me," because, "unless you attribute all and everything to free will, as the Pelagians do, the contradictions in Scripture still remain." [126]

To Luther's credit, he saw immediately the problem of Pelagian free will vis à vis Augustinian inherited guilt to be the key issue of the times, and he congratulates Erasmus on getting to the point: "I give you hearty praise: alone, in contrast to all others, you have discussed the real thing, i.e., the essential point." [127] Erasmus, for his part, gives a balanced view of man's responsibility for his actions in the economy of salvation. His authorities are the Scriptures, the Fathers, the tradition of the church, the experience of human responsibility. But for Luther the essentially tolerant and balanced thought of Erasmus tended dangerously toward an ethical and Pelagian assertion of individual responsibility at expense of belief in inherited guilt. Luther's reaction was violently to reaffirm the traditional guilt-culture precepts of Augustine on the fall of man, a reaction in which he was followed by many of the major Reformers. Luther, once an Augustinian monk, remains to an exaggerated degree Augustinian in his doctrine of the fall. This is true also of Calvin, on whom, according to Wendel, "the influence of St. Augustine . . . may even be said to be unique of its kind." [128] Indeed, on certain questions, especially those involving grace and predestination, Calvin is ultra-Augustinian, and even the Father of Grace at times seems not anti-Pelagian enough for him. On the issue of predestination, Calvin does go beyond Augustine, whom Calvin was specifically accused by Albert Pighius of misinterpreting. In consequence, says Smits, Calvin "approfondit la doctrine augustinienne sur la prédestination et la providence." [129] Nevertheless, Wendel is essentially correct in pointing out that Calvin draws special inspiration from Augustine's doctrines of free will, "and in the chapters on grace and on predestination he employs all the Augustinian arguments to his purpose." [130] Interestingly, many Reformers who wished to revert to the purity of earliest Christianity began, like Calvin, by assuming an Augustinian doctrine of the fall dating from the fifth century.

We can also explain a good deal of Luther's and Calvin's initial attitude to the Roman church if we see that for them the abuses of Rome were often and characteristically linked with those elements of the church which we have described in association with enlightenment humanism. So the Reformers, in place of syncretic theories such as accompanied the Italian enthusiasm for Hermes Trismegistus, the prisci theologi, the magus, and so on, once more asserted the unique truth of the Christian revelation. In one way, the alignment of the Roman church with enlightenment tendencies of the Renaissance, particularly the syncretic and the magical, was unfortunate, for the church itself was ambiguous in its attitude to much Renaissance philosophic endeavor. For example, although a major source of attack on the syncretic theory of the prisci theologi did indeed come from evangelical Protestants like Erastus, Wier, and Lefèvre d'Etaples,[131] there were Catholic attacks also, by such as G. F. Pico and the Jesuit Del Rio.[132] On both sides the animus was against a Hermetic and magical Christianity, and, in the people we have cited, it involved a desire to separate absolutely the prisci theologi (rightly seen as the root of the evil) from the Christian revelation in the Old and New Testaments. G. F. Pico finds that one single teaching of Moses outweighs the whole of pagan wisdom,[133] and Erastus congratulates himself that his education was not "chez ces superstitieux Egyptiens" but in the Bible.[134] Although the Roman church of the Renaissance was ambiguous in its attitudes toward its illustrious philosophers, a great many of the most vehement Protestant attacks do represent Rome's most characteristic abuses uniquely in terms of enlightenment criteria of the Renaissance, such as speculation on the prisci theologi and the magus and the general tendency to equate pagan wisdom with Christian revelation.

The magus, for instance, becomes for Protestants a figure of considerable horror, and the greatest magus of all is the pope, for he, like Asclepius, is an idolater. As soon as Bernardino Ochino makes his allegiance with the Northern Reformation, he accuses Pope Paul III of being a magician.[135] Puritan Andrew Melville attacks the Roman

Liturgy as a "magic wheel of incantation," [136] an accusation perhaps derived from Calvin who says of the papists that they "display ceremonies not understood, like a scene on the stage, or a magical incantation." [137] For Calvin, moreover, the doctrine of transubstantiation is one of "Satan's tricks," and consecration is "virtually equivalent to magic incantation." [138] The Roman church, he claims, labors under *"the error of a magical conception of the sacraments,"* and in the teaching of Paul, unlike that of Rome, "we should not imagine some magic incantation, supposing it enough to have mumbled the words, as if they were to be heard by the elements." [139] Calvin's real fear is contained in this last quotation: that somehow divine life (*spiritus*) could be channeled into the elements (*materia*) by the intervention of the human mind, as the Renaissance magus espoused. Calvin insists repeatedly on God's transcendence[140] and on the fact that the soul is an essence distinct from the body.[141] Any Neoplatonist conception (and here we can point to Ficino and Pico) of the interpenetration of spirit and matter is repudiated. The clamor of some "about a secret inspiration that gives life to the whole universe . . . is not only weak but completely profane." [142] Such teachings on the world soul set up "a shadowy deity" and "drive away the true God, whom we should fear and adore." [143]

In relation to another favorite enterprise of the magus, Calvin is willing to "confess, indeed, that astronomy has some use"; but he insists that "in this deepest investigation of heavenly things there is no organic symmetry, but here is an activity of the soul distinct from the body." [144] This is diametrically opposed to the assertion of Pico that the magus is he who "wed[s] earth to heaven" [145] and that such a man should be revered as divine. For Pico the world soul holds the universe together in its inmost being: it is the source of all the motions of the cosmos and gives them order and harmony.[146] Calvin repudiates precisely such "magical" beliefs in "corporeal co-operation," claiming they produce merely idolatry or the worship of images in the belief "that some power of divinity dwells there," and the Roman church is for Calvin the seat of such idolatry par excellence.[147] The Mass "swarms with every sort of impiety, blasphemy, idolatry and sacrilege." [148] The sacrament of the eucharist "is made a hateful idol," and the pope, supreme idolater, is Antichrist.[149] All of this can profitably be seen in terms of a reaction against that widespread Renaissance cult of the magus as we have described its derivation from the *Asclepius* and *Corpus Hermeticum*. Appropriately, the one time Calvin mentions Hermes Trismegistus in the *Institutes*,[150] it is to equate him with Servetus, who was burned at the stake by Calvin as a heretic.

Nor does Calvin simply distinguish between two sorts of magic and condemn only the demonic sort. The repudiation we have cited is clearly of the "natural" or philosophic magic as described by Pico. Puritan iconoclasm in general was less a pure antiart movement than a rejection of the magus in his "natural" form as artist. As Miss Yates points out (in accord with Walker's authoritative demonstration of the same point), the power of the magician to contain the spiritus in the materia was the power sought also by the great Renaissance artists who sought to embody, like Asclepius, real spiritual truth in the material of their works.[151] This endeavor extended also to the art of poetry. For instance, in the work of La Boderie and Tyard, the magus Orpheus was a source of inspiration, and the art of the poem and that of the magical incantation are confused.[152] Significantly, Puritan iconoclasts destroyed not only statues but books containing mathematical symbols and geometrical drawings,[153] and when, before he died, Nicholas Ferrar burned all the "vain books" of literature and devotion in his library, the Puritans thought him to be burning his "conjuring books." [154] They also considered him too sympathetic to Catholicism, and the three things seemed naturally connected in their minds: Catholicism, art, and the infernal power of the magus or conjurer. As an adjunct, therefore, to a guilt-culture insistence on original sin and to a basic anti-Pelagianism, the main Reformers insisted on a guilt-culture superiority of the Christian message, rejecting, in consequence, theories which blurred the distinctions between Christianity and paganism, together with the optimistic assessments of human nature which accompanied speculation on such "enlightenment" subjects as the prisci theologi and the magus.

This brings us to the important question of toleration. Although the Reformation provided one important impetus toward its realization, religious liberty unfortunately was not the immediate fruit of a movement which did at first base itself on the probity of individual conscience. It may be, as Tulloch points out, that Protestantism soon became "extremely dogmatic"; yet "This tendency lay with it from the beginning, in its intense assertion of one side of the evangelical principle." [155] Certainly Protestant Europe in the sixteenth century gave birth to a large number of creeds, and soon there were in effect a large number of small infallible churches all as soundly opposed to the one large infallible Church of Rome as they were opposed to each other. The guilt-culture solidarity of the family unit, therefore, still remains dominant in Protestantism even though the Roman Holy Father is dispensed with: the Heavenly Father now makes his supreme and unmediated presence felt in the spirits of the elect. For Protestants the experience of solidarity is in terms of a spiritual family with which the church becomes primarily identified.

The Protestant effort to retain on the one hand the traditional sense of the church as family while on the other hand repudiating the "carnal" elements of the Roman institution explains why there was such intense interest in ecclesiology among the Reformers. [156] Perhaps their single most important innovative distinction in this area was one they consistently made between the visible and invisible churches. Wycliffe and Huss had written treatises *De ecclesia,* both of which had already broached this question, and Huss, like Wycliffe before him, had simply claimed an identification of the true church and the body of the spiritual elect. "He treats the *corpus mysticum* as belonging to an invisible realm, where all transactions between God and man take place." [157] Significantly, the implicit threat to the corporate and hierarchical visible structure of the medieval church was felt to be severe enough for Huss to be burned at the stake largely on account of his theory. Upon his *De ecclesia* were based the charges made against him at the Council of Constance which led to his martyrdom.

Luther, not surprisingly, reaffirmed Huss's crucial distinction. Indeed, for Luther the church is essentially invisible, and he is apparently the first actually to apply to it the word *invisibilis.*[158] However, like the other major Reformers, Luther also admits that there must be a visible church among which the elect are numbered though it will also contain *hypocritae* who seem to be of the elect but are not.[159] In Zwingli, Bullinger, Calvin, and Zanchi, the distinction between visible and invisible continues to be made, though it is worked out with most rigor by Calvin.[160] Admittedly, none of the Reformers denied that the church was in the world; yet they equated the true church with the invisible or spiritual body of God's elect. This is not to say, however, that medieval Christians did not know as well as Calvin the "spiritual" meaning of Augustine's City of Jerusalem. Yet, if only through the processes of history, the visible corporate structure of the medieval church with a sacramental ordination into priesthood and a doctrine of transubstantiation in the eucharist, moved it toward a high evaluation of the visible institution. In face of this, the Protestant distinction between visible and invisible, accompanied by an equally typical insistence on a priesthood of believers and consistent attacks on the "carnal" Catholic doctrine of transubstantiation, amounts to an emphasis quite different: spiritual rather than corporate.[161]

Yet the essential point is that, despite a seemingly irreconcilable controversy on the nature of the church, neither the apologists for Rome nor the advocates of Reformation abandon the fundamental guilt-culture metaphor of the church as family. The Cyprianic formula is as wholeheartedly avowed by Calvin as by Augustine, and the figure of church as mother, ruled by the Heavenly Father and nourishing and protecting her children, the elect, is constantly reiterated in the *Institutes*.[162] The Reformation conflict with Rome contests not the basic guilt-culture concepts of paternalism and family solidarity so much as the manner in which that family should be understood, especially in relation to the earthly claims of the pope as God's uniquely appointed representative.

One result of this whole argument is to make Luther and Calvin seem primarily reactionaries, reaffirming in a perhaps exaggerated, certainly ultra-Augustinian way the main tenets of the older guilt culture: a deep belief in inherited guilt and sin, a renunciation of the ethical sufficiency of the reason, a solid sense of family solidarity (in this case the family of the elect). The reaction seems equally explicit against the widespread prisci theologi and their adjuncts insofar as they anticipate enlightenment: repudiation of Hellenic self-sufficiency, rejection of religious toleration, and condemnation of the magus and his works. Yet, as with Pico, the issues are not this easily polarized. There can be no doubt that in attacking the physical institution of the Roman church, and in rejecting sacramentalism and hierarchical structure, Luther and Calvin do encourage a radical and revolutionary individualism which contributes much to the secular spirit of the new age.

In that key debate of the times, therefore, on the question of free will, neither Erasmus nor Luther is to be understood apart, for each contains within himself complementary elements in terms of which a total situation can be comprehended. In the encounter of guilt culture and enlightenment they both, like Pico, look toward enlightenment: Erasmus by asserting the human dignity of the free will and by advocating toleration; Luther by breaking with the visible paternalistic family structure of the institutional church and by promoting an unprecedented individualism. Yet each, again like Pico, is also traditionalist: Erasmus by clinging to the old structure of the visible and sacramental church; Luther by reaffirming the guilt-culture theology of Augustine.

Perhaps only in the later seventeenth century in England are the legacies of both Erasmus and Luther, as well as of Pico, brought together in a way which most logically and peaceably resolves the contradictions. In the Cambridge Platonists we find an Erasmian tolerance and a Platonist trust in reason, together with a Protestant individualism. The bonds of the institutional church are relaxed on the one hand and the guilt-culture theology of the fall played down on the other. The singular achievement of the Cambridge Platonists was to see this as a proper distribution of elements. The extremes might well be livable in their proper context, whether as dominant guilt culture, with theories of inherited guilt and dependence on hierarchy, or as dominant enlightenment with faith in man, individualism, a secular state, and religious toleration. But the collisions and tensions of the transition from one dominant mode to the other occur in a relatively brief age characterized by upheaval and civil war. We see its agony reflected in the inspired yet depressing life and writings of Pico, in the tangle of Erasmus and Luther, as well as in the profound experience of Shakespeare's tragedies. For the men of the transition, as for Oedipus, the hypothetical alternatives are equally difficult to accept. Only at the end of the seventeenth century is it finally acknowledged that toleration and belief in the ethical power of reason cannot harmoniously accompany a strong theology of inherited guilt together with a strong institutional church.

Conclusion

One way to approach the devotional poets of the seventeenth century is in terms of a hypothetical encounter between guilt culture and enlightenment. The paradoxes of the age are similar to those produced by an equivalent confrontation in the classical period of Greek civilization. In Augustine's theology of the fall and in the structure of the medieval church we find a theory of inherited guilt within a strongly paternalistic and hierarchical "family" institution. But just as the ethical consciousness of a Socrates and the developing logos principle of classical Greek philosophy forced the individual out from the bonds of family and clan, so the Florentine philosophers set in motion a similar reaction against the accepted spirituality of traditional Augustinianism. Again there were heresy trials. And again, as with Sophocles and Plato, the conflict between a deeply rooted mythology of fallenness and inherited guilt, against which human behavior must be judged, and an ethical endeavor toward an autonomy of reason admired but still feared produces in the Renaissance both profound and disturbing theology and literature.

In the Anglican poets of seventeenth-century England, inheriting the traditional Augustinian theology as well as the modifications of both Reformation and Renaissance,[163] the discovery of a "middle way" was, understandably, the prime endeavor, even though this middle way, as we have said, soon turned into a "whirling jumble." This book will indicate a path through that jumble by means of a hypothesis suggested in this introductory chapter. The conflict of the old and the new in the seventeenth century is not simply between Protestantism and Catholicism, or between Renaissance and Reformation, but between two modes of regarding the ethical nature of man, which we have described as guilt culture and enlightenment.

In terms of this distinction, the first two of our four poets, Donne and Herbert, will appear most Catholic, and their spirituality is most Augustinian in the traditional medieval sense. Yet a characteristic enlightenment challenge is also present in each of them, though in different ways. In Donne it emerges directly in terms of the Renaissance prisci theologi, especially in relation to the problem of religious toleration. In Herbert it emerges through the individualism of the Reformation doctrine of the covenant and Puritan spiritualization of the church. While we may say that Donne and Herbert remain in essence medieval, the special energy of the later poets, Vaughan and Traherne, comes not from their deep-rootedness in the traditional Augustinian guilt culture but from their enlightenment attempts to find spiritual models to replace the dogmatic assumptions of Augustine, and in both poets we find tendencies toward what might look like Pelagianism. Finally, all four poets form a distinct group, though among these so-called metaphysicals stylistic differences are a direct consequence of the theological prepossessions of their poems. This is the most satisfactory way to explain the group as the "school" they have been long recognized to form but which has consistently foiled analysis from a purely stylistic viewpoint.

Chapter Two Augustinian Spirituality
and the *Holy Sonnets* of John Donne

Saint Bonaventure's hymn, *Laudismus de Sancta Cruce*,[1] was composed by one of the foremost representatives of the Augustinian tradition in the High Middle Ages. The spirituality of the hymn offers some interesting points for comparison with the devotional poetry of John Donne, a foremost Augustinian of the seventeenth century in England. *Laudismus de Sancta Cruce* begins by directing our thoughts to the Atonement. Bonaventure reminds us of the supreme importance of the cross for salvation and advises, "to its rule your life resign" (1). The cross is our only hope and cure, our "totum remedium" (14) and we should "place its mark on everything" (3), keeping it in our thoughts at all times:

> Be you tempted or afflicted,
> Be you faint and almost vanquished,
> Be you overwhelmed in loss,
> Linger not in sloth or slowness,
> But with instant resolution
> Mark your forehead with the cross.
>
> [12]

Whether we are laughing or grieving or resting or joyful or oppressed, our meditation should remain unwearied and sustained. The hymn continues in this vein, asserting the importance of the cross and enjoining men in all circumstances to reflect upon its significance, until Bonaventure interjects a personal prayer for strength to pursue such a proper and contritional meditation himself:

> Jesus crucified, support me,
> That so long as life is in me
> I with joy may mourn Your death.
>
> [37]

As the prayer, and the hymn, conclude, the author desires actually to join Christ upon the cross:

> That with you I may be wounded,
> And may hunger to embrace You
> On the Cross till end of breath.
>
> [37]

With just such a desire for crucifixion John Donne begins, rather than ends, *Holy Sonnet* 11:

> Spit in my face, yee Jewes, and pierce my side,
> Buffet, and scoffe, scourge and crucifie mee.[2]

But Donne does not simply want, like Bonaventure, to join Christ. Rather he would like to replace Christ on the cross and make reparation by suffering, in person, for his own sins. He comes to realize, however, that this is impossible, and he must be content to face the paradox that only the innocent can atone for the sins of the guilty:

> But by my death can not be satisfied
> My sinnes . . .
> . . . .
> God cloth'd himselfe in vile mans flesh, that so
> Hee might be weake enough to suffer woe.
>
> [11. 5-14]

Where Bonaventure, then, wishes crucifixion because he understands and accepts the meaning of Christ crucified, Donne, as speaker in the poem, wishes crucifixion precisely because he does not understand. He begins with a misconception and has to arrive at a new, and proper, perspective. The process of his arrival is the poem.

These different approaches to the same subject (penitential meditation of the cross of Christ) also help to determine the different poetic qualities of the two pieces. Bonaventure's hymn might be described as "anonymous"—it is self-effacing, the author desires to do no more than offer appropriate thoughts and directions to the reader. Donne's poem is the opposite—it is highly personal because the poet records the experience of the individual in the act of meditation, in the act of arriving at understanding. Consequently, Donne's poem is also involved with dramatically examining the theology of his false position: Bonaventure's hymn accepts the orthodox view implicitly and does not need to question it, only to draw our attention to it. Again, because of our awareness of the individuality of the speaker, in Donne we are conscious of a struggle for humility which the hymn quite naturally achieves with simplicity and directness. In the *Holy Sonnet* the personality of the meditator is urgent to assert itself, and there is need to suppress the arrogance and self-sufficiency which moves the speaker to such wrong-headed "gainfull intent" (11. 12).

Yet the poems have a good deal in common, too. They deal with the same subject matter, realizing that man's sins are atoned for on the cross, and each author is moved to penitence and humility by reflection on this event. Also, both poems use techniques of affective piety, seen in their similar composition of place through imaginative application of the senses. Both authors picture themselves actually present at the Crucifixion, and even on the cross. Such techniques as affective piety and composition of place have been well explained by Louis Martz in *The Poetry of Meditation,* but more important, Martz also explains that one of the most significant medieval treatises of meditation was the fourteenth-century handbook, *Meditations on the Life of Christ,* written by the pseudo-Bonaventure.[3] This attribution links the origins of meditation techniques, so important for the devotional poetry of the later Renaissance in England, with the establishment during the thirteenth and fourteenth centuries by Franciscans such as Bonaventure and Friar John, the pseudo-Bonaventure, of a strongly Augustinian theological tradition developed in opposition to certain unruly and upstart elements in the church, chiefly Aquinas and the Dominicans. In this light it is interesting to consider Donne's *Holy Sonnets* as a synthesis of, on the one hand, a traditional Augustinianism such as we find informing Bonaventure's hymn (and which, we suggest, provides a spiritual ground plan for the *Holy Sonnets*) and, on the other hand, a characteristically seventeenth-century latitudinarian desire to repudiate the harsh doctrinal derivations from Augustine, such as were found, for example, among the Reformers. The struggle of the *Holy Sonnets,* in short, is to discover a middle way not simply between Catholicism and Protestantism (which the Anglican via media is often represented as espousing) but between the traditional guilt-culture inheritance of Augustine, represented by Franciscan spirituality, and a typically enlightenment Neoplatonist latitude. From this point of view, and in terms of the theory propounded in the previous chapter, it is interesting that Walton should describe Donne at once as "a second St. *Austine"* and as *"another* Picus Mirandula." [4]

The Franciscan Augustine

When we move to as definite a body of material as John Donne's *Holy Sonnets,* it becomes necessary to describe also a more definite embodiment of the pervasive influence of Augustine during the Middle Ages which we have dealt with in the last chapter, in broad terms, as guilt culture. It is conventional to see the main-line tradition of Augustinian theology as extending in particular through Saint Bernard and the Victorines to Saint Bonaventure and the Franciscans; and, within this grouping, the following account concentrates on Bonaventure and the English friars from Alexander of Hales to Duns Scotus, because they represent the culmination of an Augustinian tradition which was to remain effective in England even until the seventeenth century. At the same time, the fact that Franciscans felt a special relationship of indebtedness to Saint Bernard as well as to their most revered mentor Augustine helps also to keep the main lines of the earlier tradition in focus.

To some extent, the Franciscans will clearly reduplicate elements of Augustinian thought which are common to most of the other important theologians of the Middle Ages. This is especially true on the key question of original sin which, in an Augustinian form, was an assumed doctrine throughout the entire period. Even during controversies on the subject between Franciscans and Dominicans the basic positions of Augustine were not at all in question. Pelagius was anathema for Aquinas as he was for Bonaventure, and although there was dispute among the followers of these two men with regard to issues

such as the degree of cooperation between man and God in the
economy of salvation, there was no disagreement on what are for us
the basic contentions: all men inherit Adam's guilt, original sin is
remedied by baptism within the family of the church, and Pelagian
teachings on man's self-sufficiency are heretical. In short:

> Les théologiens . . . de Jean Scot à saint Thomas, et de saint
> Thomas au concile de Trente, conaissent très certainement les
> données de la foi sur l'existence du péché originel et ses suites;
> mais ils n'ont plus à les défendre: aussi, les présupposent-ils
> plus qu'ils ne les démontrent. Ils les prennent comme point de
> départ de leurs spéculations. . . . Tout ce travail va se faire en
> des mesures différentes sous l'influence de saint Augustin.[5]

Yet despite this common indebtedness, the Franciscans saw themselves as having a special devotion to Augustine. They even saw
themselves as defenders of the true Augustine against the philosophic
innovations of the Dominicans. John Pecham, Franciscan archbishop of Canterbury at the end of the thirteenth century, goes so
far as to accuse the Dominicans of neglecting the Fathers in their
infatuation for philosophy. His biographer writes:

> Taking a leaf from the book of William de St. Amour, he
> warned the pope that this was the danger of the last days, fore-
> told by the apostle; for, if the doctrines of Augustine and the
> other fathers were scorned, the whole fabric of Christian phi-
> losophy would crumble, and truth succumb to falsehood.[6]

Certainly, Bonaventure's account in *Breviloquium* (3.1-7) of the
temptation and fall of our first parents, and of the transmission of
their sin to their children, the human race, is thoroughly Augustinian
and relies throughout on Augustinian sources.[7]

> This is how mankind is corrupted by original sin. Everyone
> generated from the union of the sexes is, by the very nature of
> this birth, a child of wrath; for he is deprived of the righteous-
> ness of original justice, in the absence of which our souls incur
> a fourfold penalty: weakness, ignorance, malice, and concu-
> piscence. These, inflicted because of original sin, are matched
> in the body by all kinds of pain, imperfection, labor, disease,

and affliction. More penalties come later: death and the return to dust, privation of the beatific vision and loss of the heavenly glory, not only for adults, but also for infants who die without baptism. Of all human beings, however, these little ones suffer "the lightest penalty." [3.5.2]

The passage reduplicates Augustine's main teaching. The children of Adam inherit their father's sin and are afflicted by weakness, ignorance, malice, and concupiscence, which are relieved only by baptism and cured only by the grace of God. The final words of the passage are indeed directly from the *Enchiridion* (93.23), and it is worth noting that Bonaventure has his attention so closely on Augustine as to cite these words simply to provide an assurance later in the argument, that Augustine's strong anti-Pelagian opinions on the subject of unbaptized infants do not reflect the total view. "In his effort to bring the Pelagians back to moderation, he himself went somewhat to extremes" (3.5.6). Augustine, we conclude, is so firmly embedded that Bonaventure will go out of his way to argue for a proper understanding of his mentor even when inconvenient, and when space is at a premium, as in the *Breviloquium*.

In the rest of his brief account in book 3, Bonaventure goes on to repeat all the major Augustinian points. He describes our inheritance as "guilt deserving eternal damnation" (3.7.4). He tells us of the overturning of a proper hierarchy within the family of our first parents (3.3.1 ff.) and of transmission of their sin inherited "through the flesh born of concupiscence" (3.6.1). He repeats his statement on the necessity of grace and baptism (3.7.1), and the Pelagians are rejected as immoderate, even though Augustine was extreme in rebuking them.

In short, Bonaventure is, on this crucial subject of the fall, "le grand témoin classique de cet augustinisme qui va se développer dans la famille franciscaine";[8] and within this family, Matthew of Aquasparta,[9] for one, develops Bonaventure's views of the fall and original sin along firmly Augustinian lines, as does Peter Auriole in his *Quaestiones disputate*.[10] In turn, the lineaments of Bonaventure's position were present in the work of his Franciscan teacher, Alexander of Hales,[11] just as they are repeated in Duns Scotus[12] and the Franciscans at Oxford—men like Roger Bacon and Robert

Grosseteste simply "continuent à enseigner sur le péché originel les thèses augustiniennes de saint Bonaventure." [13]

The importance of the question of original sin for the entire Franciscan movement becomes even more obvious in the light of two internecine controversies in which Franciscans took special interest. The first involved the hypothetical question, "cur deus homo si Adam non pecasset?" [14] Why would God have become man, they asked, if Adam had not sinned? The key issue was the relationship between the fall of Adam and the Incarnation of Christ, and the lively interest shown by Franciscans in the seemingly futile conundrum which is but one minor aspect of the question at least indicates the degree to which the issues of the fall and the guilt-culture theory of the two Adams were impressed upon their minds. The second controversy concerned the Immaculate Conception.[15] Once more the essential issue was the problem of original sin, this time in relation to the Blessed Virgin Mary, and again the intensity of Franciscan interest provides evidence of a special involvement with questions concerning the fall.

Yet the basic importance of an Augustinian theory of original sin itself is not so significant as the type of spirituality it produced. The main devotional emphases, the main spiritual techniques developed among Franciscans to body forth the theological principles they adapted so wholeheartedly from their beloved Augustine, need to be described if the tradition is to be well understood. The following account of the main elements of such a tradition is based on the *Dictionnaire de spiritualité*[16] and on an account of Franciscan spirituality, written from the point of view of its influence on medieval English literature, by David Jeffrey.[17]

Jeffrey, first of all, demonstrates that Franciscans were a fundamental influence on Middle English lyric poetry. The spiritual ideals and devotion of Bonaventure (taught to him by an Englishman, Alexander of Hales) were enthusiastically developed by English friars like Roger Bacon, Robert Grosseteste, and John Pecham. Principally through Pecham's powerful position as archbishop of Canterbury, Franciscan spirituality spread widely and on a popular basis in England. Grosseteste's *Dicta,* modeled on Pecham, were also influential, and the countless unknown friars who wandered the countryside as preachers to the people often carried handbooks for sermons based on these two sources. Such handbooks survive in compilations like the *Liber exemplorum*, the *Speculum laicorcum*, and *Fasciculus morum*, and, of particular interest, the friars used verses to assist their preaching. From this origin the bulk of medieval religious lyric poetry directly stems. Moreover, in the poems, as in the devotional books, the sermon guides, and the theology, certain distinct motifs can be readily detected and read as hallmarks of a popular Franciscan spiritual tradition. First, although the Franciscans assume an Augustinian guilt-culture doctrine of the fall, they, like Augustine, were concerned primarily with man's redemption from sin. In consequence their attention is strongly drawn to the figure of the incarnate Christ. Their special interest in the Incarnation is evident, as we have seen, in the concern for the hypothetical question, "Cur deus homo, si Adam non pecasset?"; but the special contribution of Franciscan devotion on this subject was an interest in Christ's humanity in one particular aspect—that of suffering. The cross and the passion became, in consequence, a centerpiece for Franciscan devotion, and Christ's suffering is, typically, connected with the basic Augustinian view of original sin as inherited guilt. This passage by Bonaventure is characteristic:

> Man had sinned, aspiring to be as wise as God, desiring to enjoy the forbidden tree . . . and through sin the whole of mankind was infected, forfeiting immortality and incurring inevitable death. To heal man by the appropriate remedy, God-made-man willed to be humiliated and to suffer on a tree.[18]

The tree of Adam is directly related to the tree of Christ as sin to atonement, in the usual terms of the Augustinian typology. A further characteristic point is made soon after when Bonaventure remarks: "Since Christ's divine nature was beyond the reach of pain all this affected only his humanity" (4.9.8). This statement, which stresses the words *affect* and *humanity,* isolates a premise underlying the way we should make our sinful and human approach to the cross. If we are to be moved, Bonaventure implies (presumably by a sermon or a poem or a meditation on the cross), we must be moved through our senses and by the reconstruction in our imaginations of the physical details of the life of Christ as it affected his humanity.

As Martz points out, the pseudo-Bonaventure's *Meditations on the Life of Christ* is one of the seminal works in the development of the kind of affective piety which operates by stimulating the senses through imagination, and the book is in fact wholly typical of Franciscan spirituality. Certainly it develops Bonaventure's injunction to attend to the human suffering of the crucified, and the author also makes clear to us that the passion is the most important element of devotion: "If you have studiously considered the things said above on His life," he writes, "you much more diligently concentrate the whole spirit [on the passion and crucifixion] . . . for here is shown more especially this charity of His that should kindle all our hearts." [19] He then advises application of the senses, the "feeling yourself present in those places as if the things were done in your presence" (p. 387). The resulting combination of affective piety with the favorite subject of Christ's suffering is well exemplified in the following brief account of the Crucifixion:

> On all sides rivers of His most sacred blood flow from His terrible wounds. He is so tortured that He can move nothing except His head. Those three nails sustain the whole weight of His body. He bears the bitterest pain and is affected beyond anything that can possibly be said or thought. He hangs between two thieves. Everywhere are torments, everywhere injuries, everywhere abuses. [p. 334]

We are reminded also by Friar John that the source of this terrible execution is original sin: Christ (quite unhistorically) is made to ask his father to "accept, and for love of me be pleased to wipe away and remove all the old stains from them" (p. 334).

A similar intense and affective devotion to the cross can be found throughout Franciscan writings. In the final chapter of *The Mind's Road to God,* for instance, Bonaventure tells us that even the elevated state of mystical repose is achieved only "with full face . . . looking upon Him suspended on the cross in faith, hope, and charity," and we should "pass over with the crucified Christ from this world to the Father." [20] Bonaventure's *Laudismus de Sancta Cruce,* as we have seen, is another characteristic example:

Let the Holy Cross be present
In your soul and meditation:
To its rule your life resign.

[1]

The hymn develops the injunction of these opening verses: "wrap
the cross around your body" (3); "let your heart be cross-absorbed"
(6); "live within the cross so noble" (8); "lock yourself in its embrace" (8); "seek the cross and seek the nailings" (9). The entire
"labour of salvation," indeed, is "to recall the crucifixion" (22). The
"inner flavor" of the cross must penetrate "through the heart and
through the senses" (5), and Bonaventure himself forces us to apply
our senses to the composition of place:

> Now his hands and feet are riven,
> Now some bitter wine is given
> To the King in mockery
>
> Now his blessed eyes are dimming
> Now his sacred face is paling,
> As upon the cross he bleeds.

[29-30]

The hymn ends, we recall, with the author actually wishing to join
the crucified Christ on the cross, and Bonaventure makes specific the
relation between the physical horror and suffering of the Crucifixion
and man's sin. We are told simply: "Man has sinned, and for that
reason / Is the flesh of Christ now pinioned" (31).[21]

Further examples suggest themselves in plenty. Bonaventure's
Lignum vitae, the *Arbor vitae crucifixae Jesu* of Ubertino de Casale,
the *Blanquerna* of Raymond Lull, the *Stabat Mater* and *Lauda* 83
of Jacopone da Todi (in the latter, Jacopone, like Bonaventure and
Donne, wishes to be lifted onto the cross and himself crucified),[22]
all demonstrate a typical devotion to the cross. Or we could consider the poems of such English Franciscans as Friar William Herebert (*Vexilla regis proderunt; Popule meus quid feci tibi?*) and Friar
John Grimestone (*The Hours of the Cross; Popule meus quid feci
tibi?; I Would Be Clad in Christis Skin*). Finally, the Franciscans

were largely responsible for that universally popular Catholic devotion, the stations of the cross.[23]

The techniques of affective piety and the favorite motif of the passion lead to another important and characteristic subject of Franciscan piety which should be mentioned at this point, namely, a special devotion to the figure of the Blessed Virgin Mary. We have already mentioned the Franciscan debate on the Immaculate Conception as a controversy closely connected with the root question of original sin, and the Virgin herself was close to the hearts of Franciscans. I do not, however, wish to discuss in detail the nature of this readily acknowledged element of Franciscan devotion to Mary, since (primarily because of the Reformation) it is not of great importance to our poets of seventeenth-century England. But a central impulse behind it is still close to our subject, as this passage from the *Meditations on the Life of Christ* indicates. Again, the passion is being discussed:

> And all this is said and done in the presence of His most sorrowful mother, whose great compassion adds to the Passion of her Son, and conversely. She hung with her Son on the cross and wished to die with Him rather than live any longer. Everywhere are tortures and torments that can be sensed but in truth hardly described. The mother stood next to His cross, between the crosses of the thieves. She did not turn her eyes away from her Son; she was in anguish like His; and with her whole heart she prayed to the Father. [p. 335]

Mary's human example—she did not turn her eyes away, she prayed to the Father with her whole heart, she is sorrowful as she hangs upon the cross—is one with which we can easily identify and which can move us closer to picturing in our minds the crucifixion of God in human terms. The position of Mary at the foot of the cross becomes a characteristic element of Franciscan devotion and is the source of a whole range of representations on the theme, *stabat mater*. As Leon Veuthey says: "Du christocentrisme de saint François et de ses enfants a jailli tout l'amour franciscain envers Marie, lequel devait aboutir à l'affirmation de sa conception immaculée."[24] So "the Blessed Virgin Mary, swooning at the foot of the cross, became the most popular and affectual piety promulgated by Franciscan spirituality." [25] Jeffrey goes on to say:

> Under the cross, Mary becomes the dramatic representative of the contrite sinner, the secondary tragic figure with whom the contrite is invited into catharsis, and her psychological function in effecting contrition is enhanced by the claim of Bonaventure that she feels in her own body the pain of Christ's suffering.[26]

It is worth noting that Franciscans were responsible for introducing to the Liturgy not only the great *Salve Regina* and *Alma Redemptoris* but also the *Ave Regina* and the *Regina caeli*.[27] Devotion to Mary, then, becomes one of the most easily recognized elements of Franciscan spirituality, and we can see how it supports the main motif of the passion and the technique of affective piety.

In the Franciscan sermons, poems, books of instruction for preachers, and in the graphic and affective techniques by which many of their works were presented, we can now begin to detect a strong popular bias which also becomes a hallmark of Franciscan spirituality. When they came to England in 1274, the Franciscans followed conscientiously the instructions of Saint Francis that his followers preach for the "utility and the edification of the people, announcing to them vices and virtues, punishment and glory, with brevity of speech, because the Lord made His words short upon the earth." [28] Moreover, a main task which the preachers (and theologians) undertook in directing their mission to the people was to make the words of the Bible themselves available by popularizing them. One result of this concern is an unusually marked emphasis on Scripture throughout the entire Franciscan school. Friar Roger Bacon assures us: "Grosseteste and Adam Marsh invariably used the text of the Scripture for the subject of their lectures in preference to the Sentences of Peter Lombard, which later became the favourite text-book in the schools of theology." [29]

The key to understanding this emphasis on Scripture is best found in the works of Bonaventure himself. His *De reductione artium ad theologiam,* for example, is careful to place the "lumen gratiae et sacrae Scripturae" [30] clearly at the head of a hierarchy of four lights, and he insists on the very dichotomy between reason and revelation, philosophy and the Scriptures, that Aquinas tries to eliminate. In this he is not only reacting against Dominican philosophy but simply sustaining a tradition established by Francis himself, that the brothers study the sacred Scriptures carefully.[31] So Bonaventure's *Breviloquim,* "a brief summary of true theology," begins with an entire separate preface on the nature of Scripture which, after the manner of the *Reductio artium ad theologiam,* firmly establishes its primacy. Scripture, Bonaventure assures us, "deals with the whole universe, the high and the low, the first and the last, and all things in between" (Prol. 6.4). It is, to resume a familiar motif, "an intelligible cross in which the whole organism of the universe is described" (Prol. 6.4). Handbooks such as the *Meditations on the Life of Christ* follow Bonaventure's scriptural orientation implicitly by concentrating throughout on scriptural subjects for meditation. Tavard, commenting on exegesis of Scripture in Franciscan theology, concludes:

> Happen what may to the Augustinian tradition after St Thomas, a staunch party of Franciscan theologians carried on their work upon the lines adopted by St Bonaventure. Men like John Peckham, Walter of Brugghe, William of Mare and also, to a smaller extent, Matthew of Aquasparta and Richard of Middleton, vigorous theologians as they were, stood firmly by the Bonaventurian conception.[32]

Consciousness of man's fallenness, meditation on the cross and affective use of scriptural subjects are themselves ineffective, however, if they do not evoke a contritional response, and in the manner of all Augustinians, perhaps the main concern of the entire Franciscan program lay in the conversion of the will. Their preaching, their poems, and their theology were directed primarily at moving their audience to repent, and a sacrament which most interests Franciscans is, in consequence, penance. Connected with this, the Franciscans are also noted for their profound devotion to the eucharist, but repentance is the necessary "life saving plank after shipwreck" [33] which, by moving men to love properly, leads consequently to the eucharistic feast. Of the three parts of the sacrament of penance (contrition, confession, satisfaction), the first, for the Franciscans, is therefore by far the most important. In Bonaventure, "penitential sorrow conceived in the heart through compunction" (6.10.4) is prior to oral confession and the execution of satisfaction. So Alexander of Hales also singles out contrition as the central element of the sacrament:

> Respondemus: poenitentia est virtus vel gratia. Secundum unum esse est virtus, secundum alterum est gratia. Sunt enim duo effectus; unus est remissio culpae, et alter remissio poenae. Nam in contritione remittitur culpa; per confessionem et satisfactionem poena, quae etiam remittitur quandoque per solam contritionem.[34]

The emphasis of Bonaventure and Alexander is followed by Archbishop Pecham, and Jeffrey points out that the English preaching guides all have a central chapter devoted to the subject of contrition.[35] Its centrality to the popular mission is reflected in a story related by Thomas Eccleston of an English friar who "was so full of kindness and compassion that if he saw that penitents were not showing sufficient signs of repentance, he used to move them to contrition by his own sighs and tears." [36]

Theoretically, this emphasis amounts to a fairly conventional treatment of the sacrament. The Franciscans indeed do not contribute much to the theology; rather, by their peculiar stress on affective piety and consciousness of sin, they make of contrition the moving and profound emotional experience of conversion that it was for Augustine himself. The cross and passion of Christ, the blight of original sin, the *mater dolorosa,* the application of senses, all contribute to an interpretation of the sacrament of penance which stresses the element of love, of conversion of the will, of contrition.

This brings us to a final criterion. The Franciscans, naturally enough, found that a sense of human mortality which may inspire contrition could most effectively be evoked through the emotion of fear, and especially if meditation were directed to the last things, death and judgment, heaven and hell. Nor is it only as an expedient to devotion that Franciscans were concerned with last things. From the beginning, the Franciscan order had been apocalyptically oriented: "The Rule itself (I, *Reg.,* 23,16) and the great *Dies Irae* attest to this expectation." [37] A. G. Little comments on the apocalyptic element in Bartholemew of Pisa in these words:

> It represents . . . an idea that was present in the minds of many Franciscans—that their Order stood at the beginning of a new epoch in the world's history—an idea which was connected with the real and spurious writings of Joachim of Fiore. Joachim influenced Franciscan views of history and its relations to Scripture in many ways.[38]

Indeed, with the remarkable figure of Joachim of Fiore the surrogate Franciscan interest in the apocalypse came to a head. His prophecies included the prediction of a third age which would come about the year 1260 and would be ushered in by the rise to power of a series of antichrists. The third age would be a reign of peace, however, administered under the Holy Ghost by spiritual men leading a monastic life.[39] Joachim's expectation of an apocalyptic introduction to the third age exerted a strong influence on his fellow Franciscans. It can be traced even to such as Grosseteste and Adam Marsh at Oxford.[40] Certainly, Franciscans remained fond of a conception of themselves as leaders of souls through apocalyptic destruction. They apparently had much to do with the making of illustrated apocalypses, where they are "often depicted . . . among the saved at the Last Judgment" [41] and as leading the saved into paradise. This emphasis on the salvation of souls clearly connects the motif of last things with "Holy Fear" and with contrition. This connection is plain, for instance, in *Lauda* 45 of Jacopone da Todi, "How God Appears to the Soul in Five Ways," where the first of the five ways is described as "the state of Holy Fear." The poet goes on to connect "Holy Fear" specifically with contrition:

> The first Way, God comes to me
>
> . . . .
>
> Wounds me with contrition's sword,
> Love's harbinger to be.[42]

And in *Lauda* 1, "Of the Blessed Virgin Mary, and of the Sinner," fear of the last things, death and hell, is linked with recovery from sin:

> Then take, for a healing draught,
> Fear of the coming of death.
>
> . . . .

Then, for a potion, drink
The solemn terror of Hell:
In that dark prison, O think!
Lost souls forever must dwell.
So surely, thy heart will swell,
And cast the poison away! [43]

Even Bonaventure, in that final chapter of *The Mind's Road to God*, reminds us of the "burning passion" of Christ in terms of our own death, for "he alone truly perceives it [the passion] who says, 'My soul rather chooseth hanging and my bones death.' " [44]

This outline leads us, tentatively, to a set of criteria in which a style of Franciscan devotion—a quality of sensibility, a type of spirituality—is outlined. We can consider six headings:

1. A prepossession with a guilt culture and Augustinian doctrine of original sin as the source of all sinfulness and as the cause for the suffering, and perhaps the Incarnation, of Christ
2. Particular interest in the cross as the central motif for devotion, because it relates directly to the curse inherited from Adam
3. Development of affective piety, evoking through the senses specifically biblical themes
4. Devotion to the Blessed Virgin Mary as an aid to affective piety, particularly in relation to the human nature and suffering of Christ
5. Emphasis on contrition as the central element of the sacrament of penance
6. Affective use of meditation on last things (*a*) to inspire man with a sense of his fallenness and (*b*) to move him toward contrition.

This outline of Franciscan spirituality presents an account of the most significant embodiment of the theological tradition of Augustine in the Middle Ages. Its foundation, as we have seen, is the Augustinian view of the fall and original sin. In developing from this basis a sophisticated spirituality which attempts both to keep alive the spirit of Augustine himself and also to make it available as a systematic meditative piety, the Franciscans present us with the

central and most important spiritual manifestation of guilt-culture
theology in the Middle Ages.

John Donne: Augustinian

Turning now to Donne, it is difficult to resist not only that Augustine
was his mentor in thought but that traditional Augustinianism was
also the very mode of his spirituality. First, Donne's overwhelmingly
favorite nonbiblical authority is Augustine, but Donne also gives
enormous authority to Bernard, who is his next favorite nonbiblical
author to Augustine, after, perhaps, only Chrysostom. This is significant, for "no figure is of greater influence on Franciscan spirituality" [45] than Bernard, and as one turns to Franciscan sermon after
sermon one finds the same priority as in Donne—Augustine first,
then Bernard.[46] Even the *Meditations on the Life of Christ,* Augustinian in spirit, uses Bernard exclusively as glossator. Donne's
similar reliance on these two writers would seem to provide some
evidence of his inclination toward the tradition they represent.

Second, it is hard to ignore the stress Donne places on the fall, and
his obsession with sin. This is evident in the striking emphasis he
places on the penitential psalms, and, notably, he draws our attention specifically to Augustine in this context:

> So also hath there beene a particular dignity ascribed to those
> seven Psalmes, which we have ever called the *Penitentiall
> Psalmes;* Of which S. *Augustine* had so much respect, as that he
> commanded them to be written in a great Letter, and hung
> about the curtaines of his Death-bed within, that hee might give
> up the ghost in contemplation, and meditation of those seven
> Psalmes.[47]

The specific link made here between Augustine and penance accords
well with the main lines of the tradition we have outlined. But it is
much more than a chance relationship made in passing, for Donne
consistently returns to both Augustine and the penitential psalms
for inspiration. As the editors of his sermons point out, "an undue
number of Donne's sermons are devoted to four of the Penitential

Psalms," and "in many other sermons there is too much emphasis on sin and its punishment." They go on to "wonder whether Augustine's influence on him was altogether healthy" (*Sermons* 10.357-58). Certainly an Augustinian sense of the "corrupt root" of fallen human nature, of man the *massa peccati,* is oppressively strong in Donne's characteristic descriptions of original sin, for instance:

> Miserable man! a Toad is a bag of Poyson, and a Spider is a blister of Poyson and yet a Toad and a Spider cannot poyson themselves; Man hath a dram of poyson, originall-Sin, in an invisible corner, we know not where, and he cannot choose but poyson himselfe and all his actions with that; we are so far from being able to begin without Grace, as then where we have the first Grace, we cannot proceed to the use of that, without more. [*Sermons* 1.293]

Nor can we ignore the centrality for Donne of the Atonement and the cross. Coleridge draws our attention to this when he writes: "The cross of Christ is dimly seen in Taylor's works. Compare him in this particular with Donne, and you will feel the difference in a moment." [48] And we have Donne's own words in vindication of Coleridge, that "the first *Character,* that I was taught to know, was the *Crosse* of CHRIST JESUS" (*Sermons* 8.77). We may also remember such powerful passages on the Atonement as that from the closing of *Deaths Duell,* where an intense and affective meditation on the passion leaves us (as in *De Sancta Cruce* and *Holy Sonnet* 11) "in that *blessed dependancy,* to *hang* upon *him* who *hangs* upon the *Crosse*" (*Sermons* 10.248), or such poems as *The Crosse* (which, according to Helen Gardner, is a defense of the cross as a proper, traditional subject for devotion),[49] and *Goodfriday, 1613. Riding Westward.*

Donne also was familiar with authors representative of the main lines of the Augustinian tradition: Augustine, Bernard, Hugh of Saint Victor, and such Franciscans as Bonaventure, Franciscus de Arriba, Petrus Aureoli, Duns Scotus, Petrus Galatinus, Nicholas of Lyra, Miguel Medua, Francesco Panigorola, and Bernardino Ochino, once a Franciscan, who developed Augustinian spirituality toward the lines of the Northern Reformation. We should remember too that the techniques of affective piety to which Donne is undoubtedly in some sense indebted derive from the spirituality of pseudo-Bonaventure's *Meditations*. Also, as a hypothetical point, it may not be fanciful to suggest that Donne the Anglican, sensitive to the traditions of his national church, should favor a spirituality as distinctly English as that which we have been describing, for "with the exception of St. Bonaventure—and he was taught by Alexander of Hales—all the greatest and most original Franciscan scholars of the Middle Ages were natives of Britain." [50]

Granted, Donne's devotion to the Virgin is not so enthusiastic as it was among Franciscans, but it is easy to understand in the England of James and Charles why this most characteristic of Roman devotions should be suppressed. Even so, for a Protestant, Donne does demonstrate notable feeling for Mary. His *La Corona* is based on the rosary (and a version probably Franciscan in origin), and *A Litanie* addresses a stanza to "The Virgin Mary" which in a variant reading bears the more Romanist title "Our Ladie." [51] As Evelyn Simpson says, "in various ways he showed that the pull of the older associations was strong upon him," [52] and it is sometimes easy to feel for Donne (as for Herbert) that he remains more silent on the subject of the Virgin than he would if the politics of religion had been different. At least one modern critic feels that Ben Jonson was nearer the truth than he imagined when he said of Donne's first *Anniversary*, "If it had been written of ye Virgin Marie it had been something." [53]

Finally, there has been some recent critical interest in Donne in terms of the influence of Augustine which helps this argument. William Halewood's *Poetry of Grace,* for instance, argues that Donne's interest in conversion is related to the Calvinist Augustine and to the Reformation insistence on the inexplicability of God's converting power as a means of ending rebellion and bringing man into harmonious relation with God. Halewood agrees that Donne insists on differences with Calvin and wants to restore the link between *fides* and *caritas* that Luther broke,[54] but concludes that the *Divine Poems* nevertheless reflect the direct influence of Reformation interpretations of Augustine in their prepossession with rebellious selfhood and sudden reconciliation.

The central point of Halewood's argument is certainly true— Donne's Protestantism heightens his sense of "self" and of reconciling grace. But I am interested here in the fuller picture which Halewood also acknowledges. The skepticism about Calvin and the interest in linking *fides* and *caritas*, together with the intense prepossession with Augustine and with conversion, can be further illuminated from the perspective which I bring to bear—the Franciscan Augustine, mediated to the Northern Reformation.

The work of Richard Hughes is also influential.[55] He suggests that Saint Bernard is the ultimate model for Donne's devotion to Mary in *La Corona* and that Donne develops, starting from *A Litanie* and going through the *Anniversaries*, a "myth" based on the Augustinian idea that the image of the Trinity in man is severely damaged by original sin but can be restored by meditation. Donne's ideas are developed, says Hughes, from Saint Augustine, Saint Bernard, and Saint Bonaventure. But Hughes implies an eclecticism rather than a tradition, and what he is pointing to is surely no "myth" but more simply the spiritual tradition we have outlined. Indeed, Hughes's summary fits readily with what we have described as Franciscan spirituality:

> It is a concept that was developed by St. Augustine in both the *Confessions* and, in much greater detail, in his disquisition on the Trinity, was further refined by St. Bernard, and was given brief but lucid treatment by St. Bonaventure in his treatise on *The Journey of the Mind to God*. Given Donne's early and continuing attraction to Augustine and Bernard, it's not surprising that he should have availed himself of the concept, which envisions the Trinity as being reflected in the faculties of reason, imagination, and will; that reflection being blurred as the result of original sin; but that entire image being recoverable through meditation and God-directed exercise of all the faculties.[56]

With regard to the *Holy Sonnets* in particular, Hughes suggests that they develop the above Augustinian myth and are moreover based on an Augustinian view of history which is left incomplete because of difficulties Donne was having with the Reformed doctrine of imputed grace. The main emphases of the poems are on the passion, on man's flawed nature, and on repentance.[57] Hughes's suggestions, if read in light of the foregoing analysis of Franciscan spirituality, corroborate the view that Donne was influenced by such a tradition.

From another point of view, Dennis Quinn has dealt with Donne's sermons in terms of Augustinian preaching techniques. Quinn's argument seems to me conclusive as he demonstrates that Donne owes fundamental allegiance to Augustinian principles of scriptural exegesis, which are developed mainly through Saint Bernard. Quinn also mentions a Franciscan, Fray Diego de Estella (d. 1578), as a key figure who may have influenced Donne in keeping the traditions of Augustine alive through the Renaissance.[58] Both Quinn's argument and that of Hughes indicate how Donne was in some sense influenced by the Augustinian tradition in his *Sermons* and *Divine Poems*. A complete work on this subject, however, is yet to be written. The present examination of the *Holy Sonnets* at best indicates the direction such a study might take.

The Holy Sonnets: Augustinian Devotion

More striking than the suggestions on how Donne might have been in touch with the traditions of Augustine in the Middle Ages is the conformity of the *Holy Sonnets* themselves to the total spirituality we have outlined. When we look at the suggestions critics have made with regard to the unity of these poems we find, even more than in Hughes's suggestions, that aspects of this same spirituality are indicated without the critics synthesizing their perceptions within it as a whole. For example, Miss Gardner in her edition sees the *Holy Sonnets* as being "penitential" and on "last things," with three occasional poems. Mr. Peterson, arguing the impossibility of clearly distinguishing between such motifs, reads the poems as a sequence demonstrating Anglican contrition as distinct from Catholic attrition.[59] According to the spirituality we have described, it is indeed important to see contrition at the center of the poetry, and the sort of contrition that throws emphasis on proper experience of sorrow based on love of God rather than the attrition satisfactory to the confessional, as Alexander of Hales points out. We would also expect such contrition to be described in terms of the passion which makes satisfaction for Adam's sin, inspires humility and penitence, with some meditation on the fearful proximity of last things. This conflation of motifs is what we do find throughout the *Holy Sonnets*.

First, as Martz has made clear, affective piety is a central technique throughout Donne's *Divine Poems* and is frequently used in the *Holy Sonnets* also to evoke biblical scenes—for instance, Revelation:

> At the round earths imagin'd corners, blow
> Your trumpets, Angells, and arise, arise
> From death, you numberlesse infinities
> Of soules,
>
> [7.1-3]

or Crucifixion:

> Spit in my face yee Jewes, and pierce my side,
> Buffet, and scoffe, scourge, and crucifie mee,
>
> [11.1-2]

or sometimes to stimulate fear of last things:

> Oh, my blacke Soule! now thou art summoned
> By sicknesse, deaths herald, and champion;
>
> [4.1-2]

> This is my playes last scene, here heavens appoint
> My pilgrimages last mile[.]
>
> [6.1-2]

In each case, as Martz says, "the moment of death, or the Passion of Christ, or the Day of Doom is there, now, before the eyes of the writer, brought home to the soul by vivid 'similitudes.' " [60] Donne, moreover, maintains a marked fondness for scriptural allusion, as the notes to Helen Gardner's edition adequately demonstrate. Therefore, not only do his poems show the influence of affective piety, itself frequently demonstrated in evocation of biblical scenes, but as a whole the poems reveal a deep interest in the Bible, so often alluded to as a direct source of inspiration.

Second, a graphic awareness of the contribution of Christ's blood sacrifice is one of the most distinctive themes of the *Holy Sonnets,* and for Donne, certainly, the cross is always close to the forefront of this awareness. "Marke in my heart, O Soule, where thou dost dwell, / The picture of Christ crucified, and tell / Whether that countenance can thee affright" (13.3-4). Here, on the model of Friar John's *Meditations,* the imagination is deployed and the senses stimulated to picture the event on which the Atonement rests. The scene is seldom far from our minds as we read the *Holy Sonnets.* "The Sonne of glory came downe, and was slaine" (15.11), and it is the death of "this Lambe" which "with life the world hath blest" (16.5). The "blood" that "fills his frownes, which from his pierc'd head fell" (13.6) is the same blood in which man must wash himself, paradoxically to make his sinful or red soul white with purity (4.13-14). "When I was decay'd," Donne avers, "Thy blood bought that" (2.3-4), and the poet himself wishes to be crucified as we have seen earlier, "For I have sinn'd, and sinn'd, and onely hee, / Who could do no iniquitie, hath dyed" (11.3-4). The final mystery of our salvation lies in the tremendous act of a "Creator, whom sin, nor nature tyed" but who made of himself a blood sacrifice "For us, his Creatures, and his foes" (13.13-14).

The intimate link between the bloody suffering of the cross and the fallenness of man, the connection suggested by the Franciscan formula, "Cur Deus homo si Adam non pecasset," is also constantly in Donne's mind, as we have seen in *Holy Sonnet* 11 where the poet began by wishing to endure the cross himself, because his own sin had made such suffering necessary. Such conviction of man's unworthiness naturally causes the *Holy Sonnets* to be deeply concerned with original sin. Certainly, Donne's awareness of the disastrous consequences of the fall is ubiquitous. Like man in Augustine's *City of God,* the poet is a treasonous pilgrim (4.2-3) who is enthralled to "the world, the flesh, and devill" (6.14), the trinity of afflictions consequent on original sin and renounced at baptism. His soul is "like an usurpt towne" (14.5) held by the devil since the fall, for although we are created by God we are "stolne" by Satan (15.12), and only the "Sonne of glory" (15.11) can unbind us. Until then, Donne sees that through the fall "my feebled flesh doth waste / By sinne in it, which it t'wards hell doth weigh" (1.7-8), that "black sinne hath betraid" him in body and soul "to endlesse night" (5.3), and that of his own volition he has only "sinn'd, and sinn'd" (11.3), yet further confirming his thralldom to Satan. He remembers the tree in the Garden of Eden "Whose fruit threw death on else immortall us" (9.2) and asks why mere human reason should have made original sin so disastrous for man, only to discover that the question it-self is an arrogant conceit of a reason already flawed by the fall (9.9). The only answer, as the poems repeatedly affirm, is atonement won on the cross.

A principal struggle of the poet faced with such awareness is, as Peterson suggests,to maintain an attitude which is properly contri-tional, neither arrogant nor servile, proud nor falsely humble. In his pursuit of such propriety Donne in the *Holy Sonnets* is consequently concerned to define repeatedly an attitude to contrition and penance. Indeed the center of many of the poems lies in a specific attempt of the poet to address himself directly to this question of contrition:

> Yet grace, if thou repent, thou canst not lacke;
> But who shall give thee that grace to beginne?
>
> [4.9-10]

> Teach mee how to repent; for that's as good
> As if thou'hadst seal'd my pardon, with thy blood.
>
> [7.13-14]

> Onely thou art above, and when towards thee
> By thy leave I can looke, I rise againe.
>
> [1.9-10]

In these characteristic lines (and in each case they are critical to the poem's resolution), we find an effort to define the paradox within which a balance may be preserved between fallenness and the desire to love God and repent. In such humble awareness of one's total dependence on grace, tempered by a disposition to sorrow in love of God, the contrite heart can realize grace. As Peterson points out, such contrition (based on love of God), rather than attrition (based on fear of last things), informs the *Holy Sonnets* as penitential poems.

The final criterion is the motif of last things, and in Donne the urgency of the predicament of unregenerate man (as with the Fran-ciscans and Augustine himself) is frequently made present to our awareness by allusion to the terrifying proximity of death and judg-ment: "deaths doome" (4.5) is something that constantly preys on Donne's mind. He pictures himself "summoned / By sicknesse" (4.1-2) to face judgment in terror. The anticipation of the apocalypse, when angels' trumpets blow from "the round earths imagin'd corners" (7.1) and the legions of the dead arise to find either heaven or hell, is for him a powerful and terrifying image. He sees himself a sinner poised on the brink of hell (8.4) and constantly tormented by the thought of death that will come like a thief in the night: "What if this present were the worlds last night?" (13.1), he asks. Perhaps this is his "playes last scene" (6.1), even the "minutes last point" (6.4) before "gluttonous death" (6.5) will hurl him in terror to "see that face" (6.7) which will command him to heaven or hell.

To complete the analysis we should at least raise the question of supposed threefold meditation structure in the *Holy Sonnets*. This theory has been influential and is germane in the present context because, as we have said, a seminal treatise for such patterns of meditation is the work of the Franciscan Brother John. If Donne, as is doubtful, did use Loyola's *Spiritual Exercises* in the *Holy Sonnets*,[61] we should remember also that Ignatius adopted the earlier Franciscan treatise as his model. But surely Donne's supposed interest in trinal structures derived at least partially from a source affirmed by Donne himself. In the sermons we are told repeatedly of trinities to be found in all things (so why not poems?), an insight which, for Donne, derives from Augustine and is supported, significantly, by Bernard:

> It is true that S. *Augustine* sayes, *Figura nihil probat,* A figure, an Allegory provides nothing; yet, sayes he, *addit lucem et ornat,* It makes that which is true in it selfe, more evident and more acceptable.
>
> And therefore it is a lovely and a religious thing, to find out *Vestigia Trinitatis,* Impressions of the Trinity, in as many things as we can. . . . Let us therefore, with S. *Bernard,* consider *Trinitatem Creatricem,* and *Trinitatem Creatam,* A Creating, and a Created Trinity; A Trinity, which the Trinity in Heaven, Father, Son, and Holy Ghost, hath created in our soules, Reason, Memory, and Will. [*Sermons* 3.144-45]

The *Holy Sonnets,* then, centrally concerned with contrition and the twice-born experience of regeneration, stressing the centrality of the cross to salvation and using techniques of affective piety to stimulate fear of last things as well as awe of the crucifixion itself, and informed throughout with a profound sense both of the fallen nature of man in Adam and of the link between Adam and the blood sacrifice of the Atonement, not only confirm interests well attested in Donne's other theological writings but, in the quality of the experience they offer, are what we have described as traditionally Augustinian. Even Donne's interest in threefold structures, if it does have any spiritual significance in these poems as some have argued, may also be related specifically to Augustinian inspiration.

John Donne: Latitude Man

As we can see from the initial comparison of Donne with Bonaventure, the *Holy Sonnets* can not be reduced so readily to the Augustinian criteria. Professor Battenhouse has pointed out that Donne the theologian frequently expresses himself in terms which modify the assumptions of traditional Augustinian theology,[62] and, we suggest, this aspect of the theologian appears in the poems. This is particularly true if we read Battenhouse's evidence in terms of a typical enlightenment challenge to the bases of Augustinian guilt-culture spirituality. For Battenhouse, the latitudinarian Donne believes with the humanists that ancients may be saved (*Sermons* 4.78-79), that all churches have some share in the divine light,[63] and censures Augustine for going too far against Pelagius (*Sermons* 7.203). Bonaventure had also thought the anti-Pelagian Augustine to be immoderate, but, as Battenhouse sees it, Donne's attitudes at times not only court Pelagius but are couched in terms which clearly prefigure the Cambridge Platonists. Battenhouse quotes Donne's assertion that divinity is "supernatural philosophy" and goes on to say: "Indeed, he tells us in *Biathanatos* that Christianity is 'above all *other* Phylosophies' —thus implying the notion (essentially Pelagian?) that faith is a matter of doctrines." [64] "Donne's emphasis," he continues, "falls strongly on natural religion of a Platonic variety," a point which reinforces an earlier assertion that Donne "in many ways anticipates" the attitude of the Cambridge Platonists.[65] Nor are such assertions without support. Pico, for instance, is the source of Donne's optimistic contention in *Essays in Divinity* that man is the great exemplar of the universe, "the Epilogue, and *compendium* of all this world, and the *Hymen* and Matrimoniall knot of Eternal and Mortall things," [66] and like Pico and the Renaissance Platonists, Donne maintained an interest in the relations between Christian inspiration and the prisci theologi, that hypothetical and Neoplatonist tradition which, philosophers thought, extended from Moses and Hermes Trismegistus through Plato and Plotinus to the fifteenth-century Florentine scholars. In the spirit of Ficino, Donne asserts in *Biathanatos,* "I have comfort in *Trismegistus* axiome, qui pius est summe philosophatur," [67] a statement later repeated in a sermon. Trismegistus, Zoroaster, Plato, and "some other Authors of that Ayre," says Donne, have given "clearer, and more literall expressings of the Trinity, then are in all the Prophets of the old Testament" (*Sermons* 8.55). This is why, in another sermon, he can claim:

> You shall not finde a *Trismegistus,* a *Numa Pompilius,* a *Plato,* a *Socrates,* for whose salvation you shall not finde some Father, or some Ancient and Reverend Author, an Advocate. In which liberality of Gods mercy, those tender Fathers proceed partly upon the rule, That in *Trismegistus,* and in the rest, they finde evident impressions, and testimonies, that they knew the Son of God, and knew the Trinity. [*Sermons* 4.78]

In a well-known passage which develops the latitudinarian implications of this attitude to the ancients, Donne sees the whole church in Platonist terms, with various denominations each containing an aspect of the truth which reflects a higher synthesis:

> You know I never fettered nor imprisoned the word Religion, not straightening it friarly *ad Religiones factitias* (as the Romans call well their orders of religion), nor immuring it in a Rome, or a Wittenburg, or a Geneva; . . . they are all virtual beams of one Sun. [68]

In passages such as these, acknowledging a tradition of inspiration among the pagan philosophers (especially the Platonists) which is sufficient even unto salvation, in the refusal to extend the damning effects of original sin to the ancients and children, in the willingness to see all churches as beams of one sun, we detect a latitude of both spirit and language, and we may also discover in this side of Donne's theology a sensibility approaching, as Battenhouse suggests, the Cambridge Platonists. To them also the prisci theologi, the language of Platonism, the universalism of the church and continuity of religion and philosophy, are essential.

Yet for Donne, who cherished such latitudinarian ideals and, as Evelyn Simpson says, "preached toleration in an age which demanded rigid conformity," [69] it was a cause of conflict to discover the most appropriate vocabulary for such a theology in the language of Ficino and the Florentine syncretists, tending to deemphasize the fall while affirming the probity of the ethical will. On the one hand, as we have seen, Donne's *Holy Sonnet* 11 has marked affinities with the traditionalist Bonaventure's *Laudismus de Sancta Cruce,* but it is unlike it too, and precisely the consciousness within Donne's poem of an enlightened self-assertive and ethical will marks it off from Bonaventure's hymn. A third poem will make the opposition clearer. Again by an Anglican, like Bonaventure's *Laudismus de Sancta Cruce* and Donne's *Holy Sonnet* 11 it deals with the Crucifixion. But it offers quite a different experience from either Donne or Bonaventure:

> Then scoffingly they bend the Knee,
> And spit upon his sacred Face;
> And after hang him on a Tree
> Betwixt two Thieves, for more Disgrace.
> With Nails they pierc'd his Hands and Feet,
> The Blood thence trickled to the Ground:
> The Pangs of Death his Countenance sweet
> And lovely eyes with Night confound.
>
> . . . .
>
> O wicked sin to be abhorr'd,
> That God's own Son thus forc'd to die!
> O Love profound to be ador'd;
> That found so potent Remedy!
> O Love more strong than Pain and Death,
> To be repaid by nought but Love,
> Whereby we vow our Life and Breath
> Entire to serve our God above! [70]

In this poem we have neither the pathos nor humility of the *Holy Sonnet* or the hymn, nor do we have penitence or any urgent sense of the uniqueness of the Atonement. We perceive only a gesture at affective piety, and of a very conventional sort. The poem, though the rhythms and imagery recall *Laudismus de Sancta Cruce,* lacks both the ardent quality of Bonaventure's simplicity and the passionate complexity of Donne. If we ignore for a moment the uniqueness of the different sensibilities of our three poets, on little reflection it becomes clear that Henry More, the Cambridge Platonist, understands the Crucifixion from within a different philosophic tradition than Bonaventure and Donne, as he indicates in his preface "To the Reader, Upon the first Canto of Psychozoia":

> I shall not be blamed by any thing but ignorance and malignity, for being invited to sing of the second Unity of the Platonicall Triad, in a Christian and Poeticall scheme, that which the holy Scripture witnesseth of the second Person of the Christian Trinity. As that his patrimony is the possession of the whole earth ... yet the Platonists placing him in the same order, and giving him the like attributes, with the Person of the Sonne in Christianity, it is nothing harsh for me to take occasion from hence to sing a while the true Christian Autocalon, whose beauty shall adorn the whole earth in good time.[71]

The "true Christian Autocalon" is a different subject for meditation than the crucified Jesus. Consequently, More's dying God is more an exemplar than a human person, and although More does refer in his poem to the physical details of the passion, they have an emblematic rather than an actual force. The poet remains far from embracing the physical cross itself, as Donne and Bonaventure do. He is moved rather to a dedication of love on a more abstract level and one which, we feel constantly from his writings, is increasingly desirable as it transcends the sordidness of physical reality. We should not be surprised that More very rarely writes about the Crucifixion at all. The "true Christian Autocalon" derives from a divine cosmic principle adapted from the Platonists, and man's soul too has its place in the total scheme of emanation:

> Wherefore mans soul's not by Creation,
> Nor is it generate, as I prov'd before.
> Wherefore let't be by emanation

(If fully it did not praeexist of yore)
By flowing forth from that eternall store
Of Lives and souls ycleep'd the World of life,
Which was, and shall endure for evermore.[72]

This approach to man, toying as it does with Platonist preexistence
and interpreting the fall as a declension from higher to lower degrees
of reality, rather than a fracture of human nature rendering man
abject and dependent on grace, is radically different from the guilt-
culture view of man implicit in Donne and Bonaventure. More does
not see Adam's mind and will as tragically and pathetically broken
by the fall, and his meditation on the cross consequently misses the
note of humility and penitence. For More, God's love should be re-
paid with man's love, and God has shown he loves man, "whereby,"
says More, without trouble, "we vow our life and Breath / Entire to
serve our God above!" The position More assumes about the nature
of fallen man and his redemption is the enlightenment, philosophic,
and optimistic position expressed by Plotinus, for whom the fall is
also part of a necessary "down-going or away-going" [73] from the One,
and its "vice" simply "an ignorance or lack of measure in the soul"
(1.8.8). What we find in More and Plotinus is far removed from the
theological and less optimistic position of Augustine, where reason
is certainly not enough and the "corrupt root" merits only eternal
damnation. Man is saved by the grace of God alone.

More's enlightenment thought being Platonic, its genealogy is
clear. It derives from Plotinus through Ficino and the Florentine
Neoplatonists. Significantly, the Cambridge school to which More
belonged is best known for pioneering a theology of latitude, of eccle-
siastical broad-mindedness and nondogmatic toleration, and also it
found the Church of England the most favorable intellectual environ-
ment to develop such ideas. As Battenhouse has demonstrated,
Donne is one of the early founders of this tradition. So, if we could
distinguish between our three poems by calling Bonaventure's hymn
spiritual, Donne's sonnet theological, and More's poem philosophic,
we might suggest that the peculiar energy informing the *Holy Sonnets*—and the stridency that occasionally mars them—expresses an
effort persisting throughout Donne's theology, and one which has not
been adequately described, to discover a middle way between the

guilt-culture spirituality represented by Bonaventure and the enlightenment philosophy represented by More. The *Holy Sonnets*, composed at a critical period in Donne's life when he was debating a possible career in the church, reflect the tensions of the young Renaissance latitude man attempting to express himself in the mold of older models of devotion despite aspirations to achieve new. In him we find a direct confrontation of guilt culture and enlightenment.

We have examined the traditional Augustinian side of Donne's *Holy Sonnets* in some detail and should now indicate more fully the antithetical presence of the "philosophic" Donne in these poems. Primarily it resides, as we have said, in the sense we get of that "gainfull intent" which distinguishes *Holy Sonnet* 11 from Bonaventure's hymn and which reflects the sense of an ever-assertive and constantly uncomfortable rationalizing mind, chafing before the self-abnegation required of it. As Helen Gardner points out, there is an inordinate insistence in these poems on the first personal pronoun, which gives us a strong sense of the presence of the speaker. For instance:

> Take mee to you, imprison mee, for I
> Except you'enthrall mee, never shall be free,
> Nor ever chast, except you ravish mee.
>
> [14.12-14]

Yet in lines such as these we may feel an oppressive sense of the poet's self-conscious individuality which threatens even to usurp the priority he wishes to give to God. The first four lines of *Holy Sonnet* 6, for example, contain this (not atypical) catalogue of personal doubts and worries—"*my* playes last scene," "*my* pilgrimages last mile," "*my* race," "*my* spans last inch," "*my* minutes last point"—which inevitably tends to steal the poem away from the humble and central request of line 13, "Impute me righteous." Donne certainly experiences difficulty in submitting himself to God's will, in acquiring that selflessness which, Bonaventure says, is a question of "grace, not instruction; desire, not intellect," and which imposes "silence on cares, concupiscence, and phantasms." [74] This is the opposite to the sin of speculation which Augustine condemns in the *Confessions* as "*lust of the eyes*" and describes as "a certain vain and curious desire, veiled under the title of knowledge and learning." [75] With Donne, just such a sin threatens the quality of "anonymity" we discovered in *Laudis-*

mus de Sancta Cruce. It is the "immoderate desire" he finds also in Pico, the enlightenment strain of learned and self-assertive optimism which makes Pico welcome man as the "magnum miraculum," the great miracle able to choose his own destiny. Indeed *Holy Sonnet* 12 recalls these very words of Pico's. Donne wonders, "Why are wee by all creatures waited on?" (12.1). Then he strikes an attitude perhaps self-pitying and certainly indicative of that urge of his speculating mind to question:

> Weaker I am, woe is mee, and worse then you,
> You have not sinn'd, nor need be timorous.
>
> [12.9-10]

He concludes:

> But wonder at a greater wonder, for to us
> Created nature doth these things subdue,
> But their Creator, whom sin, nor nature tyed,
> For us, his Creatures, and his foes, hath dyed.
>
> [12.11-14]

There is a significant ambivalence in these lines. The "greater wonder" may well be the fact of the Incarnation, but the comparative "greater" implies that man, despite his sinfulness, is himself a "great wonder," or "magnum miraculum," forerunner of the "philosophic" man of the Cambridge Platonists or the "Great and Wonderfull Miracle" [76] of Thomas Traherne who also adduces the prisci theologi and the language of the philosophers to prove the "infinit Dignity" of human nature.[77]

This reading of *Holy Sonnet* 12 could almost be taken as an index of the total experience we find in these poems. We respond first to a traditional spirituality but are disturbed by a secondary awareness of an alternative response. The note of disturbance is introduced by a variation of attitudes: sometimes by the implied rebuke of self-pity —"to (poore) me is allow'd / No ease" (3.12-13); or a more straightforward aggressiveness—"Thou hast made me, And shall thy worke decay?" (1.1); or a candid acknowledgment of the reality of both sides of the coin—"In prayers, and flattering speaches I court God: / To morrow I quake with true feare of his rod" (19.10-11). We may feel too that there is often something uncertain, even flawed, in the quality of the total experience which the *Holy Sonnets* offer. There is perhaps too much of the showy and flamboyant sinner, too much effort behind the humility that only makes us acutely aware of the assertive and sinful self when what the poem wants to do is suppress it. Yet we have perhaps come to admire the *Holy Sonnets,* like some of Michelangelo's statues, despite these flaws and even partially because of them. The contorted and impassioned logic, the witty paradox, the flawed spirituality and note of sensationalism are compelling.

We find preserved in Donne's *Holy Sonnets,* then, the lineaments of a spirituality which is traditionally Augustinian and peculiarly English. In a larger context we may venture that it is a spirituality shared by such poets as George Herbert and Francis Quarles but not by poets like Henry More and Thomas Traherne, who are nurtured by another tradition—a philosophic tradition of the Renaissance from which developed the moralism that replaced the traditional modes of devotion still dominant, though challenged, in Donne. Certainly in the later poets motifs such as the cross, the Augustinian fall, the fear of death and hell are much attenuated. Henry Vaughan, we shall see, is a pivotal figure, a bridge between the poetry of Donne and Herbert and that of More and Traherne. But in Donne, of all the seventeenth-century devotional poets who shared the same struggle, the effort to define himself was most strenuous and most fiercely impassioned. As Mrs. Simpson remarks, "His theology was too medieval in some respects and too modern in others." [78] Yet the ways in which Donne's *Holy Sonnets* are medieval have scarcely been adequately described. Although they are clearly poems of their times, they do belong firmly within a definable and distinctly medieval Augustinian spiritual tradition. This, despite their idiosyncratic qualities, affords the most satisfactory explanation of the spiritual unity which underlies the *Holy Sonnets.* In them the confrontation of guilt culture and enlightenment is the conflict of two types of inspiration—the "spirituality" of Saint Bonaventure and the "philosophy" of Henry More: the conflict of traditional Augustinian piety and the enlightened ideals of the latitudinarians.

Chapter Three Augustinian Spirituality
and George Herbert's *The Temple*

Donne and Herbert

The turbulence of the *Holy Sonnets* contrasts the comparative assurance of Herbert's *The Temple*. The drama of Donne's poetry, which is, in one respect, a consequence of his speculative mind in conflict with traditional modes of devotion, relaxes into the more delicate and refined harmonies of Herbert's art. Their meditations on death, as Martz points out, reflect the differences. "In all Herbert's poems on death there is no trace of fear or horror at the prospect, but a calm, mild acceptance of the inevitable, often approaching the whimsical and jesting in tone." [1] For instance, in his poem *Death*, Herbert writes:

> But since our Saviours death did put some bloud
> Into thy face;
> Thou art grown fair and full of grace,
> Much in request, much sought for as a good.[2]

Herbert's reflection is quite a contrast to Donne's deliberately evoked horror in the *Holy Sonnets* of the "feebled flesh" which "doth waste / By sinne in it" (1) and is imminently "summoned / By sicknesse, deaths herald, and champion" (4). Or consider Herbert's *The Reprisall*, which meditates the problem of grace in relation to the sacrifice of Christ: "I Have consider'd it, and finde / There is no dealing with thy mighty passion" (*Works*, p. 36). The tone is, from the beginning, reflective, and the fact that there is "no dealing" does not excite undue anxiety. True, as the poem progresses, working through the paradoxes of salvation, the emotion intensifies until the climax of the fourth stanza:

> Ah! was it not enough that thou
> By thy eternall glorie didst outgo me?
> Couldst thou not griefs sad conquests me allow,
> But in all vict'ries overthrow me?

Yet even here the reproof is gentle, rather than anguished or truly aggressive. It anticipates the perfect resolution of the closing lines:

> though I can do nought
> Against thee, in thee I will overcome
> The man, who once against thee fought.

The confidence here complements the mood of the opening lines, just as the assurance of the conclusion explains their tranquillity. Herbert never loses sight of the fact that "The man, who once against thee fought," the sinner of the first stanza, the first Adam, is redeemed "in thee," in Christ, the second Adam, his real and providential counterpart. In contrast is Donne's *Holy Sonnet* 2, which also considers the problem of grace and the Atonement. Like Herbert, Donne begins mildly, but unlike Herbert he begins with a positive rather than a negative statement:

> As due by many titles I resigne
> My selfe to thee, O God.

This claim, however, belies the developing realization in the poem that it is not at all within Donne's power to resign himself. Because the speaker does not acknowledge at the beginning what he must realize at the end, the poem becomes increasingly fraught with strain and anxiety. The ending is in violent contrast to Herbert's *The Reprisall:*

> Oh I shall soone despaire, when I doe see
> That thou lov'st mankind well, yet wilt' not chuse me,
> And Satan hates mee, yet is loth to lose mee.

Herbert's poem graciously confirms what it began by acknowledging, that even in resigning himself to God, man's will is not sufficient. Donne's poem must discover in anguish that the desire for self-resignation is a self-willed desire, and his poem consequently ends by denying what it set out to affirm. The resulting contrast in tone is striking—Herbert's relative mildness and assurance against Donne's terror of despair.

Other poems revealing this basic difference come easily to mind. Herbert's *The Holdfast* could be read with *Holy Sonnet* 16, *Judgement* with *Holy Sonnet* 7, *The British Church* with *Holy Sonnet* 18, *Vanitie* 2 with *Holy Sonnet* 13, or *The Agonie* with *Holy Sonnet* 11. In *The Agonie,* for instance, Herbert deals with the Crucifixion almost as an allegory of sin and love and exploits a typological convention of Christ as the grapes in the winepress of the cross. A complex set of analogies and correspondences sustains the second and third stanzas, where the pressing of the grapes on the cross, the "presse and vice" (*Works*, p. 37) of sin, also yields the blood, or wine, of redemption, which is love. *Holy Sonnet* 11 also deals with the Crucifixion, but the typological and analogical imagery is largely missing, except for the closing comparison with Jacob, which is made quite explicit in the text. Donne's effect comes less from a complex articulation of conventional images than from a violent personal identification with the Crucifixion evoked by daring application of the senses. Yet the difference here between Donne and Herbert, distinct as it is, would seem in the end to be one of degree rather than kind, of sensibility rather than doctrine. Donne's violence and strain, his turbulence and drama, contrast with Herbert's assurance.

This fairly consistent distinction between the two poets has been explained by Martz in terms of the influence of different meditative techniques: Donne's poetry is Jesuit, and Herbert is indebted to Saint François de Sales.[3] This suggestion is original and illuminating, though in broader terms of the theological traditions shared by our poets and the challenges and alternatives which they faced we might suggest another, and complementary, viewpoint. In Donne's *Holy Sonnets,* as we have seen, the encounter of a naturally Catholic and Augustinian consciousness with the ideals of Renaissance latitude makes for bold and violent conflict. Herbert, for his part, is a more assuredly Protestant theologian than Donne, as his acceptance of the typically Calvinist doctrines of predestination and the Covenant attests. In this acceptance we find a main reason for the differences between his poems and Donne's.

The evidence for Herbert's Calvinism is largely circumstantial but is no less convincing for that. Walton, for instance, tells us that Herbert engaged in a debate with Bishop Andrewes concerning *"Predestination,* and *Sanctity of life."* [4] Andrewes's position, though the documents are lost, would be Arminian and closer to Donne than to Herbert who argued the case for predestination. In another controversy, Herbert has, significantly, no quarrel with the Puritan Andrew Melville concerning his teaching on God or the learned divines he favors—Peter Martyr, Calvin, Beza—but only with Melville's attack on sacred rites. We may conjecture that Melville's Calvinism did not displease Herbert and that the predestination he argued against Andrewes was a Calvinist brand. *The Temple,* moreover, shows a fascination with predestination, with the election of the righteous who will inherit the kingdom. *The Water-course* is a striking example, especially in the closing lines which deal with God,

$$\text{Who gives to man, as he sees fit,} \begin{cases} \text{Salvation.} \\ \text{Damnation.} \end{cases}$$

[*Works,* p. 170]

Herbert's view of such a determinism extending into history itself is found in *The Church Militant,* where the church moves on predestined lines toward judgment. In short, as Summers has it, *"The Temple* shows that Herbert believed as strongly in predestination and the doctrine of the Covenant of Grace as he believed in the significance and beauty of the ritual."[5] For the true believer, however, belief in the Covenant (paradoxical though it may seem in our times) often yields assurance and trust. It is a John Donne, who cannot accept the assurance of such a Calvinism and is drawn rather to the Arminianism of Andrewes, for whom the problems of doubt are crippling. For Donne, the language and ideals of the Protestant latitude man complicate the traditions of medieval devotion within which he is working. For Herbert, who is also Augustinian and medieval in the main lines of his devotion, a fascination with Calvinist predestination affords his poems those qualities which most readily distinguish them from Donne's.

Herbert and the Augustinian Tradition

As far as Herbert's traditionalism is concerned, he is firmly rooted in that mainstream Augustinian spirituality we have described in the previous chapter. With Donne it was possible to demonstrate from his prose writings his highly developed interest in Augustine. Herbert has left no theological documents comparable to Donne's, and the task of establishing the sources of his thought is consequently more difficult. The most striking attempt has been that of Rosemond Tuve. Her argument is more than enough, as she says, "to keep the continuity" of the medieval traditions she outlines "unbroken at least as late as Herbert." [6] Briefly, what Miss Tuve establishes is that Herbert's poems rely heavily on the Liturgy, that he used the Sarum missal and breviary, the *Speculum Christiani*, the *Speculum humanae salvationis* and *Speculum Sacerdotale*, sermon collections like Mirk's *Festial*, and collections of hymns such as those of Prudentius and Venantius Fortunatus. He also used popular medieval lyrics which did not go out of print in the seventeenth century and the *Biblia Pauperum*, which was well known in countless editions and was, in the Renaissance, "virtually a handbook of iconographical convention" (p. 29).

One result of all this, Miss Tuve concludes, is that Herbert shares the conventions, the style, and the tone of much medieval lyric poetry. The originality of so-called metaphysical style is largely a reflection of our own inability to perceive the conventions it assumes, and the "secret of Metaphysical wit lies in a reading of life (of the nature of truth and of knowledge) inherited through at least the ten or twelve preceding centuries" (p. 136). Miss Tuve's controversial test case is *The Sacrifice*. The poem belongs with a type of medieval lyric in which Christ complains to his people from the cross. Such poems are based on the liturgical offices of Holy Week, and "most obviously . . . in the *Improperia* or Reproaches of Good Friday" (p. 24). In *The Sacrifice*, the central theme of man's ingratitude, of Christ's suffering, the ironic contrasts, the terse understatements that reflect the liturgical text, the dramatic presentation and the use of refrain are all elements shared by countless medieval lyrics of this type. The ironic metaphysical antitheses used to present human ingratitude, for example, are found everywhere in the medieval lyrics

—for instance, this *Popule meus quid feci tibi?* poem, patently a lyric of the same sort as Herbert's:

> Heilsum water i sente þe
> out of þe harde ston;
> & eysil & galle þu sentist me,
> o þer ʒef þu me non.[7]

Herbert writes:

> They give me vineger mingled with gall,
> But more with malice: yet, when they did call,
> With Manna, Angels food, I fed them all:
>> Was ever grief, etc.
>
> *[Works,* p. 34]

In each poem the tone of reproach is identical, and each poet effects a typological contrast between the Old and New Testaments, more specifically between Moses and Christ. Just as Moses clave the rock, so Christ's side is pierced with a spear, and the "Heilsum water" issuing from both is in contrast with the "eysil & galle" of man's ingratitude. The typology in the lyric is implicit but unmistakable when the Old Testament significance of water and rock is dealt with, as here, in relation to the Crucifixion. In Herbert, a strikingly similar contrast is effected. The manna which was fed to the people under Moses, a type here of Christian communion (and again implying a parallel between Christ and Moses), is in contrast to the vinegar and gall of human malice. The witty antitheses, the implicit typology, the tone of rebuke, the shared "popule meus" tradition obviously relate both poems to the same traditional sources. The refrain poem *Popule meus quid feci tibi?* of Friar William Herebert provides examples like this:

> Vor vrom egypte ich ladde þe,
> þou me ledest to rode troe.
> My volk, what habbe y do þe?
>
> *[XIV,* p. 17]

against Herbert's

> Without me each one, who doth now me brave,
> Had to this day been an Egyptian slave.

They use that power against me, which I gave:
Was ever grief like mine?
[*Works*, p. 27]

or,

In bem of cloude ich ladde þe;
And to pylate þou ledest me.
My volk, etc.
[*XIV*, p. 18]

against Herbert's

Herod and all his bands do set me light,
Who teach all hands to warre, fingers to fight,
And onely am the Lord of Hosts and might:
Was ever grief, etc.
[*Works*, p. 29]

The range of these similarities is not in any way limited to *The Sacrifice*, though there it is particularly striking. Richard Rolle's *A Song of Love-longing to Jesus* shares with Herbert's *Dulnesse*, for instance, a convention deriving no doubt from the *Song of Songs* where the beloved is described as "white and ruddy." Rolle writes, meditating the beloved on the cross:

Whyte was his naked breste, & rede his blody syde,
Wan was his faire face, his woundes depe & wyde;
[*XIV*, p. 101]

while Herbert says,

Thou art my lovelinesse, my life, my light,
Beautie alone to me:
Thy bloudy death and undeserv'd, makes thee
Pure red and white.
[*Works*, p. 115]

Not only the wit of the imagery and the play with the colors red and white is shared but the whole meditation on the cross through application of the senses, and above all the note of wistful yet ardent longing which each author expresses. The central desire of Rolle's poem,

"Send wil to my hert anly to covayte þe" and "sett me in stabylte" (*XIV*, p. 99), is precisely that consistently expressed wish of Herbert's for peace of mind and rest in God, as he says in *Dulnesse:*

> Lord, cleare thy gift, that with a constant wit
> I may but look towards thee[.]
>
> [*Works*, p. 116]

The sentiment is very close to that of Rolle just quoted, "Send wil to my hert anly to covayte þe."

Another traditional theme—that of writing in the stony heart—occurs in Herbert's *Sepulchre* (*Works*, p. 40) and *The Sinner:*

> Yet Lord restore thine image, heare my call:
> And though my hard heart scarce to thee can grone,
> Remember that thou once didst write in stone.
>
> [*Works*, p. 38]

This has readily recognizable medieval analogues, for instance:

> Ihesu þat hast me dere I-boght,
> Write þou gostly in my poȝt,
>
> . . . .
>
> For þogh my hert be hard as stone,
> ȝit maist þou gostly write þer-on.
>
> [*XIV*, p. 114]

Again, not only the image but the typological and iconographical reverberations help establish the total similarity of tone. In each case the idea of restoration of nature by grace (in Herbert "thine image," and in the lyric the gift that is "dere I-boght") moves our mind to the Atonement and to the rock as stony heart, out of which Moses brought water, as Christ brings grace. As Miss Tuve says, "In their setting Herbert's images, like the medieval ones, are potent and direct; they are not naïve and they are not over-ingenious; they are simply the natural flowering of symbolic writing" (p. 129).

We could develop these parallels further, in terms of lyrics like *A Song of Mortality* (*XIV*, p. 96) or *The Vanity of Life* (*XIV*, p. 68), which recall poems of Herbert's such as *Mortification* (*Works*, p. 98) and *Vanitie 2* (Works, p. 111), or in terms of details of style and tone, such as Rolle's sudden expostulation to Christ as "My dere—worthly derlyng" (*XIV*, p. 95), recalling Herbert's intimacies of the same sort: "Ah my deare, / I cannot look on thee" (*Works*, p. 189). There are also the characteristic, though seemingly quaint, tricks of the anagrammatical type, as in Friar Herebert's *Ave Maris Stella*, where we are reminded that the "Ave" "turnst abakward eves nome" (*XIV*, p. 20). This is simply made more elaborate by Herbert's *Ana-*$\left\{{\text{Mary} \atop \text{Army}}\right\}$ *gram* (*Works*, p. 77). I am concerned here, however, basically to reinforce Miss Tuve's conclusion and to stress the most basic spiritual affinities between Herbert and the medieval lyricists, which are often largely a matter of tone and rhythm as well as of symbol and imagery. A passage of Miss Tuve's on this point will make an apt summation:

> It would be especially tempting to remark the Yeats-like, ritual-istic, modal changes in an identical refrain when it occurs in differing contexts (an effect found in various medieval poems as well as in Herbert's). Or to demonstrate the effect of the basic structure provided by the liturgical text—flat, unelaborated statements of antitheses generally found from one like verb or noun. Or to study the curious mingling of hardness with pathos, metrically conveyed (quite independently, of course) in the Herbert and the Middle English poems. The patient, consider-ing, accusatory rise and fall of "óthĕr géf thu m̂e nón" is pre-cisely similar to the tone, especially in the final cadence, of many lines in Herbert: "The tree of life to all, but onely me," "My face they cover, though it be divine." ... Many such minute but fascinating similarities are due simply to similarities in *genre* and inspiration. [Pp. 40-41]

I wish to affirm these similarities between Herbert and the med-ieval religious lyrics because it is particularly interesting, in terms of our earlier speculations about traditional Augustinian spirituality and its mediation by Franciscans, that as much as 85 percent to 90 percent of medieval lyric poetry written in England before the Black Death was of Franciscan origin. In 1940 R. H. Robbins had already attributed 66 percent of medieval lyric poetry written before 1350 to Franciscans,[8] and Jeffrey's researches have now suggested the considerably higher figure.[9] Moreover, as I indicated briefly in the last chapter, the poems themselves are developments of specifically Franciscan preaching methods and are closely related to Franciscan preachers' handbooks. It is remarkable, but no coincidence, that very many of the popular handbooks and materials adduced by Jeffrey as Franciscan should be the very materials adduced also by Miss Tuve in her discussion of Herbert's traditionalism.

The Franciscans, as we have seen, directed their mission to the common people. Saint Francis himself had suggested the use of songs for preaching, and his suggestions were adopted by his followers.[10] It has long been recognized that Franciscans were the first in England to use vernacular verse in their sermons (p. 271), and Wycliffe's denunciation of the friars singles out this very use of poetry:

> For freres in her prechinge fordon prechinge of Crist, and prechen lesyngus and japes plesynge to þe peple. . . . For þei docken Goddes word, and totteren it by þer rimes, þat þe fowrme þat Crist ȝaf it is hidde by ypocrisie. [P. 272]

Probably because they were in the vernacular, few Franciscan sermons actually survive, but, as we have seen in chapter 2, a rash of preachers' handbooks and chronicles were written mainly as a result of John Pecham's *Lambeth Constitutions,* in which, as Jeffrey shows, the influential Franciscan archbishop "employs Franciscan standards" (p. 287) as a model for the instruction of preaching clergy. In combination with Robert Grosseteste's *Dicta,* the example of Pecham's *Constitutions* caused a "considerable boom in the production of preaching manuals" (p. 287), and the authors of these manuals seem mostly to have been Franciscans. The *Fasciculus Morum* is one example. Jeffrey points out that it is ascribed in some of the twenty-one manuscripts to the Franciscan Robert Silke (p. 291). Its divisions into discussion of the vices and virtues recalls the *Lambeth Constitutions,* and it makes specific reference to the Rule of Saint Francis. It also includes poems for the use of the preacher, and the most important of these are lyrics dealing with the passion and Crucifixion, exactly as we would expect in the Franciscan spirituality outlined in the last chapter. The *Speculum Christiani* is described by Jeffrey as the "best example of the Franciscan preaching manual which was organized to fulfill both the preaching ideal of St. Francis and the orders of the Franciscan Archbishop of Canterbury" (p. 307). Pecham's *Constitutions* are the basis of the prologue and the first four divisions of the *Speculum Christiani*, and again it uses poems centering on the Crucifixion to promote repentance and contrition. Other examples are the *Speculum laicorum*, compiled by an English friar in the archepiscopate of John Pecham and widely known and used until the seventeenth century (p. 289), or the *Speculum Sacerdotale*, another sermon collection which uses verse and which Jeffrey again ascribes to Franciscan authorship (p. 287). Other popular books of instruction, such as *The Lay Folks Catechism*, also show clear Franciscan influence.

From such a background the main body of Middle English religious lyric poetry in the vernacular issues, and in it we find the characteristic spirituality—the application of the senses, particular interest in the passion as atonement for original sin, a singular devotion to Mary, a liturgical and scriptural emphasis, an apocalyptic interest in the last things, and all centering on the stimulation of contritional response. "If the corpus of Middle English lyric poetry is rich in examples of Franciscan Biblical 'translation' and contrition spirituality it also offers examples of their adaptation of the vernacular poetic medium to liturgical and catechismic ends in the spirit of Pecham's *Constitutions* and early Franciscan preaching handbooks" (p. 361).

From Miss Tuve's establishment of Herbert's indebtedness to Middle English lyric poetry alone, it would now be possible to make a claim for the survival of traditional Augustinian spirituality as evidenced by Franciscan devotion, not only in the learned theological tradition which we have described for Donne but in a popular English tradition which extends as far as Herbert's *The Temple*. The case is even more substantial when Miss Tuve is seen so effectively to adduce as influential on Herbert not only the Liturgy but also such popular compilations as the *Speculum humanae salvationis*, the *Speculum Sacerdotale*, the *Biblia Pauperum*, and the *Festial* of John Mirk who, although a Dominican, was educated by Franciscans and whose manual of instruction for preachers, according to Jeffrey, reflects not only Pecham's *Constitutions* but also the spirituality of Mirk's own training. But perhaps the key case for our linking of Jeffrey's argument with Miss Tuve's lies in the nature of the *Biblia Pauperum* and the *Speculum humanae salvationis,* those two virtual "handbook[s] of iconographical convention" which are cited on every page of Miss Tuve's argument. The *Biblia Pauperum* receives most emphasis, and we should look at it closely. Although the authorship (not surprisingly in view of the multiplicity of the relevant traditions) has been designated anonymous, it is possible to demonstrate strong Franciscan influence, especially in the forty-leaf blockbook versions. The *Biblia Pauperum* is at one with the mass of Franciscan "specula" and of preachers' handbooks and popular compilations of devotion which are in turn the fountainhead of the bulk of medieval religious lyric poetry.

The Biblia Pauperum

The most attractive and recent edition of the *Biblia Pauperum* is by the Corvina Press from the Esztergom blockbook of forty leaves.[11] This forty-leaf blockbook was the most popular version, and a large number of original copies survive. That it was also widespread in Europe seems clear from the fact that there are ten other editions extant, from diverse origins, in which "the woodcuts are bewilderingly similar." [12] Miss Tuve, appropriately, uses the forty-leaf blockbook in her work on Herbert. For the modern enthusiast there are several facsimile editions,[13] and in the present argument, although the Corvina Press version is our first choice, we refer also to the 1859 facsimile, edited by J. Ph. Berjeau, for the simple reason that the introductory argument is faulty on a number of critical issues and can thus effectively direct our attention to what these issues are. But if we look at the *Biblia Pauperum* in no matter what edition of the blockbook of forty leaves, certain basic principles of construction are obviously related to the Franciscan spirituality we have already discussed.

The book is, first of all, an attempt to promulgate the central teachings of the Bible in popular form. The Latin text is used and explained visually by means of woodcut illustrations and by short verses. The fact that Latin is included would indicate that originally the book was for preachers, since lay folk could not speak Latin.[14]

The central panel depicts one of the main events in the life of Christ, and panels on the left and on the right depict Old Testament scenes which typologically relate to the central subject. The book follows the order of events in the central panel, so that it is essentially a series of meditations on the life of Christ. The Old Testament scenes do not themselves follow any particular order, other than that dictated by the center. Directly above the central panel is a fourth engraving depicting two prophets who comment, with words written on scrolls, on the central scene, and directly below are two more prophets who comment on the central scene with sentences from their prophecies. Immediately under this bottom panel is a verse which again explains the central illustration, and on either side of the bottom panel are further verses which also relate to the central subject. In the blank space on either side of the top engraving is a short prose passage which explains the Old Testament woodcut directly underneath and again relates it to the central subject. In all the illustrations the dress and details are contemporary. More briefly, and in more technical language, each composition consists of "one anti-type, two types and four prophets. Three *tituli,* two *lectiones* and four sayings of the prophets provide the explanation to each group of pictures." [15]

Elements of Franciscan spirituality are immediately evident, even from the format of the *Biblia Pauperum.* The book is, first of all, a set of meditations on the life of Christ and is obviously analogous to the seminal work of the pseudo-Bonaventure, the *Meditations on the Life of Christ.* Both are illustrated books and attempt to popularize the life of Christ by means which will fully engage the senses of the reader. In the *Biblia Pauperum* the woodcuts with their contemporary details and verses perform such a function.[16] The fact that verses are used of course invites comparison with the preachers' handbooks and with the Middle English religious lyrics, themselves designed to fulfill exactly such a function as the poor man's Bible. The passion too is of paramount importance, and from Gethsemane to the entombment there are nine plates dealing with the subject, which is almost one quarter of the whole book. The cross, moreover, is central to the design of each page, since the arrangement of the panels themselves is obviously cruciform. At the center of the cross which thus appears on every page is an event from the life of Christ, and the implication is surely that every other event foreshadows the crowning achievement of the Atonement. A Franciscan prepossession with the cross and the events of the passion is thus fully realized. (See plates 1-4.)

Devotion to Mary is also a marked element of the xylographer's spirituality. Mary appears in the central panel of as many as fourteen of the forty leaves of the Esztergom blockbook, and, as the editor emphasizes, the color blue is reserved exclusively for her. "Two hues of blue are to be found, a light shade of blue and a dark Prussian blue. Both were used exclusively for colouring Mary's cloak." [17] It seems clear that Mary has a uniquely favored place in the theological scheme of this version of the book, and, as in Franciscan piety, she draws our attention particularly to the human nature and suffering of Christ.

Interest in the text of Scripture is another characteristic of Franciscan spirituality which is exploited. The prophets speak from the Bible itself, and the prose of the top left and right corners is careful to cite chapter and verse, which are then applied to the subject of the central panel. The specifically scriptural content of the writing on the page is high, and the techniques of the sensual evocation of Scripture by illustration and verse are characteristically Franciscan. Finally, in the last four panels of the book, which are on apocalyptic subjects, the characteristic interest in last things, heaven and hell, is evident.

We may conclude that the attempt to make popular a series of meditations on the life of Christ, the reverence for the text of the Bible, the application of the senses seen in the woodcuts and verses, the prepossession with the cross and emphasis on the passion, the devotion to Mary, the typology, and interest in apocalypse, all together correspond to the main hallmarks of Franciscan devotion. Elizabeth Soltész writes, "in the Middle Ages the *Biblia Pauperum* originated as a handbook of poor clerics and friars" [18]—she does not, however, point directly to Franciscans.

But there is evidence even more conclusive. We might start from Berjeau's assumption that "it is pretty certain that the author or copyist of this text was not the artist who made the designs." Berjeau claims that variation between drawings and their Latin explanation "shows sufficiently that the artist did not understand the literal meaning of the Latin text." He cites four such variations, two of which seem to me to be quibbles, namely, that "in the left-hand subject, page xxxvii, Dathan and Abiram are swallowed up by the earth, with houses, 'domibus,' but not with tents 'tabernaculis,' as in the text," and that "in the right hand subject of page xxxv nothing indicates that a fire from heaven, 'ignis veniens de celo,' consumed the sacrifice of Elias." [19] In Berjeau's first case, "tabernaculum" can mean a place of worship as well as a tent, and our xylographer has shown buildings which are obviously churches falling down as well as houses. Anyway, there is no reason why the xylographer, who is concerned to depict contemporary scenes, should not use contemporary buildings instead of tents. After all, his readers did not live in tents. (See plate 1.) The second case seems even more of a quibble. That the xylographer, and his readers, knew the fire was from heaven is patently obvious from the typology of the other two panels, where the tablets are given to Moses and the Holy Ghost descends upon the apostles. By analogy, the fire also comes from God, and the point is made clear by the way in which the design isolates the handing down of the tablets, the descent of the Holy Ghost, and the sacrifice of Elijah in the top half of the available space, so that it is extremely difficult not to read them all as types of divine intervention from above. It is simply difficult to draw a fire with flames consuming the sacrifice (upward) and at the same time coming (downward) from heaven. (See plate 2.) When fire is shown descending, on page xxxviii, to destroy Sodom and Gomorrah, the consuming aspect is not represented. (See plate 1.) We may suggest also that the rising flames that consume the sacrifice of Elijah are iconographically different from the descending flames that destroy. Flames rising represent charity; inverted flames represent death.

Berjeau's other two objections have more substance. "In the right-hand subject of page xxxiv, where Elias is taken up to heaven, the chariot is not surrounded by flames, although the text says 'in cum igneo,' " and "in the right hand subject of page xxxix, is seen an angel, not the Deity, 'dominum mixum scalae,' leaning on Jacob's ladder." [20] The reason for these two variations, however, is not that the illustrator did not understand the Latin but that he deliberately used details peculiar to Franciscan hagiography and tradition. First of all, it is significant that Elias is transported, for the paralleling of the two great luminaries of the Franciscan order, Saint Francis and

Saint Anthony of Padua, with the two Old Testament prophets Elijah
and Elisha is a commonplace of Franciscan hagiography. "A rather
remarkable pattern of correlation between miracles performed by
St. Francis and his follower, the famous preacher and thaumaturgist
Anthony of Padua, and miracles performed by Elijah and Elisha,
respectively, may be traced in the early biographies." [21] Elijah fore-
tells a plague (2 Chron. 21:12-15) and so does Francis (*Brother
Leo*, p. 93). Elijah fasts forty days (1 Kings 19:8) and so does Francis (*Fioretti*, chap. 7). Elisha is called to service under Elijah (1
Kings 19:19), Anthony is called to service under Saint Francis. Elisha is a great preacher, Anthony is the first famous preacher of the
Franciscans. Just as Elisha healed a leper (2 Kings 5:1-19), so does
Anthony (*Leggende Antoniae*, pp. 74 ff.). Examples can be multiplied. Jeffrey concludes: "occasional parallels of this sort are not an
unusual feature of mediaeval hagiography, but I know of no other
such extensive correlation."

Turning to the *Biblia Pauperum* we find the Old Testament panels
frequently figuring Elijah and Elisha. Page 11, on the resurrection
of Lazarus, has, as the Old Testament type on the left, an illustration
of the dead body of the widow's son before Elijah and, on the right,
the widow's son restored to life by Elisha. Page 14 has the children
of the prophets coming to meet Elisha, and on page 19 Elisha proph-
esies incredible plenty in Samaria. On page 22 Jezebel endeavors to
compass the death of Elijah. On page 23 the children mock the
prophet Elisha. On page 34 is Elijah in the chariot of fire, and on
page 35 Elijah's sacrifice is consumed by fire from heaven. That these
representations of Elijah and Elisha are specifically Franciscan cannot be doubted for two simple reasons. First, the illustrator frequently
dresses his Old Testament prophets as Franciscans. On page 35 the
Elijah who watches his sacrifice consumed by God's flames is a Franciscan friar (see plate 2). The Elijah who is taken off to heaven in a
chariot is again dressed as a Franciscan (see plate 3), as is Elisha
who is mocked by the children on page 23 (see plate 4). And there
is another detail which is conclusive. In the depiction of Elisha
mocked by the children, not only is Elisha dressed as a Franciscan
but he has a nimbus about his head. In medieval art, Old Testament
figures are not usually given a nimbus except, as here, where they are

types of Christian saints. Certainly in the *Biblia Pauperum* this generalization holds true. There can be no doubt that the xylographer wished to show Elisha as a type of Christian saint; and who more appropriate for the Franciscan artist than Saint Anthony?

This brings us back to the fiery chariot and Berjeau's objection that it is represented not with flames but with four wheels. First of all, this is Elijah's chariot, and Elijah, dressed as a Franciscan, is a type of Saint Francis who is riding heavenward in the chariot of the order of Franciscans which he founded. Such an interpretation is not farfetched but would be timely in context of the antifraternal polemics of the fourteenth century, when friars were accused specifically of being *gyrovagi*. The similarity between a *gyrus* and a *rota* did not escape comment, and Friar John Pecham deals with it when he argues that not all wandering is *girovagacio,* citing the example of Paul. He says rather that friars are the chariot wheels of the Lord:

> Religiosi igitur pro fratribus elemosinas petituri, sicut Paulus pro collectis faciendis per se et per alios laboravit . . . aut predicaturi populo vel bonum ecclesie alitur procurantes, non sunt girovagi appellandi sed rote Domini, quas rapit vite spiritus euntes et redeuntes in modum fulguris coruscantis.[22]

It would seem, therefore, in reply to Berjeau's objection that the xylographer did not understand the Latin text, that in fact the xylographer was representing not simply Elijah going heavenward in a chariot of fire but Saint Francis borne along on the wheels of the Lord, the chariot of his wandering Franciscans. The xylographer passed up the flames around the chariot simply to make its four wheels absolutely plain.

Similar Franciscan tradition is the answer also to the objection that instead of God the xylographer depicts "an angel, not the Deity, 'dominum mixum scalae' leaning on Jacob's ladder." Even here Berjeau fails to see that there are three angels, not one, and what the illustrator is representing is a version of the six-winged seraph which appeared to Saint Francis in his celebrated vision on Mount Alverna, crucified, as a type of Christ. (See plate 5). This vision in turn became the subject of the widely read treatise of the Franciscan Saint Bonaventure, *The Mind's Road to God.* Bonaventure begins by explaining Saint Francis's own vision of the six-winged seraph, the type of Christ. He goes on to say that "the symbol of the six-winged Seraph signifies the six stages of illumination, which begin with God's creatures and lead up to God, to Whom no one can enter properly save through the Crucified." [23] The stages of this mystical ascent are compared specifically to Jacob's ladder: "Since, then, we must mount Jacob's ladder before descending it, let us place the first rung of the ascension in the depths" (p. 10). The ascent itself, following the stages of the seraph's wings, is a "threefold progress," for "our mind has three principal aspects. One refers to the external body, wherefore it is called animality or sensuality; the second looks inward and into itself, wherefore it is called spirit; the third looks above itself, wherefore it is called mind" (p. 8). The basic threefold scheme is further divisible: "Since, however, all of the aforesaid modes are twofold—as when we consider God as the alpha and omega . . . hence it is necessary that these three principal stages become sixfold" (p. 9). Bonaventure also makes clear that the threefold division is a type of the Blessed Trinity itself: "Following the order and origin and comportment of these powers, we are led to the most blessed Trinity itself." "When, therefore, the mind considers itself, it rises through itself as through a mirror to the contemplation of the Blessed Trinity —Father, Word, and Love—three persons coeternal, coequal, and consubstantial: so that each one is in each of the others, though one is not the other, but all three are one God" (p. 26). So the six-winged seraph, which divides into three, not only represents the human mind but "represents in three ways the most blessed Trinity" (p. 26).

Here we have the basic materials necessary for understanding the xylographer's true intent in the *Biblia Pauperum*. Jacob's ladder is a specifically Franciscan depiction of the mind's ascent to God. The three angels represent not only the faculties of the mind on various stages of the ladder but the Blessed Trinity itself, as well as, by their cruciform shape, that favorite subject of Franciscan devotion, the cross. The same motif is used on page 12 where three angels appear to Abraham who is pointedly dressed as a friar. A full commentary on the plate is contained in a passage near the end of *The Mind's Road to God* which makes clear the connection of Saint Francis's vision to the faculties of the contemplative mind (which, as we see, recall the Trinity), to the representation of the suffered Christ, and to the motif of Jacob's ladder:

> That was shown to the blessed Francis when, in the transport of contemplation on the high mountain—where I thought out these things which I have written—there appeared to him the Seraph with the six wings nailed to the cross, as I and several others have heard from the companion who was with him when he passed over into God through the transports of contemplation and became the example of perfect contemplation, just as previously he had been of action; as another Jacob is changed into Israel, so through him all truly spiritual men have been invited by God to passage of this kind and to mental transport by example rather than by word. [P. 44]

The xylographer did not misunderstand the written words he was illustrating. He is far from omitting God, as those who have eyes to see will acknowledge, and his contrivance in this plate is sophisticated. Just as the nimbus on Elisha makes him a type of the Christian Saint Anthony, so the God of Jacob prefigures the Trinity.

It is not necessary at this point to conduct an extensive examination of the *Speculum humanae salvationis,* the other important popular medieval book which influenced Herbert's poetry. It too is a handbook of popular devotion, with illustrations and verses of the type of the *Biblia Pauperum,* and it has long been acknowledged that there are intimate links between the two books. "The *Speculum humanae salvationis,*" writes Berjeau, "bears so strong a resemblance to the *Biblia Pauperum,* that it may be said to be the work of the same engraver." His opinion was anticipated by Camus and by Ottley,[24] and Soltész draws our attention to the same fact of common inspiration.[25] There can be little doubt that the spirituality of both books springs from a common source, at one with the extensive collection of specula which emerged in the later Middle Ages as a result of Franciscan zeal.

It can, I think, be fairly concluded on the authority of Miss Tuve's arguments and the discoveries of Jeffrey concerning Middle English lyric poetry, together with the evidence here presented with regard to the *Biblia Pauperum* and the *Speculum humanae salvationis,* that the medieval tradition on which George Herbert's devotional poetry predominantly draws is (as with the *Divine Poems* of John Donne) primarily Augustinian, mediated to the Renaissance through a devotional tradition, mainly Franciscan.

The Temple: Augustinian Devotion

As with Donne, there has been a certain amount of recent critical interest in Herbert from the point of view of the influence of Augustine, but there has been no systematic treatment of the subject. In 1954 Malcolm Ross had already talked of Herbert's "Franciscan sensibility," [26] and in 1959 Rosemond Tuve's fine essay on "George Herbert and *Caritas*" directed attention to Augustinian influence on the poems, noting also Herbert's fascination with the Incarnation and passion.[27] Arnold Stein has more recently found Augustinian aesthetics useful for a study of Herbert's lyrics,[28] as has Michael P. Gallagher for a study of his rhetoric.[29] Certainly, in terms of the criteria outlined in chapter 2, the influence of traditional Augustinian spirituality is as striking in Herbert's poems as in Donne's. Both authors are deeply concerned with an Augustinian view of original sin in its connection with the Atonement. Both write what Ross calls a "poetry of Crucifixion," [30] using similar techniques of affective piety, especially to evoke the cross. Both are deeply influenced by the Bible and are concerned with the movement of the mind to conversion and repentance. Both are fond of apocalyptic imagery, and in Herbert, as in Donne, we find that devotion to Mary, though suppressed, is not easily rejected.[31]

The yield of these emphases on Herbert's poetry is obvious. To change the order of approach slightly, it is first of all clear that his poems are firmly scriptural. As Herbert avows in *Discipline,*

> Not a word or look
> I affect to own,
>   But by book,
> And thy book alone.

> [*Works,* p. 178]

Such pieces as *The Pearl: Matt. 13:45, The Odor: 2 Cor. 2:15,* or *Coloss. 3.3* and *Ephes. 4.30* bear in their very titles the scriptural subjects on which they are based. The *Holy Scriptures* I demonstrates, moreover, the ardent feeling which accompanies Herbert's concern for the Bible:

> Oh Book! infinite sweetnesse! let my heart
> Suck ev'ry letter, and a hony gain
> Precious for any grief in any part.
>
> [*Works*, p. 58]

For, "Who can indeare / Thy praise too much?"; "Thou are joyes handsell: heav'n lies flat in thee, / Subject to ev'ry mounters bended knee" (*Works*, p. 58). The Latin poem on the same subject, *In S. Scripturas,* demonstrates this same fervent devotion:

> Sacratissima charta, tu fuisti
> Quae cordis latebras sinúsque caecos
> Atque omnes peragrata es angiportus
> Et flexus fugientis appetitûs.
>
> [*Works*, p. 411]

Throughout *The Temple,* there are countless individual lines and metaphors inspired by the Bible, such as the winepress in *The Agonie* by Isaiah, chapter 63, or the long poem *Providence* by Psalm 104 (in the Authorized version entitled "A meditation upon the mighty power, and wonderful providence of God"). The allusion in line 22 of *Businesse,* "And two deaths had been thy fee" (*Works*, p. 113), is to "the second death" or damnation of Rev. 20:6, and the odd description in *The Pearl* of "the head / And pipes" (*Works*, p. 88) may be explained from Zech. 4:12, the "two olive branches, which through the two golden pipes emptie the golden oyle out of themselves."

Such examples can readily be multiplied, as a brief glance at Hutchinson's notes to the Oxford edition will soon attest. But Herbert's deep knowledge and love of the Bible are also made present through the typological techniques which inform his work at every turn. Some poems, indeed, assume a knowledge of the Scriptures on which they depend before they will even reveal their meaning. *The Bunch of Grapes* is a good example. The conceit of the title depends on the reader recognizing the story of Num. 13:23, where the Israelites journeying toward the promised land accept a "cluster of grapes" as a sign of fulfillment. The bunch of grapes of the Old Testament is thus, in the poem, a sign of Christ "the true vine" (John 15:1), a type which becomes commonplace, for instance, through the *Biblia Pauperum* where the bunch of grapes borne on a pole is a figure of regeneration. The same metaphor is used again in *The Agonie,* where the crucified Christ is put in the winepress of the cross, "wrung with pains" for our sins, yet producing "that liquour sweet and most divine" (*Works,* p. 37) of our salvation. In *Peace* we are meant to recognize in the lines, "There was a Prince of old / At Salem dwelt" (*Works,* p. 125), the biblical figure of Melchisidec, "King of Salem, which is, king of peace" (Heb. 7:2), who is a type of Christ, since he "brought forth bread and wine" (Gen. 14:18). In *Jordan* the allusion in the title is to Elisha's advice to Naaman to cleanse himself in Jordan (2 Kings 5:10), which thus becomes a type of Christian grace. *Joseph's Coat* depends on our recognition of the typological relation of the story of Joseph, sold by his brothers, his coat torn and sprinkled with blood, his body put into a well, and that of Christ sold by his disciple, the coat of his flesh torn with nails, and laid in a tomb. The parallels are again familiar to readers of the *Biblia Pauperum* or the *Speculum humanae salvationis. The Sacrifice* is another poem replete with a series of types and dense with allusions which assume a deep knowledge and love of the Bible, and other examples could readily be found to illustrate the literal truth of those lines of the *Holy Scriptures* 2:

> Thy words do finde me out, & parallels bring,
> And in another make me understood.
>
> [*Works,* p. 58]

The prepossession with Scripture is not, as we can already see, an unimaginative one, and, following the traditions of the Franciscan spirituality to which we are concerned to relate him, Herbert's application of the senses is a wholly characteristic technique for evoking the scriptural basis of his poem. Thus, in *The Sacrifice* Christ talks directly from the cross, his rebuke to mankind informed not only by the logic of his argument but by the pathos of the situation itself, which we are forced to meditate by Herbert's composition of place:

> Lo, here I hang, charg'd with a world of sinne,
> The greater world o' th' two; for that came in
> By words, but this by sorrow I must win:
> Was ever grief, etc.
>
> [*Works*, p. 33]

Similar dramatic immediacy underlies the effectiveness of, for example, *Longing,* where we are involved in the experience of spiritual aridness by the poet's deliberate stimulation of the senses:

> My throat, my soul is hoarse;
> My heart is wither'd like a ground
> Which thou dost curse.
> My thoughts turn round,
> And make me giddie; Lord, I fall,
> Yet call.
>
> [*Works,* p. 148]

In *Redemption* the situation is again presented dramatically to involve us in the ironies of the pilgrim's unenlightened search for grace. The whole host of familiar details from contemporary life, which contribute to the effect of Herbert's poems in general, may also be conceived, on the model of the illustrations in the *Biblia Pauperum* and the example of the Franciscan preachers of the Middle Ages, as deliberate applications of the senses by meditation on the creatures, which are in turn referred to a higher end.[32] But, as Herbert says:

> Starres are poore books, & oftentimes do misse:
> This book of starres lights to eternall blisse.
>
> [*Works,* p. 58]

The glory of nature is the book of the creatures which must be referred to the higher authority of Scripture. Yet the creatures are not denied. A posy of flowers provides a meditation on human mortality (*Life*), as do infants' swaddling clothes, a young boy's bed, the music in which a young man takes delight, the "house and home" (*Works,* p. 98) of the family man, and the fireside chair of an old person, by providing, in each case, a chilling analogy to funeral appurtenances (*Mortification*). Elsewhere, a pulley provides a metaphor for providence that dictates man's restlessness on earth (*The Pulley*), sin as a sycamore tree (*The World*), and a game of bowls represents God's unaccountable ways to man. "My thoughts are all a case of knives" (*Works,* p. 90), writes Herbert, "Wounding my heart," and elsewhere he is "a blunted knife" (*Works,* p. 37). The ways of grace put "new wheels to our disorder'd clocks" (*Works,* p. 64), and, in perhaps the best poem of all, a collar represents the bonds between God and man, sometimes felt as restrictive, sometimes realized as providential.

Application of the senses, then, is a basic technique in Herbert's poetry, whether through dramatic composition of place, or use of familiar and homely detail, in the manner of the illustrations of the *Biblia Pauperum* or the *Meditations on the Life of Christ.* Herbert's attitude to the creatures is, moreover, explicitly traditional. We are told in *Mattens:*

> Indeed mans whole estate
> Amounts (and richly) to serve thee[.]
>
> [*Works,* p. 63]

Yet there is a danger that man will study heaven and earth to the exclusion of "him by whom they be" (*Works,* p. 63). The creatures are, in Bonaventure's term, an inferior light and must be referred to God,[33] as the closing stanza of *Mattens* indicates:

> Teach me thy love to know;
> That this new light, which now I see,
> May both the work and workman show:
> Then by a sunne-beam I will climbe to thee.
>
> [*Works,* p. 63]

Herbert's poetry also conforms to traditional Augustinian spirituality in its remarkable emphasis on the passion of Christ, and particularly the motif of the cross. For Herbert, the Crucifixion and the blood sacrifice enacted there are at the center of countless poems. In his Latin verse there is a group of twenty-one poems specifically on *Passio discerpta,* the events of the passion. Through characteristic application of the senses, we are invited to meditate in detail subjects such as the bloody sweat (*In sudorem sanguineum*), the pierced side (*In latus perfossum*), the spitting and mocking (*In sputum et conuicia*), the crown of thorns (*In coronam spineam*), the slaps (*In alapas*), the scourge (*In flagellum*), and the cross itself (*Cristus in cruce*). In *The Temple, The Sacrifice* is of course a prime example of a poem based on a meditation of the cross, as is *Redemption*, which turns on the pilgrim's realization that the grace he so seeks is found in the one place he least expects to find it, among "a ragged noise and mirth / Of theeves and murderers" (*Works*, p. 40) at the cross. *The Agonie* is an elaborate conceit on the cross as a winepress from which the blood of salvation issues as wine, and even in *Easter*, a poem which celebrates resurrection, our attention is soon focused on the event that makes celebration possible:

> The crosse taught all wood to resound his name,
> Who bore the same.
> His stretched sinews taught all strings, what key
> Is best to celebrate this most high day.
>
> [*Works*, p. 41]

The poem entitled *The Crosse* is about the nature of human affliction but directs our attention also to the great exemplar of patient suffering before which all protest becomes quiet. In *Good Friday*, the opening lines draw our attention to the cross and the bloody sacrifice:

> O My chief good,
> How shall I measure out thy bloud?
>
> [*Works*, p. 38]

The poet continues to meditate "The whips, thy nails, thy wounds, thy woes" (*Works*, p. 39), which alone will dispel sin. Elsewhere Herbert is fascinated by the coincidence of Good Friday and his birthday and composes a Latin poem on the subject which again focuses on the cross:

> Cvm tu, Christe, cadis, nascor; mentémque ligauit
> Vna meam membris,harula, téque cruci.
>
> [*Works*, p. 434]

Another Latin poem, *De signaculo crucis*, protests the puritan repudiation of the sign of the cross: "namque vestra crux erit / Vobis fauentibúsque, vel negantibus." Other pieces, like *The Thanksgiving, The Reprisall, Affliction 2, Church-lock and key, Unkindnesse, Conscience, An Offering, The Bunch of Grapes*, and many more, deal with the passion and Atonement. It is, in short, hard to read far in *The Temple* without acknowledging the persistence of Herbert's devotion to the cross.

Finally, in connection with the meditation of the cross and the contritional response it so clearly invites, there is a constant concern for last things. Poems like *Mortification, Life, Decay, Vanitie 1, Miserie, The Quip, Vanitie 2, The Dawning, The Flower* are examples, from a list which again could be much extended, of a recurring meditation on death and human mortality found throughout *The Temple*. The recurring message behind Herbert's reflections on death is that they should inspire us to look beyond the grave, by the grace of God, repentant:

> Man, ere he is aware,
> Hath put together a solemnitie,
> And drest his herse, while he has breath
> As yet to spare:
> Yet Lord, instruct us so to die,
> That all these dyings may be life in death.
>
> [*Works*, p. 99]

Most important, in relation to the motif of last things and an inspiration to a contrite disposition, is the deliberately apocalyptic ending of *The Temple,* which recalls the conclusion of the *Biblia Pauperum.* Just as the *Biblia Pauperum* ends with a traditional series of meditations on judgment, hell, and the glorification of the elect, so Herbert concludes *The Temple* with a series of poems entitled *Death, Dooms-Day, Judgement, Heaven,* and *Love 3.* In each case the apocalyptic emphasis is characteristic of the traditional spirituality from which both the *Biblia Pauperum* and *The Temple* emerge. And here, as in Herbert's most characteristic poems, we also experience a turning, a conversion of the will—"My deare, then I will serve" (*Works,* p. 189)—in which the sinful self is overcome. This humble, essentially penitential, conversion characteristically issues for Herbert into the love feast, the eucharist, which, as Ross has demonstrated, is a particular fascination for the author of *The Temple.*[34] In consequence, there is an assurance in Herbert's treatment of death issuing into predestined communion, which, as we have seen, is absent in Donne.

The combination of Miss Tuve's argument with Jeffrey's is fruit-
ful, therefore, for the understanding of Herbert's poems. Herbert's
art is clearly indebted both stylistically and thematically to Middle
English lyric poetry and the popular spirituality which surrounds it,
and the vast bulk of medieval religious lyrics are Franciscan in origin,
as are many of the handbooks and guides for preachers such as Miss
Tuve cites. The examination of the important *Biblia Pauperum* confirms the link and promotes the conclusion that Herbert shares in the
fullest manner that Augustinian spirituality of the Middle Ages as
it was mediated by the Franciscans, defenders and promulgators of
the true Augustine. The poems of *The Temple* confirm this conclusion. This Augustinian tradition, therefore, essentially links Herbert's
poems of *The Temple* with the *Divine Poems* of John Donne. Both
authors are basically medieval, and both reflect the prepossessions of
a guilt-culture spirituality based on Saint Augustine. Yet neither man
can be called simply medieval, and one measure of each poet's uniqueness lies in the way he rises to the challenges of his own times in
terms of the medieval traditions he inherits. In Donne we have examined the contribution of latitudinarian idealism, and in Herbert
we have suggested that the Reformation doctrines of predestination
and the Covenant account for some of the key differences between
his poems and Donne's. To this aspect of Herbert we now direct our
attention.

Chapter Four George Herbert and Juan de Valdés: The Franciscan Mode and Protestant Manner

For a fuller explication of *The Temple* it is illuminating to consider the relationship of Herbert to Juan de Valdés, harbinger of the Reformation in both Spain and Italy. Valdés was also influential in the early Reform movement in England, and Herbert knew of him at least from Nicholas Ferrar's translation of the *Divine Considerations*,[1] on which Herbert wrote a commentary.[2] Significantly, both Herbert and Valdés inherit Franciscan and Augustinian backgrounds, and each is faced with the problem of reconciling such a background with characteristic Reformation doctrines of the Covenant, justification by faith, and predestination.

The example of Valdés, who forged a middle way between Protestant Luther and Catholic Spain, was considered ideal by early Anglican theologians, and, in the Caroline church, the pursuit of this ideal survived most splendidly at the community of Little Gidding where Valdés was translated. The degree to which the Ferrars adapted the main lines of Valdesian thought to their community and the degree to which it in turn influenced Herbert have been largely ignored. But the comparison of Herbert to Valdés is significant, partly because a direct influence is probable and certainly because the parallel theological and spiritual problems of Herbert and the Valdesians illuminate some of the most important religious issues of the times.

Herbert and Juan de Valdés

The commentary on Nicholas Ferrar's *Divine Considerations* is a useful guide to Herbert's opinions on Valdés. It is clear from the start that Herbert's attitude is not one of unqualified acclaim. He disagrees, for example, with Valdés's view of Scripture when it appears that Valdés wants simply to subordinate the Bible to the Holy Spirit. Herbert is evidently cautious about what might turn out to be anarchism implicit in Valdés's strong insistence on the spirit.

Yet Herbert insists also that Valdés is "a true servant of God" and wonders that "God in the midst of Popery should open the eyes of one to understand and expresse so clearly and excellently the intent of the Gospell in the acceptation of Christs righteousnesse (as he sheweth through all his Considerations)" (*Works,* pp. 304-5). Herbert is moved by "the great honour and reverence which he [Valdés] everywhere beares towards our deare Master and Lord" and by the "setting his merit forth so piously, for which I doe so love him." Herbert also admires the *Considerations* for their "many pious rules of ordering our life, about mortification, and observation of Gods Kingdome within us" (*Works,* p. 305). This isolation of the questions of righteousness, the merits of Christ, mortification, and the inner experience of spiritual regeneration ("Gods Kingdome within us") is wholly characteristic of the covenanter and predestinationist theology which Herbert himself espoused and about which Valdés's theology also revolves.

Joseph Summers's argument that Herbert "attempted to read Valdesso charitably" but was basically out of sympathy with much of what he found is therefore one-sided.[3] There is no teaching, for example, in the *Divine Considerations* that men are perfected in this world, which Summers claims is one of Valdés's basic assumptions.[4] Valdés insists time and time again that men grow to perfection "litle by litle" and never achieve it in this life.[5] Herbert, for his part, does not hesitate to use the concept of perfection (and in a looser manner than Valdés ever does in the *Divine Considerations*) when he argues that "holy Scriptures have not only an Elementary use, but a use of perfection, and are able to make the man of God perfect" (*Works,* p. 306). Although Herbert may be justifiably cautious of antinomian tendencies in Valdés, and although he is clearly grieved by the Spanish Reformer's tendency to exalt the spirit above the letter, his attitude amounts to far less than repudiation. Even the most blunt statement of disagreement—"there is no more to be said of this Chapter but that his opinion of the scripture is unsufferable"—is modified by the significant observation that Valdés's "owne practice seemes to confute his opinion, for the most of his Considerations being grounded upon some text of scripture, shewes that he was continually conversant in it" (*Works,* pp. 317-18).

Herbert characteristically talks as if a difference in degree rather than kind separates his position from that of Valdés. He "slights the Scripture *too much,*" he·has "*too slight* a regard" (*Works,* pp. 306, 317; my emphases) for Scripture, and one doubtful teaching in the 32d *Consideration* is cleared up, says Herbert, if we read *Consideration* 33 (*Works,* p. 310). Herbert himself sums up the gist of Valdés's whole teaching on the Scriptures when he remarks in a commentary on the 32d *Consideration:* "Indeed he that shall so attend to the bark of the letter, as to neglect the Consideration of Gods Worke in his heart through the Word, doth amisse." (*Works,* p. 309).[6] Herbert's English good sense and Valdés's Spanish mysticism are not simply incompatible: indeed, Herbert's spirituality, and for good reasons as we shall see, is close to that of Valdés. Although there are differences, there is a more important underlying agreement, and an understanding of Valdesian thought provides some considerable illumination of Herbert's poems.

Finally, I am not forgetting that Ferrar's translation of the *Divine Considerations* was completed in 1632, by which time Herbert was no doubt well advanced in his work on *The Temple.* There is no telling how long Ferrar was engaged on the translation, and the following argument really concerns the reasons why Ferrar undertook to translate Valdés at all: probably because the Valdesian ideal spoke so strongly to the Little Gidding community as it was already established. But Valdés has remained a largely unknown writer among critics of literature in our period, and an exposition of his thought, its background and style, is appropriate at this point.

Valdés: The Augustinian Background

The problem of Valdés's Lutheranism, his Erasmianism, and of the native Spanish contribution to his theology is a vexed one. Valdés was introduced to Erasmian thought at the University of Alcala, where he studied as an undergraduate, and the early *Dialogue on Christian Doctrine* shows clear influence of the Dutch humanist. Not only does the form of the discourse recall the Erasmian colloquy, but Erasmus himself is cited as an authority.[7] Marcel Bataillon characterizes the work as a "moderate Erasmian catechism" [8] but goes on to affirm that "an irreversible movement" sets in between the *Dialogue on Christian Doctrine* and Valdés's next important work, the *Alfabeto Christiano*. This firmly "separates Valdés from Erasmus," [9] and in the transition from the *Dialogue* to the *Alfabeto*, affirms Mergal, "Erasmus disappears." [10]

At the University of Alcala, however, Valdés was introduced to more than Erasmian humanism and biblical scholarship. Alcala was the foundation of Cardinal Ximines de Cisneros (1436–1517) and was intended by him to promote an energetic program of reform which he hoped to effect within the church. Cisneros, claims Bataillon, "dominates so clearly the religious life in Spain during the twenty years which precede the outbreak of the Reformation, that we cannot do otherwise but to transport ourselves to his time if we want to understand the attitude of Spain in facing the Protestant revolution." [11] Granted his central significance, it is of primary importance to us that Cardinal Cisneros was a Franciscan (provincial, indeed, of his order), for his university reflects the ideals of the hardcore Franciscan spirituality through which, like so many great Franciscans, he hoped to check the worldly abuses of the church.

First (and despite the fact that he founded a university) the main drive of Cisneros's mission was popular. He encouraged not only translation of traditional devotional writings into the vernacular but translations of the Bible as well. The list of works thus made available to unlearned audiences is an impressive and, in some respects, a familiar one.[12] There is, as we might expect, a considerable literature based on the life of Christ. Some examples are: the *Vita Christi*, by Ludolfo de Sajonia (Alcala, 1502–3); *Vita Christi*, by Maestro Francesco Eximeniç (Granada, 1496); *Vita Christi fecho por coplas,* by Fr. Iñigo de Mendoza (Zamora, 1482, 1483, 1492; Seville, 1506); *Retablo del cartuxo sobre la vida de nuestro redentor Jesu Christo,* by Juan de Padilla (Seville, 1513, 1516, 1518; Alcala, 1529).

Bonaventure is also well represented, as are the apocryphal works ascribed to him, including the favorite *Meditations on the Life of Christ,* published in Valladolid in 1512 as *Meditaciones sobre la vida de Nro. Redemptor y Salvador Iesu Christo.* Other Bonaventuran or pseudo-Bonaventuran translations are: the *Soliloquio* (Seville, 1497; Burgos, 1517; Alcala, 1525); *Forma novicorum* (Seville, 1520); *Doctrina cordis* (Toledo, 1520, 1525); *Espejo de disciplina* (Seville, 1502). Another favorite was also rendered into Spanish, the apocryphal Augustinian *Meditaciones, soliloquio y manual* (Valladolid, 1511, 1515; Alcala, 1526).

Selections from the Holy Scriptures were made available in the *Epistolas y Evangelios* (Toledo, 1512, 1523, 1535; Seville, 1526), and the *Epístolary Evangelivs, siquier liciones de los domingos e fiestas solennes de todo el anyo e de los santos* (Zaragoza, 1495; Salamanca, 1498). Both of these are liturgical compilations of the type we have seen made popular by Franciscans in fourteenth-century England, and Cisneros's program included too, as we might expect, a popular Hours of the Blessed Virgin, the *Horas de Nuestra Señora* (Paris, 1495, 1499, 1502, 1507, 1509).

There were translations also of Boethius (the *Consolación* appeared in Seville in 1497, 1499, 1511, 1518, 1521; Tolosa, 1488) and of the Augustinian and Boethian *De los remedios contra próspera y adversa fortuna,* of Petrarch (Valladolid, 1510; Seville, 1513, 1516, 1524; Zaragoza, 1518). Last but not least there was, in the popular *speculum* tradition, the *Speculum humanae vitae* of Roderigo Sánchez de Arévalo (Zaragoza, 1491), and Cisneros himself drew up a popular catechism to assist priests in the instruction of their congregations.

Even a brief review of the program put into operation by Cisneros will show how wholly characteristic it is of Franciscan spirituality. There is a strong emphasis on Bonaventuran and traditional Augustinian theology, and on a high contemplative ideal never divorced from a passionately active concern with a popular mission. The Scriptures and the life of Christ are of primary importance to Cisneros, and meditative aids and translations to make these available to the unlearned are of key importance.

Cisneros insisted too that a proper knowledge of Hebrew, Greek, and Latin was necessary for a responsible approach to the Scriptures. Consequently, an Erasmian emphasis on textual studies was strong at Alcala,[13] where it was espoused by Valdés and, despite the doubtful phrases of certain *Considerations,* was not to be abandoned by him for the rest of his life.[14] In short, the university program is a "magnificent manifestation, in cultural form, of Cisneros' Evangelical-Franciscan spirit," [15] and the ethos of traditional Augustinian and Franciscan spirituality was absorbed at Alcala by the young undergraduate, Juan de Valdés, who, even though he was not studying for the priesthood, was required to dress and behave like a clerical student.[16]

A further aspect of Valdés's background needs to be mentioned briefly at this point, namely, the mystical movement of the Alumbrados, which scholars agree in some sense influenced Valdés's theology and which is also closely connected to the Spanish Franciscans. The name Alumbrados (the "enlightened ones") covers a variety of spiritual phenomena, and in its loosest sense indicates a revival of mysticism in sixteenth-century Spain, stressing the experience of personal illumination in a soul dwelling intimately with God. A number of theories have been suggested to explain the Alumbrados,[17] but it is generally agreed that they were inspired by the ideals of Cisneros's popular Franciscan evangelism. Here we can adduce the valuable evidence of Pedro Ruiz de Alcaraz, a heretical and major figure of a branch of the Alumbrados known as the *abandonados* or *dexados.*[18]

Alcaraz was tried and eventually executed by the Inquisition. In the early days of his imprisonment, however, he felt the authorities were simply laboring under some misapprehension about the nature of his thought and, when this had been cleared up, he would be released. Consequently, in an early letter (1524), he explains in some detail the origins of the movement to which he belonged.[19] He says that the Alumbrados were actually started by Franciscans, and he names Fr. Francesco Ocaña and Fr. Francisco Olmillos. He goes on to explain how his own position differed from the orthodox Franciscan one and how he had clashed with the order. Later, under pressure, Alcaraz admits that the chief, indeed the only, direct source of his own peculiar religious ideas was Isabel de la Cruz. Isabel, herself subjected to the Inquisition, was a member of the third order of Saint Francis and, according to Alcaraz, had developed her ideas from specifically Franciscan sources.[20]

Although obviously influenced and motivated by the Franciscan reform of Cisneros, both Isabel and Alcaraz must obviously have gone beyond the limits of what the established church considered orthodoxy in the pursuit of their own ideals. Neither Ocaña nor Olmillos aroused the suspicion of the inquisitors, even though their criticism of the church was overt. The key issue on which Isabel and Alcaraz (and after them Valdés) transgressed was the doctrine of justification by faith. The term itself is never used by Alcaraz, being a particularly Lutheran formula, but it appears everywhere in Valdés, as it does in the Valdés-inspired *Beneficio di Christo,* and in the works of Bernardino Ochino. To the Inquisition this whole group of writers seemed singularly dangerous, and for the inquisitors, we might say, the root error was already present in the central passionate conviction of Isabel and Alcaraz—that one could find absolute assurance of salvation only by abandoning oneself directly to the love of God. Isabel's teaching involves a clear distinction between faith and works. Her "idea of 'God's love,' " writes Sanjuan, "and the believer's 'freedom in God's love,' was a radical religious idea which undercut the power of ecclesiastic authority in matters of doctrine, biblical interpretation and Christian life." [21] The function of the church as mediator of grace through the sacraments was therefore implicitly questioned by Isabel's position.

The further habit of the Alumbrados' meeting in small groups in private homes where the Bible was read and discussed (something to which Alcaraz was in particular dedicated)[22] was likewise a dangerous confirmation of a tendency of "spiritual" religion to bring to bear a "spiritual" church emphasizing the body of the elect rather than the visible hierarchy of the corporate institution. Although Valdés himself did not overtly challenge the church universal, his spiritual teaching on the "sons of God" justified by faith alone did threaten the visible church simply by implicitly opposing it to a spiritual church.[23] Prelowski states succinctly that the probable author of the Valdesian *Beneficio di Christo,* Don Benedetto, "had crossed over the line when he made the belief in 'sola fede' the distinguishing mark between true and false Christians, and when he abandoned the conception of the universal church in favour of the invisible community of the elect, who were truly guided by the spirit of Christ." [24] And of the spiritual religion of Valdés's pupils, F. C. Church remarks simply that "in turning away from the world, they found it difficult to take the hierarchy with them." [25]

In the incipiently heretical branch of the Alumbrados, then, with which Valdés seems to have had distinct connections, we find a basically Franciscan spirituality modified by a doctrine of justification by faith and by a teaching on election by which the orthodox church felt threatened in its very foundations. But neither in Isabel nor in the unfortunate Alcaraz, nor in Valdés nor the *Beneficio di Christo,* is there yet a deliberate challenge to real and legal status of the church universal. These men had heresy thrust upon them, and in several cases their works were accepted as orthodox until the threat of Luther in the north drew attention to possibly dangerous elements at home. [26] Consequently it is extremely difficult to name Valdés or Don Benedetto a Catholic or Protestant, a Lutheran or Erasmian, a perfectionist or moralist. Their spirituality is poised on the borders between alternatives, eventually to become exclusive but for the meantime held in fragile coexistence. [27]

The Franciscan influence which was strong in Valdés's formative years stayed with him even when he was forced to flee his native Spain for Italy. At Naples, where Valdés established his celebrated circle of devotees to carry on the spiritual ideals of the Alumbrados, [28] he met Bernardino Ochino, the Observantine Franciscan who left this rigorous branch of the order to help establish the nascent Capuchin branch, of which he eventually became vicar general. [29] In his struggles with Rome for recognition of the Capuchins, Ochino was supported, indeed championed, by Vittoria Colonna, the most celebrated lady among the group of noble personages who belonged to the Valdés circle. [30] More than this, Ochino and Valdés were so drawn to each other that Valdés even supplied the famous preacher with topics and suggestions for the sermons which he delivered with apparently stirring effect to vast audiences. [31] On hearing one of these sermons, the duchess Guilia Gonzaga was moved to confess to her spiritual mentor Valdés those doubts that led to the composition for her of the *Alfabeto Christiano.* This work in turn inspired her to retire to the Franciscan monastery of San Francesco delle Monache, though, again on Valdés's advice, she did not take vows.

The spirituality of the Franciscans, therefore, influenced Valdés first through the reforms of Cisneros and the University of Alcala, next through the Alumbrados, and lastly through the Capuchin reform pioneered by Bernardino Ochino. Yet the traditional spirituality is not left unmodified by the innovations which are no less present in Valdés's thought. The revolutionary insistence on justification by faith and a tendency to spiritualize the church by regarding it as the body of the elect are no less important in creating the unique tones of Valdesian devotion, which is at once Catholic and yet imbued with the ideals of the Reformation.

Valdés: The Theology

The *Alfabeto Christiano* is a typical work of Valdés's maturity. The main techniques and motifs of traditional Augustinian spirituality are present in it, but with the modifications consequent on Valdés's emphasis on the teachings of Alcaraz and Luther concerning justification by faith and predestination. First, the *Alfabeto* is a typical manual of the sort made popular by Franciscans, being written for the spiritual direction of Valdés's friend, Guilia Gonzaga.

Throughout the book, for example, the doctrine of atonement by crucifixion is a central motif and is closely related, in the characteristic Franciscan manner, to a profound concern for and awareness of original sin. The "true cognizance of Christ consists, Signora, in knowing and considering to what purpose the Son of God came into the world; and was made man; why he suffered; and why he rose again." [32] Guilia inquires further, and Valdés continues:

You may consider, Signora, that Christ came into the world to make satisfaction for original sin. Because this having been an infinite crime in respect to God who was offended, it was necessary that the satisfaction should be infinite, and this could not be made except by God himself, who is infinite. [P. 106]

Valdés goes on to develop the typological relationship between the first and second Adam and gives us the clearest of statements of that peculiarly Franciscan concern, "cur Deus homo si Adam non pecasset?" That the image and likeness of God in man were obliterated by the fall and can only be restored by "the true physician of the soul," namely, "Christ crucified" (p. 24), is fundamental to the lesson Guilia is to learn.

The cross itself receives much attention. "And know for a certainty," Valdés tells Guilia, "that there is nowhere that we can better know God than in Christ crucified" (p. 108). If the "contemplation of Christ crucified does not disenamour you of the things of the world and enamour you of the things of God, you will be always miserably bound to created things" (p. 108). Valdés even asserts that "we can neither know, believe, nor love God, but by contemplating Christ crucified" (p. 108), and Guilia is advised that her soul should "affect to be nailed, hands and feet, with Christ on the cross" (p. 136). She is told to "turn then your soul's regard upon Christ crucified" (p. 138), and at one point Valdés makes clear (in terms which recall Bonaventure's *Laudismus de Sancta Cruce*) the importance he attaches to meditation of the cross:

I wish you to keep in your remembrance Christ crucified; carry him at all times and in every place before you for a witness of all your thoughts, words and actions, and as a shield to preserve you from the assaults that your appetites and affections will make upon you. [P. 144]

When we come to application of the senses, we first discover a modification of Franciscan practice, for Valdés's particular brand of "spiritual" devotion leads to a certain ascetic denial of the *sensualis animae motus*. Yet the Franciscan teaching on the creatures remains, though (as in Herbert's poetry) it exists in an uneasy tension with a desire to repudiate the sensual. Still, Valdés's argument is certainly filled with similitudes and graphic examples adduced to illustrate theoretical points. His teaching on the creatures is, in theory, Augustinian. Augustine, indeed, is the only source outside the Bible quoted in the *Alfabeto Christiano*.[33] The opposition Valdés consistently makes between God and the world ("either we must serve the world and despise God, or we must love God and despise the world" [p. 46]) is wholly traditional and Augustinian in tone and in sentiment. Such a distinction between proper and improper love of the creatures is the very basis of the distinction between Augustine's two cities: "Accordingly, two cities have been formed by two loves: the earthly by the love of self, even to the contempt of God; the heavenly by the love of God, even to the contempt of self. The former, in a word, glories in itself, the latter in the Lord." [34] In similar terms, in a passage where Augustine is quoted on an allied issue of justification, Valdés states that the human heart "must either love God and all things for God, or it must love itself and all things for itself" (p. 51). Self-love on the one hand results in a disorder of the affections, and in such a state a man "never knows how, or in what manner, he ought to love created things" (p. 51). On the other hand, "He who loves God performs everything he does for him" (p. 52), and "if he love anything beside God, he loves it for the sake of God" (p. 52). We are not warned against the creatures themselves but against an inordinate and selfish love of creatures at expense of a proper love of God. The point is that "we shall not depend upon, nor be so bound to created things, in which we put more confidence than we do in Christ" (p. 79).

Despite such a plainly Augustinian teaching on the use of the senses, however, there is no longer, in Valdés, the uncomplicated, direct evocation characteristic of the Franciscans. Valdés may share to the letter a Bonaventuran theory on the referral of the creatures, but, like Herbert, Valdés is particularly concerned with the Protestant problem of the self and of selfishness. This is a natural result of a Reformation insistence on the individualist doctrine of justification by faith, and it causes a special wariness of self-indulgence, whether in devotion or in poetry. Such concern produces the self-consciousness and the ascetic strain which not only characterize Valdés but also distinguish *The Temple* from the "anonymous" and un-self-conscious poetry of the medieval lyricists. Here we may also find an explanation for the decline of interest in Mary as an aid to application of the senses, a decline well exemplified in the work of both Valdés and Herbert.

Considering Valdés's background at Alcala, where textual study of the Bible was regarded as important, not surprisingly we find in the *Alfabeto Christiano* a strong scriptural emphasis. The Bible is cited with such frequency by Valdés that Guilia is made to interrupt: "You have done very well. Do not trouble yourself if you do not quote your authorities; when you shall say anything that appears difficult to me, I will ask you to prove it to me by some authority from Scripture" (pp. 34-35). It is axiomatic that Scripture is the solution of every difficult point, and if Valdés does not continue to overwhelm his text with scriptural allusions, he wants us to know it is not a case of his slighting the Bible but merely expedient to the encompassing of his argument, which, if not founded on Scripture, is nothing. Valdés's devotion to the Bible cannot be doubted even from the briefest perusal of the *Alfabeto Christiano*.

The teaching on the creatures, the consciousness of original sin, the meditation of the cross, and the devotion to Scripture are deployed to the single particular end, we are told, that Guilia "should again find God" (p. 36). Her discovery, as we see, is determined by the object of her love and by her conversion from the things of the world to God. This conversion is effected basically by faith but also, Valdés insists, by penitence. The key word is "repentance." The elect, says Valdés, are truly mortified "because they repent and humble themselves, and thus learn to mistrust themselves and to confide in God" (p. 42). Elsewhere, in his *Tract upon the Mode of Teaching the Fundamentals of Christian Doctrine*, Valdés makes it clear that repentance above all, even before justification by faith, is the basis of Christian regeneration: "*The first:* that before justification by faith, remission of sins, and reconciliation with God through Christ, be preached; *let repentance* (penitence) *be preached.*" [35] Such a movement to repentance, together with a constant and ardent enjoinment to self-mortification, is of key importance throughout the *Alfabeto Christiano*, which reduplicates exactly the Franciscan emphasis on the sacrament of penance, and particularly on the elements of contrition and repentance.

Finally, meditation on last things to promote a proper and contrite love of God is an important factor in the *Alfabeto Christiano*. Indeed the sermons of the Franciscan Bernardino Ochino, which upset Guilia in the first place and encouraged her to divulge her worries to Valdés (who had probably suggested the sermon topics to Ochino anyway), dwelled on last things. "The sermons of the Preacher have engendered this contrariety in my mind. Through them I see myself violently assailed . . . by the fear of hell and the love of Paradise" (p. 13). The fact that there is an *Alfabeto Christiano* at all stems from the very stimulation of Guilia's affections by Ochino's meditation on last things. Later, Valdés explains to her: "The Preacher, Signora, by his sermons, has awakened in your remembrance what you already had conceived of heaven and hell, and has known so well how to picture it to you that the fear of hell makes you love heaven, and the love of heaven makes you dread hell" (p. 35). There could be no more clear example of that typical Franciscan direction of the will to repentance through evocation of the last things.

The criteria we have examined—the Augustinian doctrine of original sin, the devotion to the cross, the Augustinian teaching on the creatures, the insistence on repentance and conversion, the profound interest in Scripture, and the meditation on last things to stimulate love of God—are the underpinning of Valdés's devotion and clearly mark it as a strongly Franciscan-inspired manual of instruction. In terms of Valdés's background, it is reasonable that this should be so.

The elements, however, which led the Inquisition to place Valdés on the Index while they ignored other Franciscan materials, such as the writings of Osuna, are no less present and no less important to the structure and meaning of the *Alfabeto Christiano*. The most significant of these elements is the doctrine of justification by faith and the degree to which it is insisted upon throughout the work. Valdés is very forthright: "to be a Christian person, is to be justified," he writes, "and no one can be justified except by faith, because the just live by faith" (pp. 79-80). Without faith, he says elsewhere, "no one can please God" (p. 78). Valdés also makes clear what he means by faith and its sharp division from works.[36] "But understand that when I say faith I mean to speak of that faith which is alive in the soul, acquired not by industry, nor human contrivance, but by means of the grace of God communicated with supernatural light" (pp. 74-75). Without the unmerited grace of God we cannot have faith to be justified, "and if not justified, then not saved" (p. 70). Faith alone "announces remission and pardon of sin by Christ" (p. 30), and the faith which "soothes and pacifies the conscience" (p. 30) can alone put Guilia's troubled mind at rest.

In other writings, particularly the *Divine Considerations,* Valdés does not hesitate to avow predestination as an inevitable corollary of this teaching on justification, and his consequent theology of the election of the community of the saved who enjoy in this life a living faith in the Holy Spirit through Christ, as we have suggested, offers an implicit but dangerous criticism of the hierarchical and sacramental institution of the church. The church, for Valdés, tends to be spiritual and removed from the world. It is easy to see how the Inquisition, given the orthodoxy it was dedicated to maintaining, would find cause for suspicion in Valdés's advice to Guilia that "you will find some other persons who know the way to God and walk by it . . . and these in truth are but few, as you say, Signora, although they are not so few as you think, because their path being spiritual, they cannot be seen but by spiritual sight, nor are they possibly known except by persons who walk by the same road" (pp. 41-42). This "few" of the elect who walk in the path of the true faith bear as their witness no visible institutional or sacramental sanction; yet they form a spiritual community of their own. Moreover, these few justified by faith "have no need of many preparations for the confession" because they "confide in God" (p. 42) directly. They walk a different path from "another kind of persons who desire . . . the way of God" but who are "bound by the love of the things of this present life" and are deceived by Satan (pp. 39-40). "Hence are born superfluous ceremonies; hence arise pernicious superstitions; hence come false worships" (p. 40). In these last remarks Valdés certainly comes close to criticizing the external institutions of the church through which grace is normally mediated: the "confession," the "ceremonies," the "worships." [37]

Yet it is not possible to call Valdés anti-Catholic. Here, for example, is a passage which contains the divisive tendencies which make it so difficult to generalize about the exact nature of his theology, and which indicates both the spiritual concept of the church and the orthodox Catholic teaching on a mixed community of saints and sinners.

With the same knowledge you will believe the holy catholic Church and the spiritual communion of holy persons who are in it. Thus, you will truly know that Christ has here on earth a

> Church universal, holy by participation with the holiness of
> Christ, which Church contains and embraces good and bad, and
> which holds a spiritual union of holy persons maintained by the
> grace of the Holy Spirit. [P. 114]

Valdés countenances a "universal church" which contains saints and
sinners, but in his insistence on "the spiritual union of holy persons"
and the incipient isolation of their particular "spiritual communion"
we find the seeds of that "private and individual" religion,[38] which in
its northern forms soon dispensed with the "worships and ceremonies" as, indeed, deceptions of Satan.

The total result of this conflation of elements is complex. The traditional Augustinian spirituality of the Franciscan tradition is still
clearly recognizable throughout the *Alfabeto Christiano,* but it is
strangely altered by the new and eventually revolutionary emphasis
on elements which remained muted in the characteristic devotion of
the Middle Ages. Prepossession with doctrines of justification by
faith and the predestination of a spiritual elect produces a sense of
otherworldliness which is enforced by Valdés's strong asceticism.
Valdés's teaching on the creatures does not differ notably from Augustine's, but devotion to the Blessed Virgin Mary and other human
and sensual aids to meditation are notably held at arm's length. There
is rather an introspective concern with the self and with the direct
intervention of God in the spiritual life of the individual. In these
emphases Valdés clearly moves away from the characteristically
medieval *Itinerarum mentis in Deum,* wherein the ascent to contemplation is through a series of steps from the senses to God.[39]

In the *Divine Considerations,* translated by Nicholas Ferrar, the
broad outlines of this spirituality are repeated. First, as Herbert
noted, "the most of his Considerations being grounded upon some
text of scripture, shews that he was continually conversant in it," and
Valdés's emphasis on the Bible is obvious from the briefest perusal
of his treatise. Second, there is an equally pervasive and distinctly
Augustinian doctrine of the creatures. They are not to be dwelled
upon for their own sake but referred to God for his greater glory.
"Amongst the creatures the man that loves God, loves them most
who doe most illustrate the glory of God." [40] Third, as Curione re-

marks in his introduction to the 1550 edition of the *Considerations,*
they are full of "proper examples, and similitudes," [41] and despite
Valdés's consistent emphasis on mortification (an emphasis ac-
claimed by Herbert) his asceticism does not prevent, though it may
restrain, him from imaginatively engaging the senses of his readers
to illustrate his point. Such application of the senses provides an understanding "like to that knowledge which an ill painter gets of a most
perfect Painter, by seeing the things which he hath depainted" (p. 5).

Next, there is the uncompromisingly Christocentric nature of the
Considerations and the emphasis throughout on the cross of Christ.
"The unlearned man, that hath the spirit, serveth himself of *Images*
as of an Alphabet of Christian Pietie; forasmuch as hee so much
serves himselfe of the *Picture* of Christ Crucified, as much as serves
to imprint in his mind that which Christ suffered, and to tast, and
feele the benefit of Christ" (p. 109). *Consideration* 89 ends with
these words:

> For God will, that as the first man desiring to know, lost him-
> selfe; so wee should gain our selves, mortifying, and slaying
> every desire to know, contenting our selves only to *know Christ
> crucified,* who is to us the Tree of life, to him be glory for ever,
> *Amen.* [P. 328]

Here the central significance of the cross, the typology of the two
Adams, and the theme of atonement are entirely a traditional grouping of elements. Valdés, throughout the *Considerations,* keeps us
aware of the cross and engages in meditations on the passion of
Christ, the agony in the garden, and the crucifixion, as well as the
more general but nonetheless characteristic meditations on the life
of Christ. The significance of all this, in terms of a fifth criterion, is
to direct the mind toward that critical and Augustinian conversion
from the world to God—a conversion which involves mortification
and repentance and which is characteristically based on a strong conviction of original sin.[42] Valdés insists on the unfortunate consequences of the fall which destroyed the image and similitude of God in
man. "Our depravation and evill inclination, draws us to that, which is
altogether contrary" (p. 16) to the love of God. We must therefore
"leave the image of *Adam,* and take the image of Christ" (p. 4).

Lastly, Valdés uses the evocation of last things in the traditional manner to excite, through fear, the love of God, as is made clear in *Consideration* 45: *"Whence the feare of death proceeds in pious persons, and that it is a signe of Predestination for a man to content himselfe, that there should be another life"* (p. 152).

Beside these traditional elements which are the mark of Valdés's early training and education are the other, no less characteristic, hallmarks of his thought. First is the insistence on justification by faith and the allied doctrines of predestination and election. The characteristic language of Valdés (like Herbert) is that of the Covenant: "They who accepting the Gospell, and through the Covenant of Justification, which is by Jesus Christ our Lord, being made the sonnes of God, and having familiarity with God, know God" (p. 129). "Holinesse consisteth in the election of God" (p. 317), he writes, and "justice consisteth in believing in Christ" (p. 317). The firmness with which these teachings are insisted upon in the *Divine Considerations* is evident in this passage from *Consideration* 16:

> I know, will the pious Christian say, that God *calls* not unto him but those *whom he hath first known,* and predestinate: I know also, that *those whom he calls, them hee justifies, and them he glorifies.* And I know certainly, that he hath called me, and thereby I assure my selfe, that hee hath known, and predestinated me, and that he hath justified me, and that he will glorifie me. [Pp. 53-54]

As in the *Alfabeto Christiano,* the emphasis on justification by faith, and on predestination and election, leads directly to a preoccupation with the self and with mortification. Valdés, indeed, seems obsessed with the idea that self-regard is the ground of all sin: "they . . . who are impious doe not know but only their own proper wills" (p. 180) is the summation of his position in this regard. The sinful man "loves himselfe, and loves all things for himselfe; and pretends in every of his own matters his own proper glory" (p. 256). Men should not go "loving God for themselves" (p. 259) but "loving themselves for God" (p. 259).

The insistence on mortification leads in turn to a characteristic austerity and asceticism, as is evident from a perusal of any few sections of the *Considerations*. It leads as well to an emphasis on perfection and to an individualist, spiritual view of religion, as we have seen also in *Alfabeto Christiano*. The teaching of perfection is not, indeed, as strong as in *Alfabeto Christiano* but is still at the forefront of what Valdés believes should be the Christian's aspiration, that he "doe attend unto perfection" (p. 178). Valdés makes it repeatedly and absolutely clear, however, that perfection is not to be fully realized in this life. "By litle and litle" shall the Christian "goe augmenting in himselfe the reparation of his minde" (p. 185), but his reward of fulfillment is in eternity. Yet the aspiration to otherworldly perfection, together with the asceticism of mortification, does yield an individualist and psychologist tendency in Valdés's writing. The "certaine *inward vision*" (p. 315) is insisted upon. Physical images of Christ are useful only insofar as they enable us "to behold him with Spirituall Eyes" (p. 108). The Holy Scriptures should enable a man to "lift up his minde to pray God" (p. 109). Human wisdom is opposed to "inward sense," "the inward feeling" (p. 162) which is the mark of the Holy Ghost and which produces an *"Inward certainty"* (p. 215) of assurance: "So," says Valdés, "all men, who have the sight of their inward eyes cleare, doe know all inward things by the benefit of Christ" (p. 269), and the inward things—the personal assurance of justification, of predestination, of being among the elect "sons of God"—are important to Valdés's spirituality. In this light, as in the *Alfabeto Christiano,* many of the external observances of the church are implicitly regarded with suspicion, for in themselves they may be witness only to bad faith.

In both the *Alfabeto Christiano* and the *Divine Considerations,* therefore, we find a traditional Augustinian spirituality modified by a novel emphasis on the doctrine of justification by faith, which tends to produce a doctrine of election and a spiritual view of the church. The characteristic tensions in Valdés's work develop from those points where his traditional modes of devotion clash with his individual emphases. His asceticism and denial of the senses, for instance, seem to oppose his Augustinian teaching on the creatures. There is a consequent uncertainty: an approval of evocation by the senses of the passion, yet very little such evocation in Valdés's own writing; a desire for directness and simplicity, yet a constant use of similitude to illustrate the point by indirection; a subordination of the Scripture to the spirit, yet a characteristically Franciscan devotion to the Scripture whereby, as Herbert noted, Valdés seems in practice to confute his own theory.

Valdés and Herbert

The influence of Valdesian thought in the English church was felt before Herbert's time. It was mediated especially through Valdés's best-known disciples, the Augustinian Peter Martyr Vermigli and the Capuchin Bernardino Ochino, both of whom joined the Northern Reformation and visited England at the invitation of Cranmer. John T. Betts writes:

> The Zurich letters witness with what reverence both Archbishop Cranmer and Bishop Jewell held Peter Martyr as the master-spirit in Israel, and can it be otherwise than deeply interesting to the English reader to study the sentiments of Juan de Valdés who moulded the mind, in evangelical doctrine, of Peter Martyr, the arch-counselor of the recognised founders of the English Church? [43]

The poet Daniel Rogers, writing an epigram on Bishop John Jewell, notably includes Valdés with Peter Martyr, Calvin, Melanchthon, Luther, and John Knox as one of the greatest figures of the Reformation—"of Valdés, as an author, let all Spain be proud" ("Valdesio Hispanus scripturae superbiat orbis").[44] This interpretation distinctly links Valdés to the Protestant heritage of Jewell, which is also the inheritance of Herbert. It must be assumed, however, that the main relationship of Herbert with Valdés is through Nicholas Ferrar, who translated the *Divine Considerations*.

In the years from 1613 to 1618, Nicholas Ferrar traveled in Europe, visiting both Italy and Spain. It is "certain," says Maycock, "that his years in Italy exercised a deep influence" on Nicholas through the rest of his life. In this time of spiritual regeneration in Italy he absorbed the "interior life of the Catholic Church in Europe," [45] and the absorption was not a passive process, for Nicholas went about busily collecting a library, primarily of theological materials. These he shipped home in a large crate, and in Nicholas's own words the books were mainly devotional, "treating of the spiritual life and religious retirement." [46] Among the materials he thus collected was no doubt the *Divine Considerations* of Valdés, a book of considerable bulk and the only major work, from among those many volumes, that Nicholas actually translated.

The seeds of Nicholas's own life of "religious retirement" are already present in his early desire to collect such books as he describes. It may well be that the traditions which fed and inspired his religious community at Little Gidding are diverse and gleaned from a number of sources, but it is surprising that attempts to isolate these sources have ignored the possible influence of Valdés and his circle. Given the decided links between Valdesian theology and the Church of England already well established before Nicholas, always an ardent Anglican, took off on his travels and given that Nicholas actually translated Valdés, it would seem reasonable to look to the influence of Valdés on the Gidding community. Certainly Valdés seems to have a prior claim to the Oratorians,[47] with whom Ferrar has no specific relationship, or to Saint Macrina,[48] whose biography offers parallels but who is otherwise not particularly important to Ferrar or the Church of England in general.

Parallels demonstrating how the example of Valdés could have been accommodated to the practice of Little Gidding will enforce the point. First, both communities are made up of men and women whose reverence for the Scriptures moves them to a life of devotion and spiritual communion but one in which formal vows have no part[49] and in which an active concern for charity toward one's neighbor is expressed by an interest in his welfare and a desire to help him.[50] Second, reverence for the Bible expresses itself in terms of a marked interest in the Psalms and Gospels. At Little Gidding, John Ferrar tells us, "David's Psalms and the Gospel" are the core of the rule, and they are "Heavenly Food and Medicine" which should be committed to memory "to make use of upon all occasions." [51] Maycock's account of the rule at Gidding demonstrates that the offices and the night watches relied almost exclusively on the Psalms and Gospels.[52] That Valdés shared the same enthusiasm for precisely these books of the Bible is evident from the prefaces to his translations and commentaries where he outlines the supreme importance of the Psalms and

Gospels for Christian devotion.[53] We should perhaps note here that Valdés's enthusiasm also extends markedly to Paul, and this does not seem to be shared to any marked extent by Ferrar. But it is unreasonable to go looking for the importance of the psalms in the fourth century A.D. in relation to Saint Macrina, and the absence of vows in Saint Philip Neri's Oratorians, when the same repudiation of monastic vows and enthusiasm for the Psalms and for the Gospels are found together in Valdés, the one source actually translated by Ferrar.

Third is asceticism: we have already seen the insistence on mortification of the flesh in both the *Divine Considerations* and the *Alfabeto Christiano,* and, at Little Gidding, Nicholas was remarkable for the extent of his practice of mortification in the long night watches.[54] Fourth, learning was an important part of the exercise of both communities: as with the Valdés circle, not an unsophisticated group of people surrounded Nicholas, and the stories and anecdotes of the Little Academy (a small society for the edification and entertainment of the Gidding community) and *The Story Books of Little Gidding*[55] are full of learned allusions, of quips from history, from philosophy and other branches of learning, such as Vittoria Colonna and Marc Antonio Flamineo might have delighted to hear.

All this brings us eventually to the question of Catholicism at Little Gidding, a key criterion if Nicholas was influenced by Valdés's Franciscan spirituality. Certainly, rumors of Catholicism among the Ferrars were a cause of much scandal to English Puritans of the day. The Little Academy, for instance, was founded on the feast of the Purification of the Blessed Virgin Mary, with a woman called Mary as its leader and with one of its aims the imitation of the saints.[56] Nicholas, moreover, did not hesitate to decorate his church with the ornaments and trappings of Catholic worship, and the restoration of George Herbert's church at Leighton Bromswold was undertaken, with Herbert's permission, in the same spirit.[57] In the *Life* by John Ferrar we are told of scandal caused by Nicholas's display of the cross.[58] Also it is clear that Nicholas received Catholic visitors at Gidding, even though it was against the law. John Ferrar tells us that all sorts of visitors came in "not hundreds but some Thousands," [59] including persons of quality, scholars, Protestants, and Catholics. Nicholas never asked questions, presumably to protect himself from charges of harboring the Catholics who visited Gidding, where they were invited, as were all the guests, to join in the prayers. John tells of a close neighbor who was a Catholic and kept a priest in his house and who visited Gidding frequently.[60] He tells of three learned priests "habited like Gallants" who came to visit and talk with Nicholas.[61] The king, whose court was leaning ever more favorably in the direction of Rome, was himself interested in Gidding and borrowed the splendid concordance of the Gospels which the family had compiled, in order to have one made for his own use.[62] The same concordance, we are told in a letter to Nicholas Ferrar from Arthur Woodnorth, was highly prized by George Herbert.[63]

The connections of Nicholas Ferrar with the king, and the attitude toward Catholicism which seemed to prevail at the Ferrar community, were no doubt sufficient to relate, at least in the Puritan mind, the plague of Catholicism in the court of Charles I to the "Arminian nunnery" of Little Gidding. That a scurrilous pamphlet of that title, published in 1641, was brought before Parliament and put into wide circulation clearly indicates how Puritan attacks on the king embraced Little Gidding as well. Moreover, the figures with whom the king's Catholicism was most readily associated were Franciscans. Charles I had given permission for his French and Catholic wife, Henrietta Maria, to bring her own chaplains to England, and Henrietta chose to surround herself with Franciscans of the Capuchin branch of the order and even became a member of the third order herself. One of her chief advisors was Franciscus of Sancta Clara (the English Franciscan Christopher Davenport), who remained on good terms with many Anglican clergy and even undertook to demonstrate that the Thirty-nine Articles conformed to Catholic teaching.[64]

The Puritans were definitely wrong, however, to see in Nicholas Ferrar exactly the sort of spirituality which surrounded Henrietta Maria at Somerset House. Those Valdesian teachings on justification by faith and election, which were separated out by the Northern Reformation as the central profession of Protestants and accepted as such by the Church of England, are insisted upon vigorously by Ferrar. Despite the rhetoric and Catholic style of much of his devotion, Ferrar is dogmatically a Protestant who abhors the errors of Rome. With surprising violence in a man seemingly so tolerant, Nicholas swears to his brother that he would pull down a certain room in Gidding and build it again if he thought a mass had ever been said there.[65] A definitely Puritan asceticism and desire to mortify the things of the world led Nicholas to burn all of his books before he died.[66] As John Ferrar insists throughout his *Life,* the people of Little Gidding were indeed "Orthodox, Regular, Puritan Protestants." [67] His opinion is confirmed by the bishop of Lincoln who strongly defended Nicholas's Protestantism against malicious gossip.[68] Certainly Nicholas's deathbed confession of faith would satisfy any Puritan.[69]

What we have at Little Gidding, then, is a type of spirituality which strongly resembles what we have seen in the Valdés circle. A community of men and women, living a withdrawn and ascetic yet charitable life of devotion, are brought together by a love of the Scriptures. They stress in particular the Psalms and Gospels, admire the simple life, and are assured of justification and election by a profound and simple faith in the merits of Christ as the single means of salvation. Yet they are sophisticated and learned, drawn to traditionally sensual aids to devotion. They spend their time compiling concordances and translating books like the *Considerations* of Valdés, and they are suspected as allies of the Franciscan plague run rife at the court. Granted Nicholas's confirmed Anglicanism and the enthusiasm of the founders of the English church for Valdesian theology, it seems altogether probable that Valdesian spirituality exercised a considerable influence on Little Gidding and, through it, on George Herbert.

To complete the argument, Herbert's friendship with Nicholas Ferrar was unusually deep. Herbert committed the manuscript of *The Temple* to Ferrar before he died.[70] Ferrar undertook the renovation of Herbert's church at Leighton Bromswold. Herbert's motto, "We are less than the least of God's Mercies," appears casually in *The Winding Sheet,* one of the intimate documents of the Little Academy.[71] Herbert, we are told in a letter, highly prizes the Little Gidding concordances,[72] and John Ferrar attests with a simplicity that defies repudiation that George Herbert and Nicholas Ferrar were so close that to those who knew them "there was one Soule in twoe Bodys." [73] In his study of Little Gidding, Maycock finds it irresistible that the spirituality of Herbert and Ferrar was one and the same, that they "understood one another perfectly." [74]

Herbert: The Temple

Returning to Herbert now in the light of the theological traditions we have been at pains to outline, it is possible to suggest a more just diagnosis of his poetry than was accomplished by the last chapter alone. There we saw that the traditional aspects of *The Temple* are decidedly Augustinian and Franciscan. Now we might suggest that Herbert's spirituality is Franciscan in the manner that the spirituality of Valdés is also Franciscan. As in Valdés, and perhaps by Valdés's direct influence through the Little Gidding community, we find in Herbert a traditional Augustinian piety modified by doctrines of justification by faith, election, and predestination, but modified in such a way that the opposing tendencies are sustained momentarily in harmony. As in Valdés, we find at once a desire to mortify the self and yet to engage the senses imaginatively; a desire for simplicity and directness, yet an acknowledgment of the pedagogical usefulness of rhetorical indirection; a tendency toward a spiritual view of the church and a desire also to acclaim the church universal.

Herbert's prepossession with the Protestant doctrines of justification and election in the poems of *The Temple* is both curious and interesting. Many of the best poems certainly show a fascination with the secret interior workings of God's plan and with man's instrumentality for an end already determined. The poem *Faith* shows how, for Herbert, the consolation of faith produces an assurance and how this assurance depends on the covenant of grace:

> When creatures had no reall light
> Inherent in them, thou didst make the sunne
> Impute a lustre, and allow them bright.
>
> [*Works*, p. 51]

Grace "fills up uneven nature," and with that peculiar knack of reducing complex theology to familiar and homely metaphor, Herbert describes faith in the legalistic language of justification:

> I owed thousands and much more:
> I did beleeve that I did nothing owe,
> And liv'd accordingly; my creditor
> Beleeves so too, and lets me go.
>
> [*Works,* p. 50]

The simple but profound conviction expressed here, that faith will cancel even the greatest of debts and that such faith depends wholly on imputed grace, is of the essence of Herbert's religious experience. The feeling of "exact and most particular trust" (*Works,* p. 51) which also emerges is surely the yield of that covenanter's belief that God's plan for man has indeed been worked out.

The conviction of predestination also triggers the fine poem *Redemption* (*Works,* p. 40), with its multiple ironies and perfect dramatization. The conversational, colloquial rhythms carefully maintain the attitude of the pilgrim pursuing an utterly non-Christian course in an utterly non-Christian frame of mind, seeking his "rich Lord" to make a commercial transaction regarding tenancy. He seeks him in "great resorts; / In cities, theatres, gardens, parks, and courts," and then stumbles accidentally upon him among thieves and murderers, where the Lord, amidst the "ragged noise and mirth," grants the suit and dies.

The point is that the pilgrim, despite great effort, is brought to the Lord by no means of his own but by grace, and indeed despite his own knowledge or expectations. The carnal and legalistic understanding of his "old man" has led him to seek in the wrong places, and when he does find the Lord, the supreme irony is that his request is granted before he has time even to make it. God's foreknowledge has sought him out. Such ironies of predestination echo throughout the poem. The pilgrim is made to talk of a "new" and an "old" lease without understanding the significance of these words in the Pauline context of grace which, by the end of the poem, he is to experience.

There is a further irony in that the land is "dearly bought": the pilgrim does not realize the land is himself, and that "dear" refers to love as well as high price. Again, the "thieves and murderers" are the two thieves executed with Christ and the people who are conducting the execution, though it is doubtful if the pilgrim sees anything more than the general unruly mobs who frequent public executions.

A final, and most intriguing, irony is in the very last words of the poem—"said, and died." The suit is granted, we can see, because Christ dies. To the Christian, it is a causal relationship. But to the pilgrim it seems simply a temporal relationship—a remarkable thing for the Lord to say before dying. The significance of what is experienced—the grace of salvation through the Atonement of Christ—is not yet understood by the pilgrim as the poem ends. Grace belongs to him, and understanding will no doubt follow. The remarkable skill of the poem is in allowing us to share the patterns of predestination in which grace is offered even to the errant and the blind.

The famous *The Collar* is another poem where the seeming self-determinations of man are merely the instruments of God's fore-ordained mercy. In the very assertion of his freedom the speaker is made ironically to allude (like the pilgrim of *Redemption,* without understanding) to the very means by which his rebellion will effect the opposite of what he intends. Thus he describes his grievances in terms of thorns and blood, and, as symbols of the hedonism he desires to embrace, he talks of wine and corn. All this is in vindication of his claim to be "free as the rode." The word "rode," however, is a pun on "rood," and what the speaker does not see is his real freedom determined by the cross—the cross that involves thorns and blood and in celebration of which the eucharistic wine and corn were instituted.

The very arrangement of the prosody also reflects the main idea of the poem. Lines of uneven length and in irregular rhyme scheme seem at first to be without plan (and thus to enact the disorder of rebellion) but are resolved in the harmony of the final quatrain where Christ speaks. As he does so, the four types of line of which the poem consists are brought together in a rhymed quatrain. There has been a pattern there, but only by the intervention of the Lord do we see it. Here, as in *Redemption* and so many of Herbert's poems, the intricate patterns of God's predestination are a major concern of the poet's art.

Prepossession with the Covenant, and with the direct but intimate revelations of God's grace to the individual soul, understandably produces in Herbert, as in Valdés, a certain acute consciousness of the self and a desire to mortify it. We recall that Herbert particularly admired Valdés's teaching "about mortification, and observation of God's Kingdome within us" (*Works*, p. 305). So, in Herbert's poems, as distinct from most medieval lyric poetry, there is a fascination with the first personal pronoun. *Affliction 1* is a typical example. Highly introspective, it is a poem obsessed with "I" and "me":

> I looked on thy furniture so fine,
>   And made it fine to me:
> Thy glorious household-stuffe did me entwine,
>   And 'tice me unto thee.
> Such starres I counted mine: both heav'n and earth
> Payd me my wages in a world of mirth.
>
> [*Works*, p. 46]

"Sorrow was all my soul; I scarce beleeved, / Till grief did tell me roundly, that I lived," Herbert continues. "I was entangled in the world of strife, / Before I had the power to change my life" (*Works*, p. 47). Yet *Affliction 1* is a poem which ends by acknowledging that a paradoxical renunciation and mortification of the self is the best way to fulfillment:

> Ah my deare God! though I am clean forgot,
> Let me not love thee, if I love thee not.
>
> [*Works*, p. 48]

A similar emphasis on the self is found throughout *The Temple*, whether in the fearful meditation of *Sighs and Grones*,

> O Do not use me
> After my sinnes! look not on my desert,
> But on thy glorie! then thou wilt reform
> And not refuse me: for thou onely art
> The mightie God, but I a sillie worm;
> O do not bruise me!
>
> [*Works*, p. 83]

or in other poems like *Dulnesse, Dialogue, Home,* or *Longing*. Often the concern involves self-recrimination, as in *Even-Song*, "What have I brought thee home / For this thy love?" (*Works*, p. 64); or *Church-lock and key*, "I Know it is my sinne, which locks thine eares / And bindes thy hands" (*Works*, p. 66); or *Unkindnesse*, "I would not use a friend, as I use Thee" (*Works*, p. 93); or in the very title of the poem *Self-condemnation* (*Works*, p. 170).

The explicit connection between self-regard and sin is made clear in the poem *Miserie*. By sin man is "A lump of flesh," writes Herbert, "without a foot or wing / To raise him." He is

> A sick toss'd vessel, dashing on each thing;
> Nay, his own shelf:
> My God, I mean my self.
>
> [*Works*, p. 102]

That this disordered and sinful self should be mortified is one of the favorite themes of *The Temple*. "We must confesse that nothing is our own" (*The Holdfast, Works*, p. 143), writes Herbert, and poems like *Vanitie 1* and *2* are concerned to rebuke the false aspirations of human knowledge and glory, "for earthly joy / Is but a bubble" (*Vanitie 2, Works*, p. 111). Even the rose, most beautiful of flowers, "doth judge and sentence / Worldly joyes to be a scourge" (*Works*, p. 178), and in poems like *The Quip* and *The Pearl*, the ways of human learning and honor and beauty and glory are, in the words of another poem, "adjudge[d] . . . to tears and grief" (*Works*, p. 136). The mortification of the flesh is the subject of *Church Monuments*, as it is of the poem in fact entitled *Mortification*. As Herbert says in *Miserie*:

> Man is a foolish thing, a foolish thing,
> Folly and Sinne play all his game.
> His house still burns, and yet he still doth sing.
>
> [*Works*, p. 100]

His "passions spite" must therefore be corrected (*Works*, p. 16); he must become "all reverence and fear" (*Works*, p. 22), if he is to be "soft and supple" to the will of God (*Works*, p. 44).

Again, the concern with predestination (with the consequent emphasis on the self and mortification of the things of the world) leads Herbert, like Valdés, to a certain otherworldly spirituality. In neither writer is this tendency exaggerated, but it is there nonetheless. As with Nicholas Ferrar, Herbert's practical piety is mingled with a real tendency to withdraw from the world. As we have seen, the spirituality of Valdés led him toward a spiritual conception of the church as distinct from the church universal. The same is true of Herbert, though, again as with Valdés, his position on the subject is ambivalent. On the one hand is the devotion of *The British Church:*

> But, dearest Mother, what those misse,
> The mean, thy praise and glorie is,
> And long may be.
> Blessed be God, whose love it was
> To double-moat thee with his grace,
> And none but thee.
>
> [*Works*, p. 110]

On the other hand is the downright pessimism of *The Church Militant,* which traces the predestined course of the institutional church into sin and darkness:

> Thus do both lights, as well in Church as Sunne,
> Light one another, and together runne.
> Thus also Sinne and Darknesse follow still
> The Church and Sunne with all their power and skill.
>
> [*Works*, pp. 197-98]

Herbert's loyalty to the Anglican church seems mixed with an equally strong conviction that this, like any other institutional church, will inevitably fall to corruption and sin.

Ross has pointed out in this regard how historical and social reasons, mainly a disgust with the worldliness and corruption of the Caroline court, helped force the dilemma upon Herbert. In his retreat from the court to Bemerton, and his "renunciation of courtly and bourgeois values," [75] Herbert also finds it increasingly difficult to accept the crown as the Godgiven symbol of blessing to the institution of the Church of England. Ross points to the curiously negative use of the court throughout *The Temple* and notes that it extends to Herbert's treatment of royalism as well. "Here and throughout the poems the treatment of the wealth symbol is as hostile as the treatment of royalism is negative." [76] The poem *Peace* is an example:

> Then went I to a garden, and did spy
> A gallant flower,

> The crown Imperiall: Sure, said I,
> Peace at the root must dwell.
> But when I digg'd, I saw a worm devoure
> What show'd so well.
>
> [*Works*, p. 125]

The only positive use of the idea of kingship is that which is proper to God, but "in a completely otherworldly realm." Kingliness is proper only to heaven,

> Where ev'ry one is king, and hath his crown,
> If not upon his head, yet in his hands:
>
> [*Works*, p. 77]

We recall also Herbert's acclaim of Valdés's "observation of God's Kingdome within us."

All this helps to explain Herbert's ambivalence with regard to the church, which reflects his historical situation as a loyal Anglican and at the same time demonstrates his tendency to hold the inner world of the spirit the true ground of religious experience. "The apparent contradiction between his devotion to the 'British Church' and his fatalistic view of the church as a social institution can be resolved in a deepening sense of intimacy with God, which almost transcends the church as institution, a place of collective worship, and approaches mystical communion. By the music of the church service, Herbert is almost transported beyond churchliness altogether.

> 'Now I in you without a bodie move,
> Rising and falling with your wings.
> We both together sweetly live and love,
> Yet say sometimes, God help poore Kings.'

I say 'almost transported'—but never quite. The consciousness of tension invades the mystical moment and curbs it. He is never able to shake off a quite unmystical kind of awareness." [77] Ross's diagnosis makes the point exactly. The note of withdrawal to the inner world is there, but the practical piety and Augustinian respect for the creatures curb it, and, as with Valdés, the synthesis of those opposite tendencies accounts for much of the characteristic tone of Herbert's poetry.

The conflation of elements which we find in Herbert produces the tensions whereby (as Herbert said of Valdés) the writer's practice seems to confute his own theory. In both men, emphasis on mortification of the senses seems to oppose that typically Franciscan application of the senses whereby a point is made by way of similitude. The vivid evocation of the instruments of the passion in *Passio discerpta,* or the use of similitudes in *Mortification* or *The Flower,* contrasts the spare and ascetic ideal of *Discipline.* The ideal of simplicity, of direct colloquy between God and the soul, shorn of all pretense and vanity, is held dear by Herbert. Yet the effectiveness of rhetorical indirection, of similitude, typology, and application of the senses, is also part of the tradition he inherits. In the celebrated *Jordan* poems the two elements confront one another:

> Must all be vail'd, while he that reades, divines,
> Catching the sense at two removes?
>
> [*Works*, p. 56]

Surely it is enough to "plainly say, *My God, My King.*" Nevertheless, it has taken a poem of some elaborate indirection to arrive with such effectiveness at the ideal plain statement. Again, at the conclusion of *Jordan* 2 the "friend," God, whispers in the poet's ear and shows the vanity of "Curling with metaphors a plain intention" (*Works,* p. 102). The close, private, and individual commerce between God and the soul, effected by the grace and mercy of God despite the perverse and "long pretense" of man's own efforts, represents, to the covenanter Herbert, the essence of the election of the "sonnes of God." Yet, again, the elaborate poem is anything but direct and simple. And in *A Wreath* Herbert writes, "Give me simplicitie, that I may live," while offering "A wreathed garland of deserved praise" (*Works,* p. 185). So in *The Temple* we find those qualities so characteristic of Herbert's individual style—traditional meditation involving application of the senses, meditation of the cross, and fear of death, which is dramatic but never histrionic—together with a certain chasteness of style and tone, a directness and simplicity and assurance which can coexist with elaborate rhetorical structure and occasionally deeply felt doubt.

It is interesting that similar stylistic traits occur in Valdés, in Nicholas Ferrar, and in Valdesians like Bernardino Ochino and that critics describing the styles of these writers should independently use such similar language. In *The Winding Sheet,* Ferrar tells us, in some detail, that flourishes of wit are important, though a plain and direct style is better.[78] The style of *The Winding Sheet* itself, however, is far from plain and direct as the perusal of any few pages will attest, and the editor in his general introduction talks of a "continuous inner tension" and surface "serenity," recalling qualities which we find in Herbert's *The Temple.*[79]

Father Cuthbert, describing the early style of the Valdesian disciple Bernardino Ochino, does so in terms which might well apply to Herbert, drawing attention to the elegance and yet the simplicity, the complexity and the directness:

> Every sentence is chastely chiselled to convey the preacher's thought; a restrained emotion vibrates throughout, yet there is no blatant attempt at effect. The language is simple and direct. . . . But clothed in this eloquent simplicity, the thought compels attention; it is the living thought of one who has passed his doctrine through the crucible of his own thought and experience.[80]

To summarize, what we find in Herbert is the unique effect of old and new in coexistence.[81] In this discussion, I hope to have provided some analysis of what, in terms of theological traditions, the old and the new consist, and what are the consequences of attempting to keep them in coexistence. For Herbert, the old is the traditional Augustinian spirituality as exemplified by the widespread and popular mission of the English Franciscans. In his poetry we find all the hallmarks—devotion to Scripture and fascination with typology, dramatic techniques of application of the senses and composition of place, devotion to the cross and deliberate evocation of the blood sacrifice of Christ, a strong sense of original sin and concern for contrition, a notable use of meditation on last things to promote the proper love of God. The further irrefutable similarities between the poetry of *The Temple* and medieval lyric poetry, itself so predominantly of Franciscan origin, together with the demonstrable reliance of both Herbert and the medieval poets on similar Franciscan devotional materials, establish the continuity of this tradition of Augustinian spirituality from the Middle Ages to the seventeenth century.

The new, on the other hand, is basically the emphasis of Protestant dogmatism on justification by faith. For Herbert, a covenanter, this doctrine is of fundamental importance and leads to a prepossession with predestination and election and to a marked introspective interest in the self. These emphases are accompanied by a disenchantment with the world and a desire for mortification, which produces in Herbert a devotion of marked spiritualist elements.

But the point is that these different traditions are, for a brief moment, together, and the perfect analogy in terms of theology for what is happening in the poetry of Herbert's *The Temple* is to be found in the writings of Juan de Valdés. There too we have a theology which is basically Augustinian and Franciscan, deriving from the reform program of Cardinal Cisneros, which so resembles, in its aims and devotional materials, the Franciscan mission in England, and sustained by a continuing relationship between Valdés and Franciscan theologians and institutions.

However, from within the Franciscan order itself a particular branch of the Alumbrados, by emphasizing elements within the tradition which were always there but not exaggerated, isolated the doctrine of justification by faith as the essence of Christian salvation. The new emphasis is fully embraced by Valdés, but he did not accept, as the Northern Reformers did, that it implied a new theology. Although Valdés had to flee the Inquisition, he did not repudiate the church universal. In Valdés, for a brief moment, the opposing tendencies do remain in coexistence, and from this coexistence a certain distinctive spirituality and a distinctive style emerge.

When the old and the new separate, we have on the one hand the orthodox Capuchins such as those who came to England with Henrietta Maria, and on the other hand we have Luther and the later Bernardino Ochino. Not surprisingly, the founders of the Church of England welcomed Valdés's thought, seeing in it a possible middle road, a balance such as they desired for their own church vis à vis the Puritans and the Roman Catholics. By the time of Charles I, however, the ideal of Cranmer and Jewell was fast fading in a worldly court with papist and worldly leanings. Only Little Gidding, "the spiritual focus of all that was best and holiest in the Caroline Church," sustained the older Anglican ideal,[82] and Nicholas Ferrar, its founder, also looked with favor on Juan de Valdés. In George

Herbert, too, with whom Nicholas Ferrar had such perfect understanding, the coexistence of opposing theological traditions is maintained in a characteristically Valdesian synthesis, producing parallel states of spirituality and qualities of style. But after Herbert, the old and the new again separate. On the one hand, Richard Crashaw embraces the Catholicism of Henrietta Maria's Capuchins. On the other hand, Henry Vaughan and Thomas Traherne move toward the withdrawal and the antinomian mysticism of the later Ochino.

From our argument thus far we can state, then, that the poems of Donne and Herbert are similarly medieval, working from within the rich guilt-culture traditions of Augustine in the High Middle Ages. Yet, in his own way each poet encounters also the enlightenment challenges to such a medieval spirituality. With Donne, his engagement with the problems of latitude forces a violent conflict in the *Holy Sonnets*. With Herbert, an equivalent concern with the individualist Protestant doctrine of justification by faith produces the more refined harmonies of *The Temple*. Our examination of Juan de Valdés has suggested some important spiritual analogues for Herbert's poetry and some explanation of how the incipiently discordant elements could be held, momentarily, together. Certainly, the contribution to English theology and literature of the Spanish and Italian theologians of the Reformation period has too long been ignored, both as a source of Protestant theology and letters and also as a means of mediation into seventeenth-century England of the older traditions of Catholic devotion.

Chapter Five Henry Vaughan and the Hermetic Philosophy

In Henry Vaughan's *Silex Scintillans* there is perhaps the strongest example in all English literature of the results of one poet having influenced another. In the preface to the 1655 edition, Vaughan writes of "the blessed man, Mr. *George Herbert,* whose holy *life* and *verse* gained many pious *Converts,* (of whom I am the least)," [1] and the results of Vaughan's enthusiasm are immediately obvious to the reader of *The Temple* who turns even casually to *Silex Scintillans.* E. C. Pettet points out that approximately half the poems in Vaughan's collection bear discernible traces of Herbert,[2] and many of these deliberate borrowings are listed in Martin's edition. The debt to Herbert, as we might expect, yields a distinctly Augustinian emphasis in Vaughan's poems. But there is not only a unique case of poetic influence; there is also in Vaughan a striking example of the influence of an esoteric system of ideas. It has been long agreed that *Silex Scintillans* is somehow indebted to the Hermetic philosophy,[3] and a confrontation between the influence of an Augustinian Herbert and the influence of the *Corpus Hermeticum* is a key for understanding the important place of Vaughan's poetry in the devotional literature of the period. A third significant element in this context is Vaughan's own theology which he expresses in his prose. This has been largely ignored by critics of the poetry, but it can throw considerable light on the means by which *Silex Scintillans* attempts to synthesize Vaughan's guilt-culture Augustinian heritage with the innovative enlightenment philosophy of the Hermetists.

The importance of these three elements is not only that they remain conveniently distinct in Vaughan's work but that they represent the three main factors which often contribute to the making of poems in general: the influence of other poetry, the influence of provocative ideas, and the influence of the poet's own belief. A fourth element which holds these others together is, of course, the poet's own sensibility, by which I mean the synthesizing and creative faculty through which he converts what he borrows into the poetry which bears his own stamp. The remarkable thing about Vaughan's sensibility in this sense is its highly intuitive nature. As Joan Bennett remarks, his best poetry occurs often in single lines, and even half lines.[4] "His religious insight," writes S. L. Bethell, "is intuitional not ratiocinative, instantaneous not developing," [5] and Helen White contains both viewpoints in her perceptive statement:

> He has not the kind of mind that takes possession of his theme firmly and precisely. Rather his sensitivity outreaches his power of analysis, and his best intuitions would seem to come in a flash and all too often to vanish again when he tries to hold them or to fit their vague implications into a preconceived scheme.[6]

It is important to understand the spontaneous character of Vaughan's sensibility, because his intuitive response, in particular to the Hermetists, and not his reasoned consideration of the systematic framework of their philosophy best explains the nature of his debt to them. Critical endeavor which has concentrated on the details of sources, or on the theoretical compatibility or incompatibility of Hermetic philosophy with Vaughan's Christian theology, has not adequately explained the relationship,[7] for mainly in his intuitive moments, in those unsustained but brilliant episodes which are not ratiocinative, as Bethell says, Vaughan realizes a poetry which most truly reflects a Hermetic influence and is not primarily grounded on an Augustinian anthropology. In such moments his poems strike a distinctive note which qualitatively separates them from the fundamentally traditional devotion of Donne and Herbert. Yet throughout *Silex Scintillans* the struggle between an anthropology of traditional guilt culture and an anthropology of enlightenment (deriving in this case principally from learned Hermetism) provides the impetus for the poetry. Vaughan's resolution of the conflict may indeed mark a departure from the traditional modes of Donne and Herbert, but the matrix within which he works is the same.

Vaughan and Herbert

In view of the profound indebtedness of *Silex Scintillans* to *The Temple,* it may be useful to begin by comparing some poems by Herbert and Vaughan. Both Herbert's *Giddinesse* and Vaughan's *Man* are about sin. They show us man's inconstancy, his fickleness, his unreliability, and would no doubt have been explained in the same theological terms by each author: they deal with fallen human nature. But within the general subject matter there are poetic differences. In *Giddinesse,* when Herbert shows us the results of the fall, he does so directly, by telling us how badly man behaves:

> He is some twentie sev'rall men at least
> Each sev'rall houre.
>
> [*Works,* p. 127]

He vacillates wildly—"Now he will fight it out"; "Now eat his bread in peace"; "Now he scorns increase"; he builds a house and destroys it just as quickly, and should the chameleon nature of his mind be evident to others he would hide himself for shame. Vaughan, on the other hand, shows us the fickleness of man in his fallen state through contrast to the constancy of nature and the cosmos:

> I would (said I) my God would give
> The staidness of these things to man! for these
> To his divine appointments ever cleave,
> And no new business breaks their peace.
>
> [*Works of Vaughan,* p. 477]

Birds, bees, flowers, and even stones possess "some hid sense" and cleave loyally to their "divine appointments." Such faithfulness has, however, been lost to man, who is seen as homeless in the midst of nature, as the single "ever restless and irregular" outcast. The strength of Vaughan's poem comes from his ability to create a sense of the unseen harmonies that connect and animate the things of creation and then to present man as the one piece of grit in the mechanism—or organism. There is a consequent feeling of pity, and indeed sympathy, for man in his loneliness:

He knows he hath a home, but scarce knows where,
   He sayes it is so far
That he hath quite forgot how to go there.
                     [Works of Vaughan, p. 477]

    The central differences between these two poems might be summed up by saying that Herbert, when he writes about the fall, is mainly interested in human behavior. The subject is man's broken will, his recalcitrance, his perverted love. Herbert's treatment of the fall is perfectly in accord with his Augustinian theology and Calvinist emphasis on predestination. This is the anti-Pelagian Augustine, and the Augustine of the eighth book of the *Confessions*. For Vaughan, on the other hand, the fall is seen mainly in terms of cosmology and in the way man fails to fit into the ordered scheme of the universe. This is more like the Neoplatonist Augustine of the early dialogues, and running through Vaughan, too, is something very close to the non-Augustinian idea that nature did not fall with man. Perhaps the most notable difference resulting from these separate emphases is the sentiment of pity which is present in *Man,* as distinct from the tone of rebuke (contained even in the title) of *Giddinesse.*

    The distinction I am making in this first comparison can be developed by further examples. Vaughan's *Man,* for instance, is recognizably based on Herbert's *The Pulley* and invites comparison with it. Moreover, Herbert's poem is about man's place in the whole of creation, and he might seem to approach the "cosmological" position we are claiming for Vaughan. But when we look closer we find the shift in Vaughan's emphasis away from Herbert is the key to the particular achievement of his poem, for what Herbert is dealing with in *The Pulley* is not really the fall but the fact that man is the high point of God's creation. He has all the gifts:

    When God at first made man,
      Having a glasse of blessings standing by;
    Let us (said he) poure on him all we can:
    Let the worlds riches, which dispersed lie,
      Contract into a span.

                        [Works, p. 159]

Man is above nature, and this is why his restlessness is stressed—the poem is more about God's bounty than about man's fallenness. Vaughan, however, certainly is talking about the fall, and his point is that man is not above nature; he stresses that nature has a sort of knowledge that man does not. Vaughan has adapted Herbert's poem, but his emphasis is on man's cosmological fall rather than upon God's bounty.

The same sort of distinction can be found by comparing Herbert's *Man* with Vaughan's *Etenim* ("And do they so? have they a sense"). *Man* again is a good choice because it is a poem in which Herbert seems to come close (even closer than in *The Pulley*) to Vaughan's point of view. He writes of nature's harmony and benevolence,

> Herbs gladly cure our flesh; because that they
> Finde their acquaintance there,
>
> [*Works*, p. 91]

and we recognize something of the universe infused with sentience, with friendly consciousness, that runs through Vaughan. Herbert continues,

> The starres have us to bed;
> Night draws the curtain, which the sun withdraws;
>
> [*Works*, p. 91]

and we again recognize the interest that Vaughan takes in the benevolent processes of nature. In *Etenim*, on the other hand, Vaughan writes,

> Shall I thy mercies still abuse
> With fancies, friends, or newes?
> O brook it not! thy bloud is mine,
> And my soul should be thine;
>
> [*Works of Vaughan*, p. 433]

and we seem to recognize the bluntness and colloquial quality of Herbert's transpositions of the theological into the familiar and domestic.

Yet Herbert in his poem is, again, not telling us about man's fallenness, that man is a misfit in the world of animate nature, the world in which God is immanent. Herbert writes:

> More servants wait on Man,
> Then he'l take notice of: in ev'ry path
> He treads down that which doth befriend him,
> When sicknesse makes him pale and wan.
>
> *[Works,* p. 92]

If these lines came in Vaughan, their point would be man's unrecep-
tiveness: that man does not take notice of all the servants he treads
down, that all the servants show him up as a misfit. But this is not
Herbert's emphasis. Herbert is saying *more* than man can take notice
of, *so many* that he treads them down. The last two lines of the stanza
make this clear by calling no attention to man's unresponsiveness but
only to God's bounty:

> Oh mightie love! Man is one world, and hath
> Another to attend him.
>
> *[Works,* p. 92]

Man is a poem, like *The Pulley,* about God's goodness in placing
man at the head of nature and then so richly endowing nature to
serve him. Stanza 2 bears this out:

> For Man is ev'ry thing,
> And more: He is a tree, yet bears more fruit;
> A beast, yet is, or should be more:
> Reason and speech we onely bring.
> Parrats may thank us, if they are not mute,
> They go upon the score.
>
> *[Works,* p. 91]

The general sense is that man is the law of created things, and Herbert's plea is that God, by an added grace, should dwell with him.
There is, incidentally, an interesting crux in this stanza which involves
the meaning of the whole poem. A variant of "more fruit" in line 2
is "no fruit." [8] "No fruit" would make this sound a lot more like
Vaughan, for it would then be saying that man alone does not fulfill
his natural role. To preserve the contrast I am beginning to elaborate,
I naturally rejoice in the better manuscript authority of "more."
("No" fruit would be artistically inept anyhow—only one detail
against the general run of the poem is not a way to make an effective

point.) But the poem throughout is consistent in its emphasis. It is about the goodness of God's creation and God's bounty to man, and it steers clear of mentioning man's inadequacy, his unresponsiveness: it is not primarily a poem about sin or about the fall.

This is not to say, of course, that Herbert is less aware of the fall than Vaughan. That would be nonsense. Herbert is the poet of inner conflict, temptation, sin, and redemption, as we recall from *Giddinesse*. What I am saying is that Herbert, when he writes about the fall or about man's sinfulness, does not characteristically use the world picture to do it. Herbert's poetry on the fall is quite lacking in the idea so dear to Vaughan that man is a cosmic misfit, which we find if we look at *Etenim:*

> And do they so? have they a Sense
>   Of ought but Influence?
> Can they their heads lift, and expect,
>   And grone too? why th'Elect
> Can do no more: my volumes sed
>   They were all dull, and dead,
> They judg'd them senselesse, and their state
>   Wholly Inanimate.
>   Go, go; Seal up thy looks,
>   And burn thy books.
>
>
>   2
> I would I were a stone, or tree,
>   Or flowre by pedigree,
> Or some poor high-way herb, or Spring
>   To flow, or bird to sing!
> Then should I (tyed to one sure state,)
>   All day expect my date;
> But I am sadly loose, and stray
>   A giddy blast each way;
>   O let me not thus range!
>   Thou canst not change.
>   [*Works of Vaughan*, p. 432]

Nature here is charged with the grandeur of God, and not simply because its beauty is the end of creation but because all things are somehow aware of God's orderly control, and God's goodness. The stones and trees, the flowers and herbs and birds, the rivers and streams are filled with this consciousness. The use of "heads lift" is very striking, incidentally, for it is a purely descriptive term (with reference to flowers or birds), and it also suggests the awareness these creatures show. The one forlorn and pathetic creature who breaks the symmetry, who is "sadly loose" and strays, is fallen man. His very learning and desire to control nature only confirm his ignorance, and the "volumes" he must reject I take to be those of Galileo, Descartes, and Hobbes. In this poem the world shows a piety that man does not, and the most striking and characteristically Vaughan aspects of the poem are in those lines which create an excited apprehension of animism in nature, and a consequent feeling of pathos for man the outsider. This, altogether, is Vaughan's cosmological fall, and, interestingly, the stanza which contributes least to the general effect is, indeed, the most Herbert-like, especially in its closing lines:

> O brook it not! thy bloud is mine,
> And my soul should be thine;
> O brook it not! why wilt thou stop
> After whole showres one drop?
> Sure, thou wilt joy to see
> Thy sheep with thee.
>
> [*Works of Vaughan*, p. 433]

If the introduction of Herbert's *Man* to the discussion has complicated the analysis, I feel it still strengthens the main point that Herbert's poetic treatment of the fall is characteristically behaviorist, as distinct from Vaughan's, which is cosmological. But it may be interesting now to turn up a pair of poems on a different subject, which do not seem to offer this contrast at all, and to ask if, on closer examination, they really do.

Vaughan's *Unprofitableness* on first reading might well be taken for a poem by Herbert, and in fact it is strongly influenced by him. Vaughan is figuring his experience of spiritual dearth under the guise of a flower, which is exactly what Herbert does in *The Flower*. Vaughan's opening line, "How rich, O Lord! how fresh thy visits are!"

(*Works of Vaughan,* p. 441), is a direct echo of Herbert's "How fresh, O Lord, how sweet and clean / Are thy returns" (*Works,* p. 165). Indeed there is very little difference in idea or sensibility between the progress of the flower in Vaughan, from storms and frosts to regeneration in the blessed sunlight, and the similar progress in Herbert. The influence of *The Flower* on *Unprofitableness* is so direct that Herbert is partially the author of Vaughan's poem. Yet there may be a shade of difference. I quote Ross Garner:

> Vaughan takes on the being of the object. Herbert places the reverse emphasis on his experience, for in Herbert's poem the flower speaks as would Herbert, relishes versing, etc. In Vaughan's, Vaughan speaks as would the flower, and *his* leaves "hopeless hung." [9]

There is something in this, and certainly Vaughan's poem is a splendid example of negative capability:

> 'Twas but Just now my bleak leaves hopeles hung
> Sullyed with dust and mud.
>
> [*Works of Vaughan,* p. 441]

Vaughan has become the flower with an immediate intensity and absorption. In Herbert, on the other hand, moral and psychological terms are more directly inserted: "Offring at heav'n, growing and groning thither" (*Works,* p. 166). Garner has, incidentally, not put his point well, for of course Herbert's flower does not relish versing: it is Herbert who relishes versing, and not to see this is to miss the most powerful effect of the poem. Vaughan writes his poem wholly in metaphor, but Herbert writes his mostly in simile: "ev'n as the flowers in spring"; "as flowers depart." True, Herbert's poem does move into metaphor, and it does so at the best moments. The two finest parts of *The Flower* are the opening of the second stanza, "Who would have thought my shrivel'd heart / Could have recover'd greennesse?" (*Works,* p. 166), and the whole of the penultimate stanza:

> And now in age I bud again,
> After so many deaths I live and write;
> I once more smell the dew and rain,
> And relish versing: O my onely light,

> It cannot be
> That I am he
> On whom thy tempests fell all night.
>> [*Works*, p. 166]

At these points Herbert is writing most completely in metaphor, and poet and flower are fused, without any explicit mention of a comparison. But these lines seem to get most of their power from the very fact that the poet and flower are held apart, as simile, for most of the poem and then rush together at these moments of intensity. It seems appropriate that this should be done by Herbert, the poet we are describing by the word "behavior," with his eye on the facts of moral experience, and that Vaughan the cosmologist, the poet of immanence, of divinity present in nature, should turn himself into a flower for the duration of his poem.

Two final examples will illustrate that the distinction between behaviorist and cosmologist is also supported by some of the best-known poems of both writers on the subject of the fall and human sinfulness, which is what specifically interests us here. Clearly, Herbert's *Nature* and *The Collar* show the sinful state of man by concentrating on his rebellious and recalcitrant behavior:

> Full of rebellion, I would die,
> Or fight, or travell, or denie
> That thou hast ought to do with me.
>> [*Works*, p. 45]

> I struck the board, and cry'd, No more.
> I will abroad.
>> [*Works*, p. 153]

In Vaughan, on the other hand, such famous poems as *The Tempest* and *Cock-crowing* describe man's fallen state in terms of that sad discord between man and the rest of creation, which is the hallmark of Vaughan's cosmological fall:

> All have their *Keyes*, and set *ascents;* but man
> Though he knows these, and hath more of his own,
> Sleeps at the ladders foot: alas!
>> [*Works of Vaughan*, p. 461]

> If such a tincture, such a touch,
> So firm a longing can impowre
> Shall thy own image think it much
> To watch for thy appearing hour?
>
> [*Works of Vaughan*, p. 488]

Examples such as these could be multiplied, but enough has been said to permit a tentative generalization. When Herbert writes about the world picture, he does not use it to show the fallen state of man. When he wants to do that, he does so direct, by showing man's passions, his broken will, his giddiness, his pride, his insubordination, his ambition and decayed reason. When Vaughan writes about the world picture (which he does far more often than Herbert), that is his way of writing about fallen man, for the fall is seen by Vaughan essentially in the way man does not fit into the cosmos. In their poetry of the fall and original sin, Herbert's object is behavior, Vaughan's is cosmology.

Yet it may be objected that I am exaggerating a nuance into a contrast, for Herbert can hardly have believed that man does fit harmoniously into the world, and Vaughan must certainly have believed that man's misfitting shows itself in behavior. But I have carefully avoided introducing the poets' beliefs to this discussion. I have merely been looking for adequate ways to express the differences between the poems themselves, for what in terms of commonly held ideas is a nuance might well yield a real difference in terms of poetry. Such is the case with Vaughan's poetry of Man in relation to the work of his revered mentor, George Herbert.

Vaughan's Theology

So far we have been talking about some of the best-known poems by Vaughan, *Cock-crowing*, *The Tempest*, *Etenim*, in which we have found a characteristic approach to the subject of the fall. However, there are lines in *Silex Scintillans* which seem to be a flat contradiction of Vaughan's cosmological poetry of man. Consider this piece from *Corruption:*

Things here were strange unto him: Swet, and till
    All was a thorn, or weed.
Nor did those last, but (like himself,) dyed still
    As soon as they did *Seed,*
They seem'd to quarrel with him; for that Act
    That fel him, foyl'd them all,
He drew the Curse upon the world, and Crackt
    The whole frame with his fall.
                    [*Works of Vaughan,* p. 440]

The poem states clearly that the world did fall with man, and the fact that the world is "Crackt" and cursed and "foyl'd" would seem to deny that it is innocent and in harmony with God, while man alone is guilty and outcast. Another example is *Ascension-day,* which describes the "pure earth" and "fair woods" of Eden on the "first seventh day, / Before man brought forth sin, and sin decay" (*Works of Vaughan,* p. 482). The implication is again that man's sin corrupted the world after he fell. The description of the fall here is quite different from *The Tempest* and *Etenim,* and it is easy enough to find this sort of approach throughout Vaughan's writings. But it does not occur in his best poems. Neither *Corruption* nor *Ascension-day* is particularly recognizable as being by Vaughan at all, and neither is much better than an adequate piece of versifying. In a poet as intuitive as Vaughan, indeed, we expect unevenness, and often (as here) his poems slip off into tedious versification of his commonplace theological beliefs. Now we are clearly moving into the realm of ideas in an attempt to explain the poetic differences we have already described. To purue this we should look first at the traditionalism of Vaughan's fall theology, especially as he states it in his prose writings.

    The most important of Vaughan's prose pieces are *The Mount of Olives; or, Solitary Devotions; The Life of Holy Paulinus; The Bishop of Nola,* together with the prefaces to these works and to *Silex Scintillans.* The most useful for us is the devotional treatise, *The Mount of Olives.* Although it is not composed as a systematic meditation, it is much influenced by the many such handbooks which were popular throughout the seventeenth century. Vaughan is aware that he is adding one volume to that already well-stocked library: *"I know the world abounds with these Manuals, and triumphs over them. It is not then their scarsity that call'd this forth, nor yet a desire to crosse the age, nor any in it"* (*Works of Vaughan*, p. 140). The hint of dis-illusionment with the "world" in this statement becomes a prepos-session in *The Mount of Olives:* Vaughan was much anguished by the political chaos of his times, and one consequence is an emphasis in his treatise on the vanity of transient things and on human per-versity and mortality. Of the traditional Augustinian motifs which naturally are accommodated to his work, meditation upon last things, in consequence, receives special emphasis:

O miserable and sad mutations! (*Petrarch. de otio Rel.*) Where is now their *pompous & shining train?* Where are their *triumphs, fire-works, and feasts,* with all the *ridiculous tumults* of a *popu-lar, prodigious pride?* Where is their *purple* and *fine linen,* their chains of *massie gold,* and sparkling ornaments of *pearls?* Where are their *Cooks* and *Carvers,* their *fowlers* and *fishers?* [*Works of Vaughan,* p. 172]

This attack on the vanity of the court, which reminds us so much of Herbert, leads to a complementary affirmation: "O happy then, yea Infinitly happy is that religious liver, who is ever meditating upon the houre of death before it comes, that when it is come, he may passe through it with joy" (*Works of Vaughan,* p. 173). And Vaughan continues with detailed and evocative meditations on death, resur-rection, and judgment: "The difference betwixt the *righteous* and the *wicked,"* he claims, "is to be seen in their *death"* (*Works of Vaughan,* p. 183), and nothing can bring us sooner to good counsel than "the serious consideration of our own frailty" (*Works of Vaughan,* p. 185).

Other striking and traditionally Augustinian emphases in *The Mount of Olives* are on repentance and the eucharist, as can be seen even from the table of contents. There is a section devoted to "the Grace of Repentance, with a Confession of sins," and several sections on the eucharist: "Admonitions with Prayers and Meditations before receiving the Lords Supper"; "A particular Meditation before re-ceiving the holy Communion"; "A Prayer when thou art upon going to the Lord's Table." We are reminded throughout also of the im-portance of the Atonement, and especially of the blood sacrifice and passion of Christ, though Vaughan does not, admittedly, devote much space to the actual meditation of the cross. Finally, the traditional technique of application of the senses is important. As we have indicated, there is a good deal of emphasis on the evocation of last things, and there are a number of typical graphic meditations on events from the life of Christ. This one, for example, clearly directs the reader to application of the senses:

> Meditate with thy self what miracles of mercy he hath done for thee. Consider how he left his Fathers bosome to be lodged in a manger, and laid by his robes of glory to take upon him the seed of *Abraham,* that he might cloath thee with Immortality. Call to minde his wearisome journeys, continual afflictions, the malice and scorne he underwent, the persecutions and reproaches laid upon him, his strong cries and teares in the days of his flesh, his spiritual agony and sweating of blood, with the Implacable fury of his Enemies, and his own unspeakable humility, humbling himself to the death of the Crosse, a death accursed by Gods own mouth. [*Works of Vaughan,* pp. 157-58]

These characteristic motifs from traditional devotion are obviously enough present in Vaughan's *The Mount of Olives* and help establish, in the widest terms, its spiritual antecedents. However, the motifs we have mentioned, and especially the meditation on last things, subserve what is the single most profoundly felt fact in the work, namely, Vaughan's perception of the utterly unregenerate condition of human fallenness. Man's corruption and mortality, his perversity, his pride and self-righteousness, in short, the fruits of his original sin, are continually at the forefront of Vaughan's attention, and his view of the fall is the severe interpretation of the Reformation Augustine. This view Vaughan shares also with Herbert, whose opinions we have already seen and whom Vaughan indeed quotes in *The Mount of Olives.* Moreover, when Vaughan is describing the effects of the fall, he does so in Herbert's behaviorist terms. There is no mention whatsoever in *The Mount of Olives* of anything even approaching that typical cosmological fall which we find in the poetry. "And what else is the World but a Wildernesse," Vaughan asks, "a darksome, intricate wood full of *Ambushes* and dangers!" (*Works of Vaughan,* p. 146).

"I shall hold it no *Paradoxe* to affirme," he says, *"there are no pleasures in this world"* (*Works of Vaughan,* pp. 185-86). There is no sense here of a harmonious or sentient universe. The sinful nature of man is consistently (and evocatively) described in terms of human behavior: "A pretended *sanctity* from the teeth outward, with frequent *mention* of the *Spirit,* and a presumptuous assuming to our selves of the stile of *Saints,* when we are within full of *subtilty, malice, oppression, lewd opinions,* and *diverse lusts"* (*Works of Vaughan,* p. 182). In another passage Vaughan asks:

> What an habitation of darknesse and death wilt thou finde within me? What abominable desolations and emptinesse? What barrennesse and disorders wilt thou see there? Many a time hast thou knockt, and I have shut the doors against thee, thou hast often called, and I would not answer. Sleeping and waking, early and late, day and night have I refused instruction, and would not be healed. And now, O my God, after all this rebellion and uncleannesse, wilt thou come and lodge with me? [*Works of Vaughan,* pp. 160-61]

In both passages (and there are many others) man's unregenerate nature is described, not in terms of his being a tragic misfit in the ordered scheme of nature, but in terms of his recalcitrance, his perversity—in terms of his behavior. The Calvinist and often ultra-Augustinian opinion of human sinfulness and utter culpability and powerlessness which Vaughan repeatedly expresses ("I know, O my God, it is not in man to establish his own ways" [*Works of Vaughan,* p. 152]) leads to several outbursts which remind us of Donne when, in certain moods, he regards man from that most pessimistic aspect of the Augustinian theology he so admired:

> And now, O my God, seeing I am but Dust and Ashes, and my Righteousnesse a filthy Rag, having no deserts in my self but what should draw Everlasting vengeance, and the Vials of thy bitter wrath upon my body and soul; behold . . . my Redeemer and Mediatour in whom thou art well-pleased, hear thou him. O look not upon my Leprosie, but on his beauty and perfection! [*Works of Vaughan,* p. 145]

Or:

> But all my righteousnesse is a filthy rag, my heart neither new nor undefiled, but a nest of unclean birds, where they have not onely laine, but hatched and brought forth their viperous young ones. [*Works of Vaughan*, p. 161]

Or:

> I have come unto the bread of life, and yet am hungry; into the light, and yet am blind; unto the great Physician, and yet my Issue runs: The former and the later rain of thy heavenly Doctrine falls still without intermission upon my heart, but this bad ground yeelds nothing but Thornes and Briers . . . but in vain, O Lord, shall they cry in our Ears, unlesse thou openest and renewest our hearts. [*Works of Vaughan*, p. 149]

The Reformation insistence on the devastating effects of the inherited curse of original sin which has caused man's unregenerate nature and his powerlessness to act for good is central in these passages.

The same picture is presented in Vaughan's other important prose work, *The Life of Holy Paulinus*. The *Life* is not, however, so useful for our purposes as the devotional treatise, because it attempts to give a true historical account of the bishop's career, rather than an exposition of the author's personal habits of devotion. But certain emphases do come through as Vaughan's own. First of all, the interest in Paulinus is itself significant, for the bishop was, as Vaughan notes repeatedly, very close to Saint Augustine. "But above all, the Soules of holy *Augustine* and *Paulinus* (like *Jonathan* and *David,* or *Jacob* and *Joseph*) were *knit together,* and *the life of the one was bound up in the life of the other*" (*Works of Vaughan*, pp. 357-58). Vaughan's scholarly task of biography was, therefore, within the very ethos of Augustinian theology from its inception, and Vaughan even undertakes his account under the two characteristically Augustinian headings of Nature and Grace: "In the explication of his life I shall follow first the method of *Nature,* afterwards of *Grace*" (*Works of Vaughan*, p. 340). Moreover, the account of Paulinus's life is dealt with as a typical Pauline and Augustinian conversion.[10]

More important is Vaughan's treatment of sin, and again, as in *The Mount of Olives*, the overwhelming emphasis is on man's unregenerate nature seen in terms of his rebellious, hypocritical, recalcitrant behavior:

> The greatest part of men, which we commonly terme the popu-
> lacy, are a stiffe, uncivill generation, without any seed of honour
> or goodnesse, and sensible of nothing but private interest, & the
> base waies of acquiring it. What Virtue, or what humanity can
> be expected from a *Raymond Cabanes,* a *Massinello,* or some
> Son of a Butcher? They have one barbarous shift, which Tigers
> and Beares would blush to commit: They will cut the throats of
> their most generous and Virtuous Benefactours, to comply
> with times, and advantage themselves; Yea, they will rejoyce
> to see them ruined, and like inhumane Salvages, insult over their
> innocent and helplesse posterity. [*Works of Vaughan,* p. 363]

The contrast with tigers and bears does not reflect the cosmological
fall of Vaughan's poetry, for we are not meant to reflect on the innocence of these animals. The meaning is that the people named are
worse *even* than tigers and bears, which are the most ferocious of
beasts. Here, as throughout the *Life,* when Vaughan wants to show
human sinfulness, his method is to compare other men's behavior
with that of Paulinus.

Yet I cannot say, as I can for *The Mount of Olives,* that there is
not a single mention of Vaughan's cosmological fall in the *Life.*
There is one, and it is a flat statement of that cosmological emphasis
which recurs in the most memorable Vaughan poems. "The afflictions of man are more moving then of any other Creature," Vaughan
writes, "for he onely is a stranger here, where all things else are at
home" (*Works of Vaughan,* p. 352). However, this single statement
occurs in a place where Vaughan is enjoining us to pity suffering
humanity and lamenting that "the losing of his innocency, and his
device of Tyranny" have made man lose also the sense of pity for
other men, or even the perception of himself as pitiable. The sense of
man's fall as pitiable is accompanied here, as in the poems, by the
theory of man as the one misfit in nature. Even this is complicated,
however, for naming man "a stranger here" may merely echo Peter's
idea of the Christian as resident alien, his citizenship in heaven
(1 Pet. 2:11). Certainly, the cosmological reading is not at all the
general emphasis of either *The Mount of Olives* or the *Life,* where
the fall is characteristically a horrifying witness of human corruption
and the world is, as Vaughan writes in the preface to the *Life, "not*

worth the enjoying, it is corrupt, and poysoned with the Curse," and
we are advised, *"doat not any more upon a withered, rotten* Gourd,
upon the seducements and falshood of a most odious, decayed Pros-
titute" (*Works of Vaughan*, p. 338). Man's sinfulness is characteristically seen in terms of a fallen world, and in terms of the psychology
of his own inner rebellion.

Ross Garner has written about what he rightly calls "The Augustinian Temper" in Vaughan.[11] He points out that Vaughan's Augustinian theology is influenced by Herbert (and therefore by Calvin), and he notes the pessimistic emphases on man's unregenerate
nature throughout the poems. He then points to a recurring optimistic view about creation in Vaughan and shows that it was not an
uncommon Anglican practice to reconcile optimism about creation
with pessimism about man. I concur with Garner's view but would
now bring it a step further. Reconciliation of optimism and pessimism
concerning creation and man has always been a problem for Christian theologians, and it is of central importance to the argument of this
book that these problems were especially acute in seventeenth-century
England. Garner is therefore right to point out the special importance
of the question for Anglicans. But he has not noted what seems to
me a curious fact, namely, that Vaughan's prose writings, together
with his prosaic verse, are almost totally concerned with a Herbertian
and behaviorist fall (Garner's "pessimism"), and they are without
any sense of the cosmological fall (Garner's "optimism") which occurs only in those poems where Vaughan's poetic sensibility is at its
highest.

We have already looked at *Corruption* and *Ascension-day* for
examples of Vaughan's "pessimistic" and prosaic verse. Garner gives
the example, among several others, of *Repentance:*

> O what am I, that I should breed
> Figs on a thorne, flowres on a weed!
> I am the gourd of sin, and sorrow
> Growing o'r night, and gone to morrow,
> In all this *Round* of life and death
> Nothing's more vile than is my breath,
> Profanenes on my tongue doth rest,
> Defects, and darknes in my brest,

> Pollutions all my body wed,
> And even my soul to thee is dead,
> Only in him, on whom I feast,
> Both soul, and body are well drest.
>
> [*Works of Vaughan,* pp. 449-50]

These lines are clearly an expression of the sort of thing we have been reading in the prose. It is man in the Augustinian view, and it is behaviorist. Above all, these lines are not characteristic of what we remember of Vaughan's best skills as a poet. This is very mediocre poetry indeed. But, if the reader who knew his Herbert and his Vaughan were asked to point out the lines in *Repentance* that do sound most like Vaughan, he would (after indicating lines 2 and 3) surely point to the passage from line 31 to line 46:

> The blades of grasse, thy Creatures feeding,
> The trees, their leafs; the flowres, their seeding;
> The Dust, of which I am a part,
> The Stones much softer than my heart,
> The drops of rain, the sighs of wind,
> The Stars to which I am stark blind,
> The Dew thy herbs drink up by night,
> The beams they warm them at i' th' light,
> All that have signature or life,
> I summon'd to decide this strife,
> And lest I should lack for Arrears,
> A spring ran by, I told her tears,
> But when these came unto the scale,
> My sins alone outweigh'd them all.
>
> [*Works of Vaughan,* pp. 448-49]

Even if this too is not great, it is where the best energy of the poem lies, and the real Vaughan is present in that sense of mysterious inner activity which the poem struggles to convey—silent, unobtrusive, but perfectly adjusted, harmonious. The strangeness is caught in a peculiar use of words like "beams" and "signature," by the peculiar night processes of the "herbs," and by the sense of even stones having affections. Beside this activity of nature, man seems a little lost and pathetic.

The Timber is perhaps the best example in *Silex Scintillans* of the sort of unevenness we see in *Repentance*. It is a poem with some magnificent lines which pass into banal moralization. The division within the poem is even clear enough for us to draw a dividing line at the end of the fifth stanza. The opening twenty lines are remarkable, mainly because of the complete identification the poet achieves with the timber. As in *Unprofitableness,* Vaughan is here the poet of immanence. He actually becomes the dead tree, and the account of the attendant growths and deaths of birds and flowers achieves a real complexity when seen in relation to the spiritual life of man. There is a strong sense of the interrelated life processes of all things in nature, for all things endure and pass away in accordance with their special ends but are nonetheless connected intimately and necessarily:

> And still a new succession sings and flies;
> Fresh Groves grow up, and their green branches shoot
> Towards the old and still enduring skies,
> While the low *Violet* thrives at their root.
>   [*Works of Vaughan,* p. 497]

The new groves are as necessary as the dead timber and, in turn, as necessary as the new generation of birds to sing in harmony, as it were, with the "green branches." They are part of an inevitable interconnected process of life and death, which in the end identifies itself against eternity. These transitory things have their reality because they stand opposed to the "old and still enduring skies." Against this is the nostalgia of the next stanza:

> But thou beneath the sad and heavy *Line*
> Of death, dost waste all senseless, cold and dark;
> Where not so much as dreams of light may shine,
> Nor any thought of greenness, leaf or bark.
>   [*Works of Vaughan,* p. 497]

The words "shine" and "greenness" recall the acutely felt growth and burgeoning of the previous stanza and increase the "cold and dark" (but complementary) necessity of the dead tree. Throughout the opening twenty lines the peculiar feeling for submerged life forces gives the poem its most subtle power, and this is especially true in the remarkable response in stanza 4 of the (seemingly) dead tree to the rising storm. The poem achieves its finest complexity and power when all this is seen as a metaphor of the spiritual life.

The Timber breaks down, however, immediately Vaughan moves away from metaphor and from his poetry of immanence. After stanza 5 his method is simile, and he becomes explicit. He moralizes, and the poem collapses into mediocrity. "So murthered man, when lovely life is done," he begins stanza 6, by way of explication of the first twenty lines, and goes on to flat and tedious verse like this:

> And is there any murth'rer worse then sin?
> Or any storms more foul then a lewd life?
> Or what *Resentient* can work more within,
> Then true remorse, when with past sins at strife?
> $\qquad$ [*Works of Vaughan*, p. 498]

In the effort toward clear explication, the work loses, and does not recover, its poetry. *The Timber* as a whole is thus representative of the sort of unevenness which occurs in *Repentance,* as it does throughout *Silex Scintillans,* and it demonstrates how Vaughan's poetry can blaze forth with a momentary authority which is utterly distinctive from a background which is often commonplace and doctrinaire.

What this analysis is now working toward is an attempt to make a statement about Vaughan the poet as distinct from Vaughan the theologian, particularly on the question of sin. We are looking, not for inconsistencies in Vaughan's thought, but merely for some explanation of how his poetry in particular is used to make possible a fusion of two seemingly contrary views of man, the optimistic and the pessimistic, the cosmological and the behaviorist. Vaughan's prose most adequately reflects what, in terms of dogmatic orthodoxy, he probably thought. As he says in the preface to *The Mount of Olives,* he is giving *"sound directions and wholsome words"* to his reader, *"with holy and apposite* Ejaculations *for most times and occasions"* (*Works of Vaughan,* p. 140). In this treatise of devotion he is concerned to put the commonplaces of morality and human frailty as centrally and traditionally as possible. And it would seem that here, as well as in the prosaic moralizations which occur throughout *Silex Scintillans,* Vaughan's view of man does not differ from

Herbert's. It is Augustinian and is influenced by Calvin. Nor does Vaughan present human sinfulness differently from Herbert. His method is to concentrate on man's "giddinesse," his rebelliousness; in short, what we have called his behavior.

It is interesting, however, that in the preface to *The Mount of Olives* Vaughan makes a somewhat cryptic distinction between what he is doing in the devotional treatise and what he is doing in his poems. *"Neither did I thinke it necessary,"* he writes, *"that the ordinary Instructions for a regular life (of which there are infinite Volumes already extant) should be inserted into this small Manuall, lest instead of Devotion, I should trouble thee with a peece of Ethics. Besides, thou hast them already as briefly delivered as possibly I could, in my* Sacred Poems" (*Works of Vaughan,* p. 140). We are accustomed to describing *Silex Scintillans* as a volume of devotional poems, though Vaughan apparently makes a further distinction. But what exactly is the difference between "devotion" and "ethics" in *The Mount of Olives* and *Silex Scintillans* is not made clear in the above, curious passage. It does, however, provide at least an interesting hint of the sort of distinction I am pressing. For it is only in Vaughan's most characteristic and most striking poems, where the language of animism and the mystical sense of friendly consciousness running through the universe is felt, that Vaughan's cosmological and optimistic treatment of the fall is evident. Precisely this difference distinguishes Vaughan, as a poet, from Herbert on the subject of sin. And in his poems, which do, as Garner says, attempt to reconcile optimistic and pessimistic views of man, Vaughan in fact makes a leap to bridge the gap between a traditional guilt-culture Augustinian view of man's fall, which he believed in terms of dogma, and a cosmological view which, I will now suggest, is Hermetic.

Henry Vaughan and Hermetic Philosophy

Vaughan does not seem to have been an intensely devoted student of the *Hermetica,* but he was both a naturalist and a physician, which would certainly encourage his interest: the Hermetic magus, as we have seen, was concerned to utilize, in an empirical manner, the powers of the natural world, and Ficino's basic work on the magus, the *De triplici vita,* is a manual on medicine. Certainly, from his writings it can be concluded that Vaughan was more than casually familiar with the Hermetic philosophy. In 1655 and 1657, he translated the two treatises of Heinrich Nolle, the *Hermetical Physick* and *The Chymists Key,* and he promises in a note, appended to the first of these, to write a treatise on meteors *"according to the* Hermetic *principles"* (*Works of Vaughan,* p. 561). In *Flores Solitudinis* he makes an allusion to a teaching of Paracelsus (*Works of Vaughan,* p. 305), and in *The Mount of Olives* he refers to Cornelius Agrippa (*Works of Vaughan,* p. 176), thus showing himself at least familiar with the two most famous Hermetists of his time. Vaughan was also committed enough to Hermetic principles to write in his preface to the first translation of Nollius that, "If any will be offended with this *Hermeticall* Theorie, I shall but smile at his frettings, and pitty his ignorance" (*Works of Vaughan,* p. 548).

There is also the influence of Thomas, Henry's twin brother, who was probably the foremost Hermetic authority in England in his day. Although it remains true, and perhaps significant, that both Henry and Thomas produced their best work at roughly the same time, it is not now so clear as was once thought that they knew each other's work intimately and had spent some years (usually regarded as between 1642 and 1649) living in the same community in Wales.[12] Yet it seems clear from his commendatory poem in *Olor Iscanus* (*Works of Vaughan,* pp. 39-41) that Thomas was more than casually interested in his brother's writing, and there is another commendatory poem attached to the same volume which claims the brothers were spiritually close:

> What *Planet* rul'd your *birth?* What *wittie star?*
> That you so like in *Souls* as *Bodies* are!
> > [*Works of Vaughan,* p. 36]

Internal evidence, as critics have readily noted, seems to show that, if Henry had not actually read Thomas, both brothers were drawing on the same Hermetic source material. There are many parallels between *Silex Scintillans* and the Hermetic writings of Thomas, and one or two of the better-known examples will illustrate the point. The opening stanza of *Cock-crowing,*

> Father of lights! What Sunnie seed,
> What glance of day hast thou confin'd
> Into this bird? To all the breed
> This busie Ray thou hast assign'd;
> Their magnetisme works all night,
> And dreams of Paradise and light,
>   [*Works of Vaughan*, p. 488]

is closely paralleled in Thomas Vaughan's *Anima magica abscondita:*

> The Soul . . . is guided in her operations by a spiritual, meta-
> physical grain, a seed or glance of light, simple and without any
> mixture, descending from the first Father of Lights. For though
> His full-eyed love shines on nothing but man, yet everything in
> the world is in some measure directed for his preservation by a
> spice or touch of the First Intellect.[13]

This couplet from *Vanity of Spirit,*

> Weake beames, and fires flash'd to my sight,
> Like a young East, or Moone-shine night,
>   [*Works of Vaughan*, p. 418]

recalls Thomas in *Lumen de lumine:* "I could discover a white, weake
light . . . not so clear as that of a candle, but misty." This is followed
by a journey by the writer to the Mountains of the Moon, to which he
is conducted by Nature, whose garment smelled like the East.[14] If the
prose was not the source of the poetry here, it suggests, as Miss Mahood points out, "a complete affinity of mind between the two
writers." [15]

A good deal of critical interest in Vaughan and Hermetic philosophy has concentrated on the type of information we have just offered
in relation to Henry and Thomas. There are, for instance, numerous
articles and studies which isolate passages from Hermetism and compare these to poems from *Silex Scintillans.* There are major parallels,
such as the relation of *The Starre* to passages from *Magia Adamica*
and *Lumen de lumine,*[16] or details, such as the discussion of "greennesse" in *The Seed Growing Secretly,* which can be related to the
Hermetic *benedicta viriditas,*[17] and so on. The notes to Martin's edition of Vaughan's *Works* provide a range of such passages, and I will

not labor the point, for this sort of collection, although it has to be done, is not satisfactory in itself. It may well be asked, for instance, what difference does it make to a poem like *Cock-crowing?* To answer this we would naturally point first to the passage from *Anima magica abscondita* which, as we have seen, influences the first stanza. Then we would point to such semitechnical Hermetic words as "tincture," "magnetism," "ray," and to the fundamental idea, at least partially Hermetic, of the cock as a solary bird[18] responding to the dawn by the sort of sympathy which Ficino describes as flowing between the planets and their corresponding elements on earth. There is also Vaughan's phrase, the "house of light," in line 10, which probably derives from Thomas Vaughan's work of that name, *Aula lucis: The House of Light.*[19]

But all this, Hermetic as it may be, does not make any real difference to the seed, or ray, or magnetism, for on an open and orthodox reading of stanzas 1-3, these are already saying the sort of thing the Hermetic philosophy says. One difference it does make is to "it seems" in line 11. If this is a Hermetic poem, it is not saying, cocks crow at dawn and this almost looks like they have a direct apprehension of the Father of Lights, which is a lesson for us. It is saying, cocks crow at dawn and this is *because* they have an apprehension of the Father of Lights. Similarly, in stanza 6, if this is a Hermetic poem, the word that is affected is "if." The poem is then saying that the hearts of birds do beat for light and is drawing a lesson from what is, not from what seems. There is some difference here, but not much.

It is, we might conclude, interesting to trace the sources, but we do not have, at the end of all the research, much by way of significant generalization to describe Vaughan's overall debt to Hermetic philosophy. We could probably make some statement about certain evocative elements of Vaughan's vocabulary taken over from Hermetism. This would involve the words which do not appear, for instance, in Herbert, but which are so effective in Vaughan's "Hermetic" poems: words like "influence," "sympathy," "ray," "beam," "commerce," "tincture," "grain," and so on. And if we were now asked—What is the effect of this vocabulary, what characteristic experience does it yield in the many poems where it recurs?—we would probably reply that it is intimately related to that single most important poetic quality of *Silex Scintillans,* the sense of animism, the intense feeling of sentience in nature. The poet can feel this in stars:

> Thine hoast of spyes
> The starres shine in their watches,
> I doe survey
> Each busie Ray,
> And how they work and wind,
> And wish each beame
> My soul doth streame
> With the like ardour shin'd[.]
>
> [*Works of Vaughan,* p. 421]

Or in stones:

> Man I can bribe, and woman will
> Consent to any gainful ill,
> But these dumb creatures are so true,
> No gold nor gifts can them subdue[.]
>
> [*Works of Vaughan,* p. 514]

Or seeds:

> Dear, secret *Greenness!* nurst below
> Tempests and windes[.]
>
> [*Works of Vaughan,* p. 511]

Or birds and bees:

> Weighing the stedfastness and state
> Of some mean things which here below reside,
> Where birds like watchful Clocks the noiseless date
> And Intercourse of times divide,
> Where Bees at night get home and hive, and flowrs
> Early, aswel as late,
> Rise with the Sun, and set in the same bowrs[.]
>
> [*Works of Vaughan,* p. 477]

Or there is the poem where the Bible itself takes on the character and peculiar animistic atmosphere of Hermetism:

> In thee the hidden stone, the *Manna* lies,
> Thou art the great *Elixir,* rare, and Choice;

> The Key that opens to all Mysteries,
> The *Word* in Characters, God in the *Voice*.
>
> [*Works of Vaughan*, p. 441]

In short, Vaughan's Hermetism is closely related to the sense of God's immanence in the cosmos. Most critics of the subject agree readily with this sort of conclusion. But if we now go a step further, we recall from an earlier phase of this argument that in so many of Vaughan's best poems when the question of sin is being dealt with, this very apprehension of cosmic animism, which is basically Hermetic, links inevitably to what we have called Vaughan's cosmological fall. It should therefore be no surprise, and it is the final link in my argument, that when we turn to the Hermetic philosophy at large we should also find in it something that very closely approximates Vaughan's cosmological fall. This leaves the way open to suggest that through Hermes Trismegistus a typically enlightenment anthropology enters into Vaughan's poetry, where it effects a significant modification of his traditional guilt-culture and Augustinian spirituality.

The Cosmological Fall in Hermes Trismegistus

A Hellenic—more specifically, Neoplatonic—rationalism, reintroduced to Europe largely by certain Renaissance thinkers, is really the genus within which the *Corpus Hermeticum* is a species. In the Renaissance, Hermetic philosophy, as we have seen, was erroneously interpreted as part of an ancient tradition of divine theology handed down through Moses as well as Zoroaster, Mercurius Trismegistus, Aglaophemus, Pythagoras, and Plato. This genealogy is of immense importance for the understanding not only of Renaissance Hermetism but of Vaughan's debt to it, for the rediscovery of the Trismegistic writings is really an aspect of the broader emergence during the Renaissance of an "enlightenment" optimism about the state and nature of man which Vaughan, like the Cambridge Platonists, adapted in the seventeenth century as a latitudinarian reinterpretation of a harsh Reformation and Augustinian theology of human nature.

Although Ficino and Pico and Henry Vaughan believed in the fall, their sense of the effects of original sin swings noticeably away from the Augustinian conviction of a personal and inherited depravity, under the pull of a Platonist-oriented theology which encourages a trust in reason (rather than faith and grace) to attain to archetypal and eternal truth by its own light. One of the fundamental tenets of Ficino's anthropology, for instance, is the central position he affords man in the hierarchy of being by deliberately rereading the Plotinian hierarchy of substances, One, Mind, Soul, Sensation, Nature, Body. Man is at the center of an order consisting of God, angel, soul, quality, and body, and P. O. Kristeller points out that Ficino rearranged the Plotinian scheme in order especially to dignify the position of man.[20] One consequence of such a modification, as might be expected, is a significant decrease in the importance attached to a guilt-culture interpretation of the fall and original sin in Ficino's thought.

It is therefore appropriate that, when Ficino does talk of the fall, he should do so within a specifically Neoplatonic framework, as in the *Commentary on the Symposium,* where the speech of Aristophanes is interpreted as an analogue of the Christian fall of Man. According to Aristophanes, man has lost his "other half," with whom he was once joined, as a punishment for having tried "to scale heaven" where he "would have laid hands upon the Gods." The gods divided him in two (in the original he was a circular, "complete" creature), and, in consequence, "each of us, having one side only, like a flat fish is but the tallyhalf of a man," wandering on earth deprived of supernatural light, in search of his other half.[21] This is essentially a comic story, but at the same time compassionate, and much of its breadth of sympathy for man is retained in Ficino's commentary. Interestingly, the initiative to win back the divine light and find the other half is left very much to man himself. Of the fallen souls, Ficino says: "they are aroused by that innate and natural light which they have kept . . . to win back, by the study of truth, that divine supernatural light, that former other half of themselves which they lost in the fall." [22] But Ficino, sensing the specter of Hellenic self-sufficiency lurking behind this line of thought, does cautiously add a passage castigating those who, "arrogant and swollen with pride, as it were, so boldly trust in their own strength," and he threatens that such pride can only lead to further ill for man.[23]

There are a number of points about this interpretation of the fallen nature of man. First, there is no mention of any positive vitiation of the will or reason. Man is merely deprived of a higher light, and there is no mention of the Augustinian depraved will or of inherited concupiscence. Second, the fall is very close to what Plotinus regarded as the "fall" in the *Enneads*;[24] it is associated with the "downgoing or away-going" of the soul from a full realization of God[25] and is spoken of in terms of the descent of the soul into matter, precipitated by an act of self-will, as in Plotinus.[26] In consequence, something of the Platonic trust in reason to reassert itself, and to thrust back toward the light, is also implied. Ficino certainly leaves much more of the initiative to man than his own favorite theologian, Saint Augustine, and in consequence the part played by grace, not to mention the personal conviction of depravity and sinfulness, is much diminished.

Connected with this optimism about the natural capabilities of man we find the subsidiary machinery of the Hermetists and the alchemists and cabalists, which also encouraged man to exert his knowledge of the influences and powers that pass between higher and lower spheres of creation in order to control nature and even to tap the higher powers of the stars and beyond by means of magic. As man becomes magus he discovers, as we have seen in the *Asclepius,* that he has it in him even to be a god. Thus Pico della Mirandola can introduce into his *Oration on the Dignity of Man* the celebrated passage we have quoted earlier from the *Asclepius* as a testimony of man's excellence—"Man is a marvel then, Asclepius." [27]

Many of these attitudes are repeated in the seventeenth-century Hermetic philosophy of Thomas Vaughan, who consistently reads the fall story in the same broad terms as the descent of a higher nature into a more material state in which reason is obscured, after the pattern of the Neoplatonists:

The sum of all is this; man, as long as he continued in his union to God, knew the good only—that is, the things that were of God. But as soon as he stretched forth his hand and did eat of the forbidden fruit—that is, the middle soul or spirit of the greater world—presently upon the disobedience and transgression of the commandment, his union to the Divine Nature was dissolved; and his spirit being united to the spirit of the world he knew the evil only, that is, the things that were of the world.[28]

Vaughan tells us that this higher knowledge can be regained when the soul "doth elect" to be made one with the higher soul, upon which will follow a voluntary separation from the body and all its evils.[29] Here we once more catch sight of the Hellenic sage, and Thomas Vaughan follows the Renaissance Hermetists' elevated view of the capabilities of man with a passage every bit as daring as Pico's on the power of the magus, toward the end of which he quotes his favorite Hermetic authority, Cornelius Agrippa:

> Finally, "there is no work in the whole course of Nature, how-ever arduous, however excellent, however supernatural it may be, that the human soul, when it has attained the source of its divinity—which the Magi term the soul standing and not falling—cannot accomplish by its own power and apart from any external help." [30]

Finally, we should look briefly at the *Corpus Hermeticum* itself. The *Pimander*, or *Libellus* I,[31] bears an unmistakable resemblance to the chapters of Genesis dealing with the fall of man. This is even remarked upon by Ficino in his commentary, where he says that "in this, the first of the fourteen dialogues . . . Mercurius is seen to deal with the Mosaic mysteries." [32] The story of man's creation and fall is revealed to Hermes Trismegistus by Pimander (the Divine Mind) in a dream. First there was God alone. Then formless matter and, even-tually, a watery substance came into being. God then created the Word, called the Son of God, who worked upon the watery substance and separated out the elements. Then the Nous brought forth the Demiurge, the "Maker of things" who created the seven Administra-tors out of fire and air. But God himself created Adam—"a Being like to Himself." When Man saw the work of the Demiurge, he too wanted to create something, and so with God's permission he entered the highest sphere of heaven, into the company of the Demiurge with whom he resided as a brother. The seven Administrators fell in love with him, and he received from them something of their special char-acter. Man then looked down a stage further, to the realm of Nature. When Nature saw in him the beautiful image of God as well as the characteristics of the seven Administrators, she also became enamored of him, and he, seeing the image of God in Nature, in turn fell in love with her. So the two were joined together. Thus men are a mixture of corporeal and incorporeal. The union of Man and Nature produced seven offspring with natures corresponding to the seven Administrators, and these seven offspring were bisexual. At the end of a long period, God divided the seven bisexual men in two and bade them multiply. Pimander then advises Hermes Trismegistus how to live a holy life.

Despite their superficial resemblances, there is a distinct difference between the fall of man in the *Pimander* and the Augustinian theory of the fall based on Genesis, chapter 3. In the *Pimander* there is no sin of disobedience. Man descends to the lower spheres by his own will and is still loved by the seven Administrators. He is acting, not against God, but with God's permission, and his descent into nature is also an act of love. Nor is man created, like Adam, from the dust of the earth, but as a divine being, a "brother" of the Son of God. The "fall" of the *Pimander* is strongly Platonic. The "down-going or away-going" of the soul from God by an act of self-will is exactly what we have seen in Plotinus, and if this "fall" involves loss, there is nothing implied of the guilt or corruption of human nature associated with the Christian doctrine of an inherited curse. Finally, the division of the sexes from original bisexual creatures strongly suggests that the *Pimander* is influenced by the *Symposium,* and by the very same speech of Aristophanes that we have seen as the background of an account of the fall by Ficino.

The Hermetic fall is seen, therefore, primarily in a cosmological context, as the loss involved by the soul sinking from the higher spheres into a material, inferior level of reality. There is a certain trust that the initiative lies with man to reestablish his former divinity, a line of thought which inevitably weakens a guilt-culture doctrine of grace and promotes an appreciation of the dignity and self-sufficiency which Augustine found unacceptable and which Calvin was to react against so strongly in the Reformation. Finally, the gulf between God and man is lessened, and there is even a certain sympathy for man in his fall—something of the compassion of the delightful story of Aristophanes which is reflected in the myth of the love of Man and

Nature in the *Pimander* and in the *Commentary* of Ficino which deals with the *Symposium* story itself.

This Hermetic view of man is quite different from the view Henry Vaughan maintains in *The Mount of Olives,* but it corresponds exactly to the description we have given of Vaughan's cosmological poetry. There man also is a pathetic misfit in the great chain of the cosmos. He has lost his place, he has come down through the spheres to the realm of the material, and although he has fallen he is not depraved so much as outcast. It would seem therefore that in reading the Hermetic philosophy Vaughan responded first to an enlightenment-Hermetic view of man. Despite the fact that he would have rejected the Hermetists' ideas which are incompatible with his own Augustinian theology, as Garner argues, he was influenced by the poetry of their view of human nature, and in this context the allusions to Hermetism which critics have assiduously collected from *Silex Scintillans* make best sense. The suggestions and echoes of Hermetic philosophy are the objective correlative in language for a deeper response by the poet to a Renaissance cosmologist anthropology.

I could demonstrate this in many of Vaughan's poems. The distinct Neoplatonist sensibility and language of *The Retreate,* with its theme of preexistence, for instance, fits very well into this interpretation. In *Vanity of Spirit,* the excitement surely lies in the poet's search as magus for the secrets of nature, and not at all in the rather dour and traditional moral implied by the title. *The World* is also interesting in its rationalist's reproof of those who do not soar up into the ring of pure and endless light: they are "fools" because they "would" use no wing. Instead they live in "grots and caves," like Plato's prisoners in the *Republic. The Tempest, Etenim, Cock-crowing,* and *Man* I have already mentioned, and I would suggest that *Rules and Lessons, The Relapse, The Dawning, The Constellation, The Starre,* and *Disorder and Frailty* will also give support for my conclusions. I will confine myself to a short look at just one of these to complete the argument.

Disorder and Frailty is a poem about the soul's achieving an intuition of the divine, and about the resentment of the poet who knows the waywardness of his own spirit and the transience of the intuition. It is also a poem about the fall, grace, and redemption. The first stanza characteristically talks of man "breaking the link / Twixt thee, and me." For Vaughan, man's original sin breaks the link in creation that other creatures preserve. This is Vaughan's cosmological fall of man. As we have seen, the traditional idea of the cosmic hierarchy received a vital refurbishing with Ficino, who emphasized the position of man, placing him centrally in his scheme of five basic substances, and for Ficino, as for Henry Vaughan, the soul's unrest and homelessness on earth are of particular interest:

> We are all like Tantalus. We are all thirsty for the true goods, but we all drink dreams. While we absorb the deadly waves of the river of Lethe through our open throats, we scarcely lick with our lips a shadowlike bit of nectar and ambrosia. Therefore, a troublesome thirst continually burns us, oh we poor Tantali.[33]

Like Ficino, Vaughan tends to see man in terms of a cosmic background, and as being uniquely ill at ease in this setting. The resulting tone is one of pity or at any rate of sympathy very much like the compassion in the *Symposium* speech of Aristophanes, which Ficino interpreted as an analogue of the fall of man and which the author of the *Pimander* also used as source material when talking of his "fall." Thus in Henry Vaughan's poem man breaks the link, but the refrains at the end of the stanzas indicate the poet's attitude—"Alas, thy love!"; "Alas, frail weed!"; "Poor, falling Star!"—comparable to Ficino's "oh we poor Tantali" and the compassion of Aristophanes.

The second stanza opens on a note that is consistent with these elements and that should not surprise us in view of what we have seen of the development of the Renaissance magus. "I threaten heaven," writes Vaughan, as, in terms of a blossoming flower, he describes one of his rare moments of spiritual elation which soon withers down through the shortening rhythms of the stanza to the sad realization, "Alas, frail weed!" The cell of clay in the first line is, of course, both the earth and the poet's body, so that Vaughan here seems to be equating the "frailty" of line 2 with the body, saying that the soul, like the seed, is in a frail condition as long as it lies buried in the dark (corporeal) earth. And this, once more, suggests the Plotinian and Hermetic "down-going or away-going" of the spirit. Against the material element is the other principle of the dualism, the divine "fire and breath." It may at first be felt that the "fire and breath" refers to grace, but the following "thy bloud / Too, is my dew" seems to indicate that Christ's redemptive sacrifice is complementary to this process; the grace won by it supplements a tendency already there. In this case the "fire and breath" should perhaps be associated with the divine "seed" of stanza 4, and the use of "fire" in that stanza would seem to confirm this. We can detect in these lines a trace of the same self-sufficiency we have seen in Thomas Vaughan, the *Pimander,* and *Asclepius,* as well as in Ficino and Pico, which is alien to both Augustine and Calvin. The rest of the stanza recounts the falling off of this briefly sustained exaltation as the flower withers and falls, beaten down, with only the root left alive, "hid underground." The soul is back immersed in the body. Vaughan, significantly, chooses to describe this process as simply "the fall" in line 29 and to lament directly, "Alas, frail weed!" This return of the soul to the hindering impediment of the material element is exactly what the *Pimander* also describes as the "fall." Finally, against the all-encompassing brightness of the sun, the poet places his own "weak fire," which links back to the "fire" of stanza 2 and forward to the "fire" and "seed" of stanza 4.

Stanza 4 is an invocation, a plea for grace. The poet realizes that his own "weak fire" will always "pine and retire," that he will never blossom into full awareness unless God will "give wings" to his effort and cultivate the seed of light that is in him. The compassion at the end of stanza 3 now becomes impassioned longing as the poet begins with the exclamation, "O, is!," and imagines himself soaring beyond the infirmity of mundane disillusionment and frustration.

The dominant pattern of the feelings of the poem, then, is one of hopeful aspiration followed by a painful frustration and a puzzled compassion. Man has the seed and fire of God in him but is unable to sustain his mystical flight heavenward, for despite his yearning he is diverted by the body and vicissitudes of life. Vaughan would no doubt have explained this experience in Christian terms of the fall, as result of which the link "twixt thee and me" was broken. This fall was not to be repaired, as was the "fall" for Plotinus, by exercise of the intellect ("There will be no battling in the soul: the mere intervention of Reason is enough"),[34] and Vaughan recognizes the need for grace. At the same time, the experience of sin in the poem is less extreme than a reading of Vaughan's prose would lead us to expect.

Vaughan has a certain sympathy and compassion for the sinful and less of the desperate feeling of being totally dependent on grace that accompanies his behaviorist and Augustinian theology. He writes, "Thy bloud / Too, is my dew," and man has already within him a principle which enables him to "threaten heaven." Yet this, again, is not to underestimate the faith that informs the poem. Vaughan is aware that he needs God and that without His grace he is a "frail weed" indeed. Nonetheless, the experience is different from that of Herbert's *Giddinesse,* even though the religious framework of belief is the same. Vaughan assimilates his own experience to the life of natural things in a cosmic setting, and in his best lines he can "break and bud" into poetic awareness of the unity of all things in "The great *Chime* / And *Symphony* of nature" (*Works of Vaughan*, p. 424). He presents us with a cosmology and asks us to experience with him that God is immanent in all things. In *Disorder and Frailty* the background for such an experience derives from Hermetic and Neoplatonic sources.

We might conclude that Vaughan's theory of the fall followed Saint Augustine. But Vaughan's most successful poetry—that which blossoms into sudden awareness of the divinity of the cosmos and creates for us a sense of the animism of all creation—tends to give us a different and more latitudinarian experience of man's fallen nature and condition. While his prose seems too firmly Augustinian for the optimism about human nature that characterizes the latitudinarians, his poetry is nevertheless closer in spirit to the Cambridge Platonists than to John Donne's *Holy Sonnets.* In Vaughan's case the Hermetic philosophy gave him the necessary objective correlative for expression of his latitudinarian, cosmological view of Man, and I have attempted to show how Hermetism was able to influence Vaughan's poetry even though based on premises which might seem heretical to the orthdox Augustinian Christian. Vaughan did not primarily find a system of ideas or concepts in the Hermetic Philosophers but responded in his intuitive fashion to an enlightenment sensibility that informs their writings. His debt is best seen in terms of a conflict that endures throughout the devotional poets of the seventeenth century, between a traditional guilt-culture anthropology based on Augustine and the ethics of an enlightenment theory of man.

Vaughan, in this confrontation, is uniquely a poet of transition. Donne and Herbert remain rooted in their medieval past, but in Vaughan we read a poetry that strikes a new note. It is intermittent and faltering, but in it an enlightenment spirituality deriving from Hermetism has become the lifeblood.

Chapter Six Irenaean Theodicy and Thomas Traherne

The so-called metaphysicals have long enough been felt to form a group, and, in broad terms, the links among the four poets selected for this study are easy to establish. Most obviously, all four are Anglicans, and all are devotional poets. Within the group, Herbert knew Donne and, as a young man, copied his poems. Vaughan, as we have seen, borrowed extensively from Herbert. If Traherne did not actually borrow from the others, it is at least interesting that his poems, when they were rediscovered at the end of the nineteenth century, were thought at first to have been written by Vaughan. Similar themes and similar modes of devotion constitute one sort of continuity. Yet it is hard to think of devotional poems more unlike those of our first poet, Donne, than those of Traherne. In the *Holy Sonnets* we recall Donne's struggle to subordinate his perverse and recalcitrant self:

> Inconstancy unnaturally hath begott
> A constant habit; that when I would not
> I change in vowes, and in devotione.
> As humorous is my contritione
> As my prophane love, and as soone forgott.
>
> [*Holy Sonnet* 19]

At their best, the *Holy Sonnets* express this sort of experience of a divided mind. Beside this, we can place what is perhaps the best-known passage in all of Traherne: the third meditation from the third *Century*. It is worth quoting in full:

The Corn was Orient and Immortal Wheat, which never should be reaped, nor was ever sown. I thought it had stood from everlasting to everlasting. The Dust and Stones of the Street were as Precious as GOLD. The Gates were at first the End of the World, The Green Trees when I saw them first through one of the Gates Transported and Ravished me; their Sweetnes and Unusual Beauty made my Heart to leap, and almost mad with Extasie, they were such strange and Wonderfull Thing: The Men! O what Venerable and Reverend Creatures did the Aged seem! Immortal Cherubims! And yong Men Glittering and Sparkling Angels and Maids strange Seraphick Pieces of Life and Beauty! Boys and Girles Tumbling in the Street, and Playing, were moving Jewels. I knew not that they were Born or should Die. But all things abided Eternaly as they were in their Proper Places. Eternity was Manifest in the Light of the Day, and som thing infinit Behind evry thing appeared: which talked with my Expectation and moved my Desire. The Citie seemed to stand in Eden, or to be Built in Heaven. The Streets were mine, the Temple was mine, the People were mine, their Clothes and Gold and Silver was mine, as much as their Sparkling Eys Fair Skins and ruddy faces. The Skies were mine, and so were the Sun and Moon and Stars, and all the World was mine, and I the only Spectator and Enjoyer of it. I knew no Churlish Proprieties, nor Bounds nor Divisions: but all Proprieties and Divisions were mine: all Treasures and the Possessors of them. So that with much adoe I was corrupted; and made to learn the Dirty Devices of this World. Which now I unlearn, and becom as it were a little Child again, that I may enter into the Kingdom of GOD.[1]

First, in this passage, the "self" problem, as we see it in Donne, disappears. Traherne seems to glory in himself and in his own divine potentiality. He is the real focus of creation, the "Divine Philosopher," as he says elsewhere, who is "the most Glorious Creature in the whole World" (C. 4.5). The problem is certainly not, as with Donne, in getting himself out of the way but in getting himself into things as fully as possible. Again in distinction from Donne, Traherne shows a real interest in nature. It may indeed be hard to say how natural is "Orient and Immortal Wheat," but things like corn, dust, stones, streets, boys and girls, ruddy faces, are used to evoke an experience of joy and excitement at actually being in the world of nature, and for Traherne that means, essentially, the joy of seeing God in and through his creation.[2] When we are doing this properly we are happy, and only when we are corrupted by the "Dirty Devices" of the world do we lose the joy of the child's vision. So we must again become as a child, and the search to accomplish this is, for Traherne, the pursuit of "Felicity." Traherne, above all, manages to capture the peculiar sense of this childhood vision of felicity in his meditation, and the poetry of the passage resides in the sense of radiance and excitement that it communicates.

Traherne's writing, however, unlike Donne's, has little concrete imagery and intellectual tension. There is instead a certain diffuseness, communicated mainly by lists of words that express a generic quality of brightness—"Green Trees," "Men Glittering and Sparkling Angels," "Jewels," "Sparkling Eys Fair Skins and ruddy faces," the radiant or "Orient" wheat. There are also many abstract words, which, connected to these descriptions of color and light, create an experience which is both diffuse and visionary. The wheat, we are told, is "Immortal." The scene has somehow neither "Bounds nor Divisions," and "som thing infinit Behind evry thing appeared." There is also a sense of exuberance in the rhythms throughout the passage, which, although it is prose, in places will even scan. For instance: "The Dúst and Stónes of the Stréet were as Précious as GÓLD. The Gátes were at first the Énd of the World." The anapestic rhythm of these lines, their lightness and speed, and the levity of tone all suggest an optimism, a delight in the world which at high points reaches the visionary quality of the mystical experience.

Throughout Traherne's works, his characteristic visionary poetry tends to come, not, as we have said, by any striking occasional metaphors, but by the selection of things which are qualitatively heightened. Primary colors, precious stones, jewels, gold and silver, riches and treasures, valuables of all sorts abound in Traherne's writing. His poems progress, not by logical or predictable steps, but through an "open form," what Stanley Stewart has called an "expanded voice,"[3] and by concentrating on generic effects. By the piling up of syntactic elements in a manner which blurs space and time an accumulated force carries the reader into the experience of felicity.

The poem *Wonder* celebrates such a vision as seen by the child before the corruptions of the world set in, and all the characteristic elements of Traherne's poetry are there. To begin with, for readers in modern times there is the peculiar lack of concreteness and "tension" which at first seems difficult to come to terms with. "Harsh ragged Objects were conceald," we are told, from the view of the innocent eye, and we are naturally interested to know *what* objects and what are the particular acts that have destroyed our paradise but lurk in our decayed vision under the guise of normalcy. It may be disappointing to be told that these concealed objects are such obvious and general bugbears as "Oppressions Tears and Cries, / Sins, Griefs, Complaints, Dissentions, Weeping Eys" (*Poems,* p. 8). In terms of poetic insight about paradise, this is banal. We may notice also how the first stanza concertedly refuses to compose the place in the manner of, say, Donne, or to fix the speaker in any definite or individual predicament. "How like an Angel came I down!" says the poet. "How bright are all Things here!" "The World," we are told, "resembled his *Eternitie*," "And evry Thing that I did see, / Did with me talk." But we are given no particular understanding of how angels come down, or what eternity is like so that we may see how the world resembles it, or what sort of language the things of the world speak.

Yet (as Stewart has been at pains to point out[4]) our critical expectations ought not to dictate the method of a poem, and Traherne's *Wonder* communicates best when we cease looking for poetry on the terms of a Donne or a Herbert and allow it to generate the type of excitement we find in *C.* 3.3. *Wonder* is an effective poem if we attend to its rhythms, if we allow the breadth and openness of its texture to bring us to a sense of the bright and joyous world of the child's vision. The accumulation of words evoking color and light and joy sustains a rhythmic sense of breathlessness and elation:

> Rich Diamond and Pearl and Gold
> In evry Place was seen;
> Rare Splendors, Yellow, Blew, Red, White and Green,
> Mine Eys did evrywhere behold.
>
> [*Poems,* p. 10]

We are told of "Walls, Boxes, Coffers, . . . Clothes, Ribbans, Jewels, Laces," and the "Works of GOD so Bright and pure / So Rich and

Great," of "Joy, Beauty, Welfare," which "Angels prize," of "Health and Innocence," and "Great Wonders clothd with Glory." Images of wealth and riches abound. The works of God seem "Rich and Great," the streets "were pavd with Golden Stones," everywhere there is "Rich Diamond and Pearl and Gold," "Ornaments," "Coffers," "Jewels," and other "rich contents" (*Poems*, pp. 6-10).

Again, as in *C.* 3.3, the rhythms of the poem express and sustain the mood:

> The Skies in their Magnificence,
> The Lively, Lovely Air;
> Oh how Divine, how soft, how Sweet, how fair!
>
> [*Poems*, p. 8]

The iambic meter draws the voice to its form with almost incantatory emphasis, and the meter dictates the voice (unusual for iambs, which so readily accommodate spoken English). Even in "Magnificence," the one word which struggles to break the pattern, scanning $\smile/\smile\smile$, the temptation to follow the insistent rhythms of the whole line draws us strongly to $\smile/\smile/$. The general effect of the heightened rhythm in these lines is enforced by the many other obvious verbal effects. The combination of alliteration, consonance, and feminine internal rhyme in "Lively, Lovely," the strong rhyme of "Air" and "fair," the anaphora of the four times repeated "how" of the third line, the subtle links of alliteration, "soft"/"Sweet," and consonance, "soft"/"fair," serve to bind the metric rhythm to a total euphonic and fluid verbal texture. Throughout the poem this sense of fluidity, of buoyant yet compelling rhythm, creates an energy and movement which are a basic part of the poetry of *Wonder*. Throughout his work (though there has been no good study made of it), Traherne's prosody is one of his most effective elements.

Finally, underlying the whole of *Wonder* is a sense of optimism, of faith in man's divine potentiality, his justified delight in himself as possessor of the world, and his consequent desire to involve himself in it as fully as possible. "The Streets were pavd with Golden Stones, / The Boys and Girles were *mine*," "Joy, Beauty, Welfare did appear to *me*," the "Feinds that spoyl even Paradice, / Fled from the splendor of *mine* Eys," and "proprieties themselvs were *mine*" (*Poems*, pp. 8-10). In *Wonder*, moreover, it is clear that the child, when he is born, is innocent. "The State of Innocence / ... / Did fill my Sence," and when the speaker at first came down to earth he was "like an Angel" (*Poems*, pp. 6-8). Statements of this sort recur throughout Traherne's writings, and they have led to a good deal of debate about his theology of the fall and original sin. Traherne's writings, indeed, work around a set of main themes which essentially develop from his view of the innocent child and which together make a theology as unusual as his poetry. The pursuit of felicity, for instance, is really the search to recover the innocent vision of the child born, like Adam, without sin. But just as Adam's sin brought death and disruption into the world, so, for Traherne, the sins of men throughout history have added to that first sin to such an extent that children, even though born innocent, do not stand a chance of maintaining that innocence in a world so overwhelmed with the aggregate of human sinfulness and misery. So innocence is "ecclypsed" "by the Customs and maners of Men" (*C*. 3.7). In such a world, the example of Jesus Christ is necessary to direct men to salvation. But, for Traherne, a good deal of the burden of following that way rests with man himself, whose destiny is to become godlike, and whose potential for divinity must be realized by the full and proper exercise of the powers of human will and reason. Traherne is a strong defender of the freedom of the will and an enthusiastic reader of Pico.[5]

Such a view of man, and in particular of man's loss of innocence, accounts for a good deal of the difference between Donne and Traherne as poets. Obviously, Donne's thoroughgoing and guilt-culture Augustinianism will not countenance a view of the child, of original sin, and of man's will such as Traherne entertains. Yet there is no full-blown enlightenment view of human nature in Traherne either, for in a sense man does inherit the sin of Adam, and the fact that an atonement is necessary means that man's self-sufficiency does not go unqualified. Traherne, after all, was an Anglican who subscribed to the Thirty-nine Articles. But it is not surprising, despite these facts, that some critics, in view of Traherne's theories, have leveled against him the charge "Pelagian." There have, of course, been counterarguments which claim otherwise.[6]

The debate about Traherne's orthodoxy has, however, been based on false premises. To argue that Traherne is Pelagian is really to assume that he is not Augustinian, since the Pelagian heresy is defined in controversy with an Augustinian canon of orthodoxy. Yet Augustine's fall theology is not the only type which is consistent with the specifications of the Thirty-nine Articles that "man is very far gone from original righteousness." [7] There is another less central but important tradition which derives from the Pre-Nicene Father, Saint Irenaeus, and it is to this source that Traherne's theology is indebted.

The Background

As D. P. Walker points out, the revival of interest in the Pre-Nicene Fathers during the Renaissance is a subject which has been neglected.[8] But it seems incontrovertible that such an interest was especially marked among latitudinarian theologians, and this was especially true of the later seventeenth century in England. Thus Henry More, together with the group of friends who surrounded him, Lady Anne Conway, Francis Mercurius Van Helmont, and Joseph Glanvill, toyed with ideas of preexistence of the soul and of universal salvation,[9] theories which were derived from the heretical and Pre-Nicene Origen.[10] From the same source Peter Sterry developed a theology which also countenances the salvation of all men,[11] and Origen's defense of free will is an important element in Erasmus's latitudinarian attack on Luther.[12] As Walker points out, "Through Erasmus Origen became one strand in the liberal Arminian tradition which led to Le Clerc, the editor of Erasmus, and his Origenist answers to Bayle's Manichaean attacks on the Christian God." [13] Further, says Walker, "The theological tradition mainly responsible for the general revival of the early Fathers goes back to the platonizing syncretists of the 15th century, such as Ficino and Bessarion, who found in these Fathers the model of a method by which ancient pagan philosophy, especially Platonic and Neoplatonic, might be integrated into Christianity." [14] Thus the Cambridge Platonists, as latitudinarian theologians seeking the broadest basis for Christian belief on which all men agree, were attracted to the earliest traditions of Christian thought, and especially to the philosophic syncretism of the Alexandrians, such as Clement and Origen. In consequence Richard Baxter was led to complain of "a method of theologie" "lately revised" "by some deep students who are verst in ye Platonike Philosophie," which he went on to describe as "a mixture of *Platonisme,* Origenisme and Arianisme not having *all* of any of these, but somewhat of *all*." [15] This conflation of philosophy, Pre-Nicene patristic theology, and latitude verging on the heretical is an adequate diagnosis of the liberal theology of the Cambridge school.

It is significant also that Baxter chose to mention Arianism, for through the theology of Michael Servetus (burned by Calvin both as a Unitarian and as an antipaedobaptist) the crypto-Arianism of such seventeenth-century English scholars as Newton and William Whiston received its impetus.[16] And here we have a further connection with Pre-Nicene tradition, for the favorite authority of Servetus was Saint Irenaeus.[17] Moreover, Servetus repeatedly denounced Calvin as Simon Magus (a favorite term of contempt used by Irenaeus in his work against the Gnostics) and went on to say that Calvin's doctrine of original sin reduced man to a log or a stone. Calvin replied that Servetus's doctrine deified man and debased God (a complaint that critics have consistently leveled against Irenaeus), and Melanchthon, further vindicating the Augustinian position, complained that Servetus had completely distorted Irenaeus.[18] The use of Irenaeus's fall theology by Traherne, then, has at least this important and controversial precedent.

Irenaeus was further adduced in the cause of latitude by Erasmus, his translator, who pointed out in a preface that the Father's name meant "peace" and that men should imitate his concern for overcoming contention within the church.[19] Thus Irenaeus became part of that latitudinarian ideal of transcending doctrinal disputation which received such significant development in England during the later seventeenth century.

Further evidence of the Renaissance interest in Pre-Nicene tradition resides not only in the new translations of such as Origen, Tertullian, and Irenaeus but in the number of treatises appearing on the correct use of the early Fathers which showed a special interest in the Pre-Nicene apologists. Most widely read was perhaps Denis Pétau, whose *Theologicorum dogmatum* (Paris, 1644) provided a gloss for teachings of the Fathers and whose controversial preface in particular attempted to apologize for seeming unorthodoxies among the Platonizing syncretists.[20] More important for our case because it is quoted by Traherne is the work of Jean Daillé, *Traicté de l'employ des Saincts Peres, pour le jugement des differends qui sont aujourd'huy en la religion* (Geneva and Paris, 1632). Daillé's main claim, which is consonant with the basic position of the English latitudinarians, is that Protestants and Catholics do not disagree on fundamentals of faith; rather, the addition of unnecessary doctrines and the introduction of corruption have caused dissent and strife. For "there is no question but that the Christian religion was more pure and without mixture in its beginning and infancy, than it was afterwards in its growth and progress: it being the ordinary course of things to contract corruptions, more or less, according as they are more or less removed from their first institution." [21] It should therefore be our ideal to recover the innocence of the primitive church. For Daillé the apostolic tradition itself is the "zenith and perfection" of Christianity, but the Fathers to whom he allows main authority are to a man Pre-Nicene, and he lists them as: Justin, Irenaeus, Clement of Alexandria, Tertullian, Saint Cyprian, Arnobius, Lactantius, and Origen. [22]

Also important, though later than Daillé, is the figure of William Whiston, who lost his position at Cambridge for being an Arian and who founded a Society for Promoting Primitive Christianity. In his *Historical Memoirs of the Life of Dr. Samuel Clarke*, [23] Whiston describes the evidence which his society intended to go by, and, like Daillé, we find he admires the apostolic age as the fountainhead of Christianity, but "in the last degree" he admits the authority of the Pre-Nicene Fathers, "the Primitive Writers and Councils, especially those of the Three First Centuries; according to the different degrees of their Antiquity and Credibility." [24] Whiston's book is furthermore important in that it links for us the latitudinarian inspiration of the Cambridge Platonists with the interest in Pre-Nicene theology. Whiston draws our attention to the influence of the Cambridge school on him, lamenting the death of "Dr *Henry* More of *Christ's College*," and mentioning *"Mr Ward"* as "also my very good friend." [25] Benjamin Whichcote is mentioned later, [26] and it is clear that Whiston, himself a scion of Cambridge, felt sympathy for that latitudinarian tradition of which he was the inheritor and saw it linked to his own interest in Pre-Nicene thought.

Turning to Traherne, we can now see that he has a place among these thinkers who, in the cause of latitude, peace, and reason, sought to revive the spirit of an early Christianity and who looked to the Pre-Nicene Fathers for inspiration which was close to the apostolic tradition but also philosophic and within which ways could be found to avoid or resolve the cruxes of traditional doctrinal disputation.

Although it is one of the difficulties with Traherne that his best-known writings do not provide much evidence of their sources by way of acknowledgment or direct allusion, it has nevertheless been possible to indicate some important relationships of indebtedness. For instance, Traherne was undoubtedly influenced by the Cambridge Platonists, especially Henry More, and his theories and insights with regard to human reason (as well as much of the incidental imagery employed in their expression) derived from this source.[27] So too did his interest in Hermetic philosophy which evidences an enthusiasm shared by the Cambridge Platonists with the Renaissance Neoplatonists in the earliest and specifically Pre-Nicene traditions of Christianity in relation to Hellenic speculation.[28]

That Traherne had a particular interest in Pre-Nicene tradition, however, is evident from *Roman Forgeries*,[29] his single polemical and primarily scholarly piece of writing. There we find him, like Daillé and Whiston, concerned with the proliferation of *"frauds"* which "disguize and cover the face of *Primitive Antiquities*, which ought to be preserved most sacred and pure." [30] He quotes Daillé frequently to support his own arguments,[31] and we recall Daillé's insistence on the importance of the apostolic and Pre-Nicene traditions. Traherne also insists on the importance of the "Root and *Foundation*," warning us that "Hereticks are prone to be most busie in undermining the *Foundation*," [32] and cites, notably, Saint Irenaeus who warns against "Bolstering up of *Heresies*" by "Counterfeit Gospels." [33] Therefore, Traherne says, he will confine his discussion to the earliest Christian times: "I shall not descend into the latter Ages, but keep within the compass of the first 420 years, and lay open so many of their *frauds,* as disguize and cover the face of *Primitive Antiquities,* which ought to be preserved most sacred and pure." [34]

The important point, however, is that the entire ground plan for Traherne's enterprise in *Roman Forgeries* derives specifically from the authority of Saint Irenaeus against the heretics. In his "Advertisement to the Reader," Traherne sets up four criteria for conducting the ensuing book-length argument, and he clearly acknowledges his source of inspiration: "Irenaeus, one of the most Ancient Fathers, Scholar to S. *Polycarp,* S. *John's* Disciple, in his Book against Heresies, giveth us four notable marks of their Authors." He goes on to list these "marks," and the book then proceeds, using Irenaeus as its touchstone.

Traherne, then, was part of that latitudinarian movement in theology which centered on the Cambridge Platonists. Like them he was concerned with finding the foundations of Christian belief on which all men could agree. Like the Cambridge Platonists he was also attracted to the philosophic tradition of liberal Christian theology, and like so many other liberal theologians of the times from Erasmus to Le Clerc, he had an enthusiastic interest in a revival of Pre-Nicene theology. In Traherne's case, as in that of Servetus (who does, incidentally, closely resemble Traherne in his doctrine of man), the figure of Irenaeus was conspicuous.

It is necessary to establish this background because in Traherne's most interesting writings, the *Centuries* and *Poems,* he provides little acknowledgment of his sources. Besides, his own rare vision has often the effect of transmuting the quality of what he derives from elsewhere. For this reason the Pelagian argument has been formulated by critics. It is a hypothesis which might seem to fit the facts when the author himself leaves his theoretical precedents so undefined. But it would seem clear from the background we have described that Traherne's theological sources might well be among the Pre-Nicene Fathers of the church, and I suggest the hypothesis of Saint Irenaeus, rather than either Pelagius or Augustine, as one which will fit the facts in a most satisfactory manner.

The Fall in Irenaeus

That Traherne knew and respected Saint Irenaeus is clear from the "Advertisement" to *Roman Forgeries.* But the unusual teaching on the fall of man and original sin which forms such an integral part of Traherne's vision in the *Centuries* and *Poems* also corresponds,

both in broad outline and in detail, to a similarly unusual fall theology in Saint Irenaeus.[35]

In his *Adversus haereses* Irenaeus directs his arguments chiefly
against Gnosticism, but he is himself a theologian in the Hellenic
tradition, and, as Emil Brunner points out, he is largely Greek in
inspiration, though careful to modify this element in his thought by
a more fundamental and scriptural awareness.[36] For Irenaeus, the
fall of man is on the whole a less serious and catastrophic event than
the repeated and malicious sins of mature individuals against God. It
is possible for Irenaeus to maintain this view because for him Adam
was created in a state of childlike innocence. He was made "yet an
infant." [37] Nor is this infancy simply spiritual; it is physical too. The
Genesis story claims "they were both naked, and were not ashamed,"
and Irenaeus explains this lack of shame in terms of physical childhood, for "having been created a short time previously, [they] had
no understanding of the procreation of children" (p. 455).

Although Adam is innocent, immortal, made in the image and
likeness of God, and perfect in the spiritual equipment required for
his destiny, he has not yet grown to maturity. It "was necessary,"
says Irenaeus, "that man should in the first instance be created; and
having been created, should receive growth" (p. 522). Man is a child
who must develop to become godlike, for "we have not been made
gods from the beginning, but at first merely men, then at length gods"
(p. 522). So we should be "making progress day by day," and "ap-
proximating to the uncreated One" (p. 522), encouraged by the
promise of Psalm 82 that "Ye are gods; and ye are all sons of the
Highest." In our pilgrimage toward maturity and fulfillment, all of
creation is at our disposal, "For by means of the creation itself," says
Irenaeus, "the Word reveals God the Creator" (p. 469), "and therefore the creation is suited to [the wants of] man; for man was not
made for its sake, but creation for the sake of man" (p. 558).

But Adam was deceived by the apostate Satan, and as we are
shown in the Genesis story, he fell. The wages of his sin was death.
So, says Irenaeus, "at the first Adam became a vessel in his (Satan's)
possession," who brought "death upon him" (p. 456). In his subsequent history in the world, man has only increased the legacy of death
which is his inheritance from Adam by further sinning and becoming
increasingly apostate from God. So Satan moves "gradually to darken

the hearts of those who would endeavour to serve him" (pp. 552-53), and man, once "placed in honour, is made like unto cattle" (p. 525). Irenaeus remains insistent that sin is the result of bad moral choice, for "there is no coercion with God. . . . And in man, as well as in angels, He has placed the power of choice (for angels are rational beings), so that those who had yielded obedience might justly possess what is good, given indeed by God, but preserved by themselves. On the other hand, they who have not obeyed shall, with justice . . . receive condign punishment" (p. 518).

With this firmly ethical teaching on the will goes a similarly rationalist suggestion, found throughout the *Adversus haereses,* that sin is essentially a misevaluation of the things of this world used for our own rather than God's glory. Man who will "proceed to reckon up the sand and pebbles of the earth, yea also the waves of the sea and the stars of heaven" without proper reference to God is "insane, foolish," "since indeed he does in no one point own himself inferior to God; but, by the knowledge which he imagines himself to have discovered . . . exalts his own opinion above the greatness of the Creator" (p. 398). Conversely, a proper regard for creation leads to godliness, for "he who holds, without pride and boasting, the true glory (opinion) regarding created things and the Creator . . . shall also receive from Him the greater glory of promotion, looking forward to the time when he shall become like Him who died for him" (p. 450).

In dealing with man's sinfulness in the world Irenaeus countenances a slow drag downward throughout history. Men's hearts, we have seen, are gradually darkened by Satan, and in an interpretation of the parable of the vineyard owner's son, Irenaeus suggests that "God planted the vineyard of the human race when at the first He formed Adam and chose the fathers" (p. 515), but humanity has sunk increasingly into evil, killing the father's servants and eventually the son as well. Moreover, with the increase in experience which man gains in history comes an increase in responsibility. So for Irenaeus the sin of Cain, the first actual sin, is more serious than the sin of Adam (p. 456). Cain was mature and had the advantage of knowledge that Adam, the child, had not. We are therefore increasingly responsible the more knowledge we have, and consequently our knowledge of Christ renders us more accountable than those who do not have it. "For as He gave by His advent a greater privilege to those who believed on Him, and who do His will, so also did He point out that those who did not believe on Him should have a more severe punishment in the judgement (p. 516). As men's hearts are darkened, therefore, and they drift toward "forgetting of the true God," indulging in "adoration of [themselves] as God" (p. 553), they are all the while also increasing their guilt by multiplied sins against the Father's servants. Eventually, as one critic puts it, we have "a growth of social conditions" which themselves "lead to ignorance of God and make sin easy." [38]

The human race, therefore, needs an atonement to restore what is lost in Adam. "Thus, then, was the Word of God made man," for "God recapitulated in Himself the ancient formation of man, that He might kill sin, deprive death of its power, and vivify man" (p. 448). Unlike Paul, who also deals with Adam and Christ as the two federal heads of the human race, Irenaeus in his recapitulation theory draws our attention, not to the defeat of Adam, but rather to the closeness between Adam and Christ. So, for instance, he works out an elaborate parallel between the infancy of Adam and the similar infancy of Christ, and between Eve's virginity and that of Mary (p. 547), for it is appropriate that Christ "should be born of a woman, [namely] from the Virgin, after the likeness of Adam" (p. 548). Significantly, the Christ also becomes a child, bearing "all the tokens of a human infant" (p. 452), for the "Word of God was made man, assimilating Himself to man, and man to Himself, so that by means of his resemblance to the Son, man might become precious to the Father" (p. 544). This closeness between Christ and man, redounding as it does to man's dignity while acknowledging his fallenness, is responsible for the sustained note, in Irenaeus's theology, of an optimism which will also appear characteristic of Traherne.

While we are assured on the one hand, then, that man cannot save himself and that grace is necessary ("it was not possible that the man who had once for all been conquered, and who had been destroyed through disobedience, could reform himself" [p. 446]), yet we are assured as well that man will not be saved without proper exercise of his freedom of moral choice ("nor would the good be very much to be sought after, which would present itself without their own proper endeavour, care, or study" [p. 520]). Indeed freedom of the will is something Irenaeus insists on with real vigor, and that "God made man a free [agent] from the beginning, possessing his own power, even as he does his own soul" (p. 518) is for him axiomatic.

Finally, Irenaeus suggests, the end for which man should strive in salvation is just that quality of childlike innocence which was lost in Adam. If the unregenerate "use diligence, and receive the word of God as a graft," they may "arrive at the pristine nature of man—that which was created after the image and likeness of God" (p. 536). And through Christ's work of salvation man is indeed returned to the pristine state that characterized his original creation. "It is fitting, therefore, that the creation itself, being restored to its primeval condition, should without restraint be under the dominion of the righteous (p. 561):

The main difficulties in Irenaeus's teaching reside in the fact that he seems to envisage two directions in human development which may or may not involve a contradiction. On the one hand, we have a loss-and-recovery theory: what we lost in Adam needs to be restored by Christ. On the other hand, we have a moralistic theory according to which man should move from imperfection to perfection, and his own moral choice is of the essence of his sinfulness. Even prelapsarian Adam himself is to grow to maturity. It may be possible to resolve these difficulties as Wingren does, by adducing the example of a child deprived of the power of speech by an accident in infancy. This mishap will hinder his later, and proper, development. Yet the power of speech may be restored medically (the Atonement), in which case the child is restored to his original integrity and can then learn to speak, if willing.[39] In such a reading the balance between moralism and a theology of grace is preserved.

The problem then resolves itself into a question of the nature of our identity in Adam, and on this Irenaeus is tantalizingly ambiguous. Sometimes he speaks of Adam as the representative archetypal head of the race, and we are said to be contained "in" him in Platonist sense, as individuals who participate in a form. So Irenaeus talks of "the beginning of our formation in Adam," and "as in the natural [Adam] we all were dead, so in the spiritual we may all be made alive" (p. 527). At one point "the formation of Adam" is described by Irenaeus as an "archetype" (p. 516).

At other times, however, Irenaeus takes Adam simply to mean

everyman. In the following passage, for instance, the discussion begins by referring to the condition of man in general and then moves into a conclusion which specifically links everyman to Adam, the first man:

> He, the selfsame man who was in ignorance in times past, that is, in ignorance of God, is renewed by that knowledge which has respect to Him. For the knowledge of God renews man. And when he says, "after the image of the Creator," he sets forth the recapitulation of the same man, who was at the beginning made after the likeness of God. [p. 538]

As Wingren puts it, there is no "distinction between his various statements about Adam, the descendents of Adam, or man after Christ, etc. for Irenaeus would never have defined these different periods separately. In speaking of Adam he speaks of man, and in speaking of what Christ does for men he speaks of what Christ does for Adam; or again in using the word *Adam* or the word *man* he is always in some way referring either to himself, or to those to whom he was preaching, to all men everywhere." [40] The experience of Adam, in other words, is also the experience of everyman, at least insofar as we are all apostates from our childlike innocence to which we can return only in Christ.

Yet a further problem remains and is not fully countenanced by Irenaeus. It resides in the equation of the regenerate spirit to the innocence of Adam, which seems to imply there is no difference between the innocence of the child and that of the saint whose innocence may be deep in moral wisdom. Such a view is scarcely borne out in human experience.

These problems are worth mentioning for the simple reason that not only the main lines of Irenaeus's teaching but also the cruxes of his theory are reproduced with remarkable fidelity by Traherne. But we should also record as a conclusion to this summary that Irenaeus's theology of man, though unusual, is not a merely heretical divagation of an uncertain early Christian addled by Hellenism and marred by confusions. Charges leveled against Irenaeus are mainly that his theory of the fall is insufficient to support a theology of Atonement, that he overemphasizes the probity of the human will and underestimates the need for grace,[41] and that he is Pelagian in some of his attitudes.[42] Yet modern theologians have argued convincingly against such assertions, and it is possible to maintain and demonstrate that Irenaeus does have an adequate theory of grace and sin, even though his tendency is toward a highly ethical theology.[43] Moreover, the theologian John Hick has recently revived an Irenaean theology of man, suggesting that it provides a most convincing (and orthodox) approach to the problem of the fall and the origins of evil. Hick points out that the Irenaean approach constitutes an important minor tradition in Christian theology and that it recurs in the works of Schleiermacher (1768–1834), though, as far as he can see, it had lain dormant from Irenaeus to its nineteenth-century revival.[44] We might conclude, then, that it ought not to seem eccentric for Traherne to be influenced by a model so convincing as that of Irenaeus (who is also, as Brunner points out, the first important Christian theologian, a fact which would surely endear him to one as interested in "foundations" as Traherne). Moreover we may suggest that Mr. Hick's period of dormancy (which strikes one as odd if the theology is as important as he claims) is now interrupted at least by the figure of Traherne.

Irenaean Theory in Traherne

The first and most striking aspect of Traherne's fall theology is its vision of childhood, and, exactly as in Irenaeus, the paradisal state is conceived as one of innocence and promise such as characterizes our imagination of the child's world. "Adam in Paradice," says Traherne, "had not more sweet and Curious Apprehensions of the World, then I when I was a child" (*C.* 3.1); and in the poem *Eden,* referring to Adam, Traherne writes:

> Those things which first his Eden did adorn,
> My infancy
> Did crown.

> [*Poems,* p. 14]

This seems to confirm that Adam's innocence is, essentially, a childlike quality. Further, and again as in Irenaeus, man's destiny is to grow and to become godlike. "You must Want like a GOD, that you may be Satisfied like GOD," claims Traherne, for "Were you not made in His Image?" (*C.* 1.44). Yet even man created in God's image must grow to maturity, for "We are to be Conformed to the Image of His Glory: till we becom the Resemblance of His Great Exemplar" (*C.* 2.84). Such statements, and many others like them, recall the very similar teaching of Irenaeus that there must be a development of the created soul toward a divinization, an apotheosis of man. The "End of all," continues Traherne, "is, that Thou mightest be as GOD is" (*C.* 2.51). Moreover, and again following Irenaeus, Traherne stresses that all of creation is placed at man's disposal to assist him toward his divine destiny. In words that closely resemble those quoted from *Adversus haereses*, Traherne asserts that the world "Discovers the Being of GOD unto you" (*C.* 2.1), and "Thus the world servs to promote and Advance you" (*C.* 2.15). "Contemplat therfore the Works of GOD," we are advised, "for they serv you not only in manifesting Him, but in making you to know yourself and your Blessedness" (*C.* 2.26).

Adam, however, sinned and lost paradise, and death and deprivation followed upon his transgression. In the ensuing "Estate of Misery," says Traherne, "we hav his Fall the Nature of Sin Original and Actual, His Manifold Punishments Calamity Sickness Death" (*C.* 3.43). Traherne, like Irenaeus, notably steers clear of theories of imputed guilt and corruption of the nature of man by the original sin, such as characterize the theory of Saint Augustine. Irenaeus, as we have seen, describes the fruits of the fall in terms of an inheritance of death and sickness. Traherne's central position assumes a similar viewpoint. When he was a child, he claims, "I Knew Nothing of Sickness or Death, . . . I saw all in the Peace of Eden" (*C.* 3.2), implying that when the peace of Eden is lost it is "sickness and death" which follow in the wake of sin. Again, in the poem *Silence* we hear that neither "Ignorance / Nor Povery, nor Sickness did advance / Their Banner in the World, til Sin came in" (*Poems*, p. 46), but Traherne avoids the mention of such Augustinian consequences to the fall as an inborn stain and perverse willfulness to evil.[45] His teaching is consistently close to that of Irenaeus, which leaves the childhood vision intact in its innocence, though at a distance from God, to whom the infant must grow.

As history has progressed, however, man has become increasingly bound to sin, so that its roots have spread deep into the substance of society itself. Innocence is "ecclypsed," says Traherne, "by the Customs and maners of Men, which like Contrary Winds blew it out," and "a Whole Sea of other Matters and Concernments that Covered and Drowned it: finaly by the Evil Influence of a Bad Education that did not foster and cherish it" (C. 3.7). As the poem *Silence* puts it, the "World of Innocence" remained for the author as long as "No other Customs, New-found Wants, or Dreams / Invented here, polluted my pure Streams" (*Poems,* p. 48). Here Traherne is clearly approaching the very similar teaching of Irenaeus who also conceives of a slow drag into sin through history which makes sinfulness a matter of course for the child educated within society, so that, as Traherne says, "foolish Men" are "Grown mad with customary Folly" (*The Apostacy*). And as in *Irenaeus,* Traherne also maintains that in our superior knowledge lies increased responsibility: "God . . . gave his Son to die for them, and for me also, which are Strong Obligations, leading us to Greater Charity. So that Mens unworthiness and our vertu are alike increased" (C. 4.26). Although the child is encouraged to sin by a sort of inherited conglomerate of bad example built up among his ancestors into a tradition, so that we "follow a Multitud to do evil" (C. 4.44), it is clear in Traherne, as in Irenaeus, that sin is man's own responsibility. It is the result of bad moral choice, and Traherne exhorts us to shun "the Abominable Corruption of Men" and be willing to endure hell-fire rather "then willingly be Guilty of their Error" (C. 1.31). With an essentially ethical indignation, Traherne states: "Blind Wretches that Wound themselvs, offend me," for "Did they see the Beauty of Holiness or the Face of Happiness, they would not do so" (C. 4.20). Consequently we find throughout Traherne, as we do also in Irenaeus, the idea of sin as misevaluation. "The Works of Darkness," says Traherne, "are Repinning, Envy, Malice, Covetousness, fraud, Oppression, Discontent and Violence: All which proceed from the Corruption of Men and their mistake in the Chois of Riches" (C. 1.33). Conversely, and again as in Irenaeus, "Riches are but servants to Happiness" (C. 4.10), and to "lov in the Image of GOD" is to love his riches in proper proportion (C. 2.69). The two poems *Misapprehension* and *Right Apprehension* illustrate the point adequately.

This brings us to the question of atonement, which presents for

Traherne the same crux which we found in Irenaeus. On the one hand, Traherne states that man cannot save himself. "I cannot meet with Sin," he writes, "but it Kils me, and tis only by Jesus Christ that I can Kill it" (C. 3.51). He asks God to "Give me the Grace which S. Paul prayed for, that I may be Acceptable to the Saints" (C. 1.96). Yet, on the other hand, Traherne insists just as firmly as Irenaeus on man's freedom of will. God has "given me freedom, and adventured the Power of Sinning into my Hands" (C. 4.52). He complains that it is "not commonly discerned" "that God made Man a free Agent for his own Advantage; and left him . . . that he might be more Glorious" (C. 4.42). Traherne does not doubt that moral effort is a necessity for salvation, and in order to have the saints for companions "you must . . . make yourself exceeding Virtuous" (C. 1.82). He remarks wryly that "Nothing keeps men out of the Temple of Honor, but that the Temple of Vertue stands between" (C. 4.7). As one result of this moralism, philosophy and learning, for instance, become an essential part of the Christian's growth to righteousness, and in a long section of the third *Century* of meditations, Traherne discourses on how the glorious secrets of "Logick, Ethicks, Physicks, Metaphysicks, Geometry" (C. 3.36) led him toward the "Happiness . . . that I thirsted after" (C. 3.39) and how the Christian Philosopher may "by Right Reason discover all the Mysteries of heaven" (C. 4.81).

Difficulties that arise from this confrontation between moralism and a theology of salvation by grace are encountered in Traherne by a view of the Atonement which, just as in Irenaeus, attempts a theory of recapitulation both sympathizing with and accusing Adam and attempting to stress the closeness of Adam and Christ rather than the defeat of Adam and the corruption of the race. Clearly, the Savior comes to restore what Adam forfeited, and the typology is plain when Traherne describes Christ's cross as "That Tree of Life in the midst of the Paradice of GOD!" (C. 1.55). But more important at this point is the attempt Traherne makes to stress the closeness between Adam and Christ so that, just as in Irenaeus, the Atonement is a mark of optimism that signifies the dignity of man's nature as well as reproves his fallenness. Thus on the cross "we may see Mans Sin and infinit value" (C. 1.59). So Traherne can claim with enthusiasm that "GOD never shewd Himself more a GOD, then when He appeared Man" (C. 1.90), and about the Atonement he can write: "what an infinit Dignity Man is exalted for whom God counted none Worthy to suffer but His own son" (*C*. 2.33). An insistence on the dignity of man and the probity of moral effort in both Traherne and Irenaeus is balanced against a knowledge, Pauline and scriptural, that man's fallenness requires grace. In their doctrines of Atonement both men attempt to find a mean between these alternatives, though it may be argued against both that tendencies to moralism do threaten to gain the upper hand.

When we come to ask what, for Traherne, characterizes the condition of salvation when it is won, we again find exactly the same theory as in Irenaeus, that righteousness is essentially a return to that pristine state of childhood innocence or "felicity" which was lost by Adam. Reviewing his own progress, Traherne tells us, "I was corrupted; and made to learn the Dirty Devices of this World. Which now I unlearn, and becom as it were a little Child again" (*C*. 3.3). The process of salvation is essentially an "unlearning," a return to the innocent vision of the child. The point is made clear in a poem called, significantly, *The Return,* where Traherne writes, "To Infancy, O Lord, again I com, / That I my Manhood may improv." Traherne seems even to acknowledge that his teaching on this matter is one not usually presented. "Our Saviors Meaning," he writes, "When He said, He must be Born again and becom a little Child that will enter into the Kingdom of Heaven: is Deeper far than is generally believed" (*C*. 3.5). The statement may be read simply as a commonplace, but in the last clause there might also appear some note of reproof that there is no more widespread acceptance for this (peculiarly Irenaean) interpretation of the theme of childhood. Admittedly, Augustine's conversion was in listening to a child's voice, but for Augustine and the tradition he instituted, the child is simple and trusting rather than the possessor of innocence. For Irenaeus and Traherne, on the other hand, the "Infant-ey" is the possessor of true felicity.

Here again we run into the problem of man's relations to his first parent, and again, exactly as in Irenaeus, we find that for Traherne Adam may be both the federal head of the human race in Platonist terms and also everyman, so that generalizations made about Adam may also be applied to the speaker himself and to all other men. Certainly Adam has a historical reality for Traherne who can, for instance, project what he would have done "Had I been alive in Adams steed" (*C*. 1.65). But that men are somehow contained "in" Adam Traherne also acknowledges. In the first *Century,* for instance, he suggests that our understanding is "more real" than our bodies, then adds, "When my Soul is in Eden with our first Parents, I my self am there in a Blessed Maner" (*C*. 1.55). In this sense Adam is the archetypal head of the race. Yet there is no doubt that the word "Adam" is used also to refer to everyman. Wingren has pointed out concerning Irenaeus, as we have seen, that in using the word Adam "he is always in some way referring either to himself, or to those to whom he was preaching, to all men everywhere," and the same is true of Traherne, who can, for instance, write of childhood:

> I was an Adam there,
> A little Adam in a Sphere
> Of Joys!
>
> [*Innocence*]

And "why should you not render Thanks to God" for all the riches of creation, he asks, for "You are the Adam, or the Eve that Enjoy them" (*C*. 2.12). Again the poem *Adam* is equally about "Man" who was made "upright at the first" and also "a Man" who strays from the path by sin. "Adam," then, is both the archetype of human nature and everyman who participates in that archetype.

But if this parallelism between man and Adam exists in Traherne, and if man in salvation is restored to the paradise of childhood which he lost in the world, we may direct at Traherne precisely the same rebuke as we did at Irenaeus—that he does not adequately distinguish between the wisdom of the saint and the innocence of the child. Surely the experience of sin and the learning in philosophy and theology, which are part of the saint's pilgrimage toward regeneration, must alter the quality of childlike innocence which is rediscovered. While it is true that one cannot enter the kingdom without first becoming like a little child, we might suggest that the innocence of childhood which may be rediscovered by the wise will nevertheless be an innocence modified by the fact that it lies at the far side of experience. In the theology of both Traherne and Saint Irenaeus this distinction is at best an implicit one.

The main lines, then, of Traherne's theology of man follow the peculiar theory of Saint Irenaeus. Both begin from the unusual view that Adam's paradisal situation is that of an innocent child, a special creature of God whose fulfillment is to become godlike. In this both writers depart radically from the traditional Augustinian view that Adam is created mature. Consequently in both Traherne and Irenaeus the sin of Adam is interpreted less severely than in the Augustinian tradition, and the deliberate sins of postlapsarian men against God and nature are dealt with much more harshly than the fall of the childlike Adam. The results of the fall are described by Irenaeus primarily in terms of death and sickness, but he avoids propounding any theory of a corrupt human nature, and the same bias is found also in Traherne. Both authors agree, too, in the contention that man has increased Adam's legacy of sin and that there has been a slow declension into sinfulness with the passage of history. Both hold that the corruption of man has infected civilization, so that the customs of men are themselves an occasion of sin for the innocence of childhood. Yet for Traherne no less than Irenaeus, sin is essentially the abuse of freedom of choice, and in both authors we find a similar expression of the idea that sin is a misevaluation and that proper regard for creation leads to godliness. Both, of course, also agree on the necessity of the Atonement for the dispensation of grace, but in both we find a somewhat attenuated theory which leaves considerable responsibility with man himself. A theology of recapitulation is in consequence developed and stresses a particular closeness between Christ and Adam, so that for Traherne no less than Irenaeus the Atonement becomes a sign of the divinity of man as well as a reproach against his apostasy. Finally, both authors agree in the unusual speculation that in salvation we essentially rediscover the vision of childhood which characterizes both paradise and infancy, and in both we get a similarly metaphoric use of the word "Adam," which is applicable to the archetypal head of the race as well as to everyman.

Similarities between Traherne and Irenaeus, however, are discovered not only in the main lines of their theories, striking as these are, for there are also many incidental details which are compelling in their similarity. For instance, one cannot read far in Traherne without being struck by the unusual emphasis he places on metaphors which connote value in terms of precious metals—gold, silver, precious stones, and jewels. The quest for salvation in Traherne is constantly a search for a valuable "prize." So we must, says Traherne,

"Distinguish between true and fals Riches as our Savior doth" (*C.* 2.100). "Your Enjoyment of the World," he claims, "is never right, till you so Esteem it, that evry thing in it, is more your Treasure, then a King's Exchequer full of Gold and Silver" (*C.* 1.25). The "Corruption of men" on the other hand is in their "mistake in the Chois of Riches," and men are responsible for the creation of a "Riches of Darkness" (*C.* 1.33). "Gold Silver Houses Lands Clothes" are "The Riches of Invention" (*C.* 3.9), and there is "Madness" in those "who esteem a Purs of Gold" more than creation (*C.* 2.7). We should remember particularly that "Souls are Gods Jewels," "his Riches" (*C.* 1.15), and if we "Prize" God, the "World shall be a Grand Jewel of Delight" (*C.* 1.20). Consequently, a man's desire should be to "prize the Blessings which he Knoweth" (*C.* 4.54) and "to Prize them according to their value" (*C.* 1.12). Much of Traherne's individual quality as a poet in fact derives from the unique way in which he consistently uses such metaphors of heightened experience to suggest a rare quality of radiance and light which for him accompanies the experience of "felicity." Although one cannot claim the same poetic rapture for Irenaeus as for Traherne, it is nevertheless difficult to read the *Adversus haereses* with Traherne in mind and not be struck by the unusual insistence of Irenaeus on metaphors which are remarkably similar to those listed above—gold and silver, jewels, precious stones, and a quest for the valuable "prize" of salvation.

Irenaeus, like Traherne, distinguishes between true and false riches. "A clever imitation in glass," he writes, "casts contempt, as it were, on that precious jewel the emerald" (p. 315), which is Christianity, and the Christian philosopher's task is to distinguish the true from the false, for "a beautiful image of a king" which "has been constructed . . . out of precious jewels" (p. 326), here the Scriptures, should not be debased by false philosophers who rearrange the precious stones into some inferior representation. Yet "we ought not to think that the Deity is like unto gold or silver" (p. 433), for the riches of men are unrighteous, and "the houses in which we dwell, the garments in which we are clothed, the vessels which we use" (p. 503) are listed just as in Traherne. Yet there is another kind of "treasure" belonging to Christ and "hid in the field" (p. 496), and those "who have the Lord's money" (p. 474), says Irenaeus, are on the way to righteousness. He tells us that if we value His riches properly, God will "cover thee over [too] within and without with pure gold and silver" so that we will become "a perfect work of God" (p. 523). But communion with God is not "precious," he continues, unless sought after, and we must strive for the "prize" "so much is it the more valuable . . . so much the more should we esteem it" (p. 520). The similarity in the details of these metaphors of value and riches, distinguishing a true and a false wealth, dealing with gold and silver, jewels, and the prize of salvation, must at least corroborate our suggestion that Traherne was moved by the example of Irenaeus.

Another detail on which there is a striking correspondence between our two authors may be found in the use each makes of Gen. 1:26 as a commentary on the natural dignity of man. That man is created "in the Image and Likeness of God" is a central element in the theology of Irenaeus. Indeed, the distinctions he draws (or is thought to draw) between the two terms "Image" and "Likeness" have been a mare's nest for critics for some time.[46] It is not necessary to quote extensively from *Adversus haereses* to provide examples, since they are to be found throughout the work in profusion, but the characteristic deployment of Gen. 1:26 may be illustrated by the following passage: "But who else is superior to, and more eminent than, that man who was formed after the likeness of God, except the Son of God, after whose image man was created?" (p. 507.)

Turning to Traherne we find also that Gen. 1:26 is among his most favorite allusions, recurring as frequently as in Irenaeus, and that Traherne too uses it to argue man's dignity. A single passage will again set the characteristic tone and provide a parallel which demonstrates a striking similarity to the piece just quoted from Irenaeus: "The Image of God is the most Perfect Creature. Since there cannot be two Gods the utmost Endeavor of Almighty Power is the Image of GOD" (*C.* 3.61). The point here is not so much that the same biblical passage is used for similar purposes by both authors but that the similar optimism of the assertions, and the unusual frequency with which the allusion recurs in both authors (examples can be found on every page of both Irenaeus and Traherne), should again provide at least corroborative support for the suggestion that Traherne was influenced by Irenaeus.

As a last point we may note that those who find limitations in Traherne's view of man do so for exactly the same reasons as critics of

Irenaeus. Traherne, it is claimed, underplays the Atonement and the doctrine of grace and overemphasizes the responsibility of man in the quest for salvation. Traherne does not have a sufficient doctrine of original sin, and his position is Pelagian. It can of course be agreed that the ethical and moralistic element does loom large in Traherne's theology, but Traherne does nevertheless take a serious view of sin and the fall. His teaching on the felicity of childhood, however, might not continue to cause the difficulty it has hitherto presented to critics if it is seen, on the model of Irenaeus, that man (and Adam) is created in the first place at a distance from God—in his image but not yet actually his image—and that the fall itself is not only the inheritance of death from Adam but the apostasy of everyman from the innocence of childhood, a condition which is only rediscovered in salvation through Christ.

Conclusion

In terms of the argument of this book, it is significant that an Irenaean type of theology should come to light in Traherne: Irenaeus provides a timely solution to the problems posed by the confrontation of guilt culture and enlightenment. As mentioned earlier, Traherne's orthodoxy is not Augustinian, though he shares some of the guilt-culture elements of Augustinian anthropology which allow consistency with the Thirty-nine Articles. Thus, in a way (though it is not Augustine's way), for Traherne men do inherit Adam's original sin. They are not totally self-sufficient, and Traherne certainly is not simply Pelagian. On the other hand, there is little sense of the church as a patriarchal or family institution in the manner of medieval times, and Traherne moves even further along those lines indicated by Herbert, of spiritualizing the church and of removing it from the realm of the secular. But Traherne's roots in the traditions of his times are still strong enough for us to sense the struggle in his poems. It is remarkable, for instance, that Traherne managed to stay in favor with both the Commonwealth and the Restoration and that his seemingly Pelagian (certainly Arminian) theology also satisfied the Calvinists. Throughout his writings there is a constant tension between traditionally orthodox materials and strikingly new attitudes toward them. In his reconciliation of the apparent dilemma between Pelagianism and Calvinism, Irenaeus provided Traherne, on the one hand, with an acceptably orthodox theory of the fall but left him open, on the other, to enlightenment developments such as religious toleration, the secularization of the state, the assertion of the freedom and divinity of man's will. In the peculiar theology underlying his writings, the characteristic tensions between old and new in the seventeenth century are retained, but Traherne's novel solution yields an equally novel style, and a novel poetry. Yet the basic theological problems he faces constitute the real links with the other metaphysicals we have discussed.

I have used the phrase "Irenaean type of theology" with some deliberation. Just as the Augustinian tradition in the Middle Ages does not reproduce exactly the theology of Augustine, so Traherne's reading of Irenaeus is influenced by the many other writers he encountered from the point of view of his own times. In this sense, there is no going back, and renaissances are also reinterpretations. This is true of Traherne in relation to Saint Irenaeus, though this chapter has not been able to take adequate account of Traherne's modifications of his source but has only drawn attention to the main lines of agreement between the two writers. Besides, it remains my contention, despite the modifications, that an Irenaean type of anthropology is a fundamental building block in Traherne's theology and one for which critics have been looking to explain the unity of Traherne's thought. Moreover, the other major elements of Traherne's eclecticism can be most adequately read in terms of Irenaeus. For example, those who argue for some version of Augustinian influence (by way of Bonaventure or Arminius)[47] can be reconciled through Irenaeus with those who argue for Pelagianism. Also, Traherne's enthusiasm for Pico, for Hermes Trismegistus and the Cambridge Platonists, complements the emphasis of Irenaeus on man's potentiality to grow to be godlike, and indeed the whole "irenic" cast of his thought.

We may therefore conclude, as we began, by suggesting that it is confusing to discuss Traherne, as critics have consistently done, in terms of an orthodoxy which is Augustinian. The Pelagian heresy and scholastic discussion of "states" of human nature are foreign to the vision of Irenaeus and are not helpful for explicating the position of Traherne who assumes an Irenaean type of theology. A discussion of the theological background of the seventeenth century makes it clear that Traherne was more than likely to indulge an enthusiasm for such a teacher as Irenaeus, and we can see from *Roman Forgeries* that Traherne had indeed a special interest in this early Father. However, as with any discussion of Traherne's sources, we should add that he, more than any other devotional poet of the period, possessed a vision which was unique, and he stamped all he borrowed with the impress of his own peculiar mystical sensibility. Moreover, he was less interested than most writers of prose in the period with acknowledgment and demonstration of scholarly sources. However, Traherne found not only a comparably unique mentor in Irenaeus but a fellow spirit as well. It may be concluded of Traherne's individualism no less than of that of Irenaeus himself, about whom it was written by a modern critic, that:

He speaks in an accent strange to the ears of those instructed by the dogmatic definitions of the Councils, and in phrases which seem careless to the mind sharpened by the evangelical controversies of later centuries. This is true alike of his treatment of the Trinity, the Atonement, and of Saving Faith. Nevertheless, beneath the strange accent is the truth which the Church later enshrined as her heritage. None can take away his glory.[48]

Chapter Seven Conclusion

The terms *guilt culture* and *enlightenment* provide a hypothesis upon which is based the individual studies of Donne, Herbert, Vaughan, and Traherne. Like any generalization about cultural history which has a claim to validity, this one is both helpful and possibly misleading. It is helpful in that it offers a fresh perspective on materials normally arranged in terms of the traditional generalizations: Middle Ages, Renaissance, Reformation. It is possibly misleading because the terms necessarily impose an artificial pattern on a complex reality. Here the artifice may obscure the fact that transition from guilt culture to enlightenment was not, for the men of the Renaissance, an easy or even obvious choice between alternatives. The innovations of an enlightenment world view were discoveries, painfully realized.

The problem on which the hypothesis concentrates, however, is universal. It is the problem of evil, broached by mythologies, however primitive, and the ultimate test of theodicies, however sophisticated. It is the question, as Augustine claims, which lies at the roots of faith, and the energies and achievements of civilizations no less than of individuals can be characterized by ways in which they interpret the nature of their own fallenness, their guilt or enlightenment, their human limitations or divine potentialities. Arguing from such premises, E. R. Dodds, with brilliant success, has applied anthropological distinctions between "shame cultures" and "guilt cultures" to his reading of the Greek "Enlightenment" of the fifth century B.C. The distinctions Dodds makes, especially between guilt culture and enlightenment, can fruitfully be applied to a period of similar transition in European history, namely, the Renaissance.

In the western church during the Middle Ages, Augustine's theology of man's fall and original sin is the standard interpretation. In terms of criteria derived from Dodds, Augustine's is clearly a guilt-culture anthropology. The insistence on inherited guilt, the paternalism, the horror of sins against the Lord, the King, the Father, and the repudiation of Pelagian ethics are the key criteria of an attitude to man's fall, the consequences of which extend to the entire fabric and structure of characteristically medieval philosophies and institutions. Within the hierarchical and inclusive structure of medieval theocracy, a guilt-culture humanism reflects in medieval art the quality of life which such a culture could offer.

The universalism and inclusiveness which characterize the Middle Ages are, by the end of the seventeenth century, to all intents and purposes dispelled. In England, the death of the old order is symbolized by the execution of the king, and the most awesome sin of the guilt culture is blindly embraced. Gradually, and partially in consequence, religious toleration replaces the absolute rule of the universal church, democratic parliamentary procedure replaces monarchy, science turns from contemplation of God the Father, to whom the creatures are referred, to the exploration of earth, the Mother. Man the magus realizes his divine power over nature, and Augustinian guilt yields to Pelagian theories of human innocence and perfectibility. But the enlightenment gifts of democracy, toleration, and science are not without their awful liabilities: the illusion that man is a god to himself, the illusion that the unnatural rifling of the earth will not yield a retribution as terrible as that wrought on Oedipus, who also killed his father and performed unnatural acts upon his mother.

The present century inherits the Oedipal liabilities of European enlightenment with its benefits, but the Renaissance remains the most significant period for understanding the achievements as well as the predicaments of modern times precisely because it is the era when critical transformations took place. The historiography of the period still tends to overemphasize Burckhardt's brilliant but untenable opposition of a medieval "dark ages" to a modern and self-conscious "freedom" and "individualism," but recent studies are increasingly aware of the confused reality, and in our examination of guilt culture and enlightenment, the deep complexity and ambivalence which accompany the transvaluation of values in western Europe during the Renaissance are insisted upon. It is not simply a matter of the modern period being more "advanced" than the Middle Ages, or of it being even a thorough "enlightenment" break from the older culture. The old ways of thinking have not, even yet, surrendered their place in our world. The complexities remain with us, and no theory should oversimplify the paradoxes they present. Certainly, in the Renaissance, paradoxes abound, and we have seen them in thinkers from Ficino to the Cambridge Platonists. In this context, the conflicting energies of transformation implied in the "guilt to enlightenment" hypothesis provide an instrument for analyzing some of the paradoxes without destroying their complexity. Most important, the hypothesis allows us to interpret the devotional poets of the seventeenth century in context of the most important questions of their times and to conclude that the real unity of the group lies less in their stylistic affinities than in their concern for shared theological problems. Not surprisingly, effective devotional poetry ceases to be written in England when medieval guilt culture yields, at the end of the seventeenth century, to the enlightenment innovations we have described.

Of our four Anglican poets, Donne and Herbert remain basically traditional and medieval. Donne's Thomism has often been commented upon, but his debt to Augustine and to the Augustinian tradition (as critics are increasingly realizing) is even more fundamental. Although Donne had, of course, read Augustine deeply, his reading is notably influenced by an enthusiasm for Bernard and study of Bonaventure. Donne draws, in effect, from an Augustinian spirituality which comes down through Bernard and the Victorines and reaches a high point among Franciscan theologians who saw themselves as defenders of the true Augustine in the High Middle Ages. Not only was Franciscan spirituality enormously influential and widespread in Europe, but it has peculiarly English roots—a point of some importance to a man as concerned as Donne with tradition in relation to his own national church. Franciscan spirituality, moreover, is intimately related to the development of meditative techniques of devotion which have for some time been recognized as important to seventeenth-century poetry.

But more important, the traditional theology of the Franciscans rests on a typically medieval and Augustinian guilt-culture anthropology. The sense of original sin and inherited guilt, the profound consciousness of the two Adams and of the blood sacrifice of the cross, the stress on contrition, the fearful evocation of last things, and a basic anti-Pelagianism are the hallmarks of a program of devotion which develops from Augustinian principles and exerts a profound influence on thought and letters during the Middle Ages. As the Renaissance progresses, however, the bases of the influential Augustinian spirituality are more and more frequently challenged, and in seventeenth-century England, the devotional poets in particular record a development away from some of the main motifs of the traditional Augustinian devotion. There is a progressive decline, for instance, through the poems of Donne, Herbert, Vaughan, and Traherne, in devotion to the cross and in meditation on last things, as a growing latitudinarian sentiment eases men's minds of burdensome meditations on the inheritance and depths of human guilt.

In Donne, however, the main lines of the Augustinian tradition are faithfully preserved. Yet Donne's is not a type of devotion which we would mistake for that of a medieval Augustinian like Bonaventure. Donne, above all, is a man of his times, and the problems of his times strain upon him. He is both Catholic and Reformed, traditional and daringly speculative. Members of his family had died for a faith which he, in good faith, renounced, and of all the issues which caused him pain, the religious intolerance of his times was most hurtful. Donne, in consequence, is an early latitudinarian and anticipates the Cambridge Platonists. But speculation along such lines leads him, paradoxically, to a philosophic and moral tradition of the Renaissance which does not rest easy with the traditional Augustinian modes of devotion to which he is so deeply attached. The *Holy Sonnets,* written at a critical period of Donne's life, essentially record the experience of a basically traditional mind discovering another, and timely, attitude to the religious allegiances a man must make to be be saved.

George Herbert's poems are rooted in the same traditions as Donne's *Holy Sonnets.* They are medieval and Augustinian, and we have traced their complex roots in the older Catholic devotion by considering the popular piety of the English Franciscans and the continental influence of the Valdés circle. Herbert wrote a generation after Donne composed the *Holy Sonnets,* and although his poems are, broadly, in the same meditative mode, Herbert is more disturbed than Donne by the incipient failure in the Caroline church of an Anglican ideal which had burned bright in the minds of Elizabethans. Herbert, rejecting the court of Charles I with its worldly and Romanist leanings, turns to a radical Protestant ecclesiology which emphasizes a spiritual church of the elect rather than the solidarity of a corporate institution.

Herbert's emphasis on Calvinist individualism, predestination, and asceticism considerably modifies his traditional devotion. He is acutely aware of the individual nature of the experience of grace; yet in those poems which remain close to such a personal experience he is, paradoxically, driven to mortify the individual and personal, the "self" which is the root of sin. He desires a simplicity and directness between man and God; yet the devotional techniques he inherits encourage an appeal to God by metaphor and indirection. He evokes the creatures, yet he is ascetic.

Despite the paradoxes, however, Herbert's *The Temple* is the most wholly satisfying and assured collection of devotional poems produced in the period. Herbert achieves a devotion delicately poised between older medieval forms and a new "spiritual" ecclesiology and individualism that were key contributions of the Reformation to the coming secular age. But there is no doubt that Herbert also harks back to an earlier Anglican ideal, and in doing so, a note of otherworldliness creeps into his work. In his own day, perhaps the purest manifestation of the ideal he admired was preserved at the community of Little Gidding, and Herbert, like Nicholas Ferrar, was drawn to Juan de Valdés, the Spanish Reformer held exemplary by founders of the English church. In Valdés, we find a spirituality remarkably similar to that of *The Temple,* poised between an Augustinian and Franciscan heritage, and a Reformed emphasis on justification by faith, on predestination, asceticism, and a spiritual ecclesiology. In the cultural history of the times, the contribution of the Spanish and Italian Reformation to English thought has been too readily ignored, but in Herbert, certainly, the writings of Valdés help to explain the nature of *The Temple* in context of some of the most important spiritual problems of the age.

If Donne and Herbert are spiritually akin, it is often felt that Henry Vaughan, though decidedly in the same tradition, strikes a new note in the devotional poetry of the period. He is closer, in his best inspiration, to Traherne than to even his mentor, George Herbert. In some ways, Vaughan is also the most interesting of the four writers, because the transitions we are describing are present in his work in such exemplary ways. An Augustinian anthropology obviously provides the substance of Vaughan's theory of man, which is clearly expressed in his prose and reflected in his devotion to Herbert. But in his best poems, Vaughan's Augustinian anthropology yields to the vision of a cosmological fall through which he records an experience of man less austere, more tolerant, more optimistic. It is not surprising that these qualities should be intimately related to Vaughan's interest in the Hermetic philosophy, for the *Corpus Hermeticum* is at the center of those typically enlightenment innovations of the Renaissance which surround the cult of the magus and the theory of prisci theologi. In Vaughan's best poems, in consequence, a latitudinarian and typically enlightenment experience of man's nature finds expression and assumes a centrality which it never managed, to achieve, for example, in Donne. Although Vaughan's spirituality is still grounded on the solid rock of the older ways, he strikes from it an unmistakable and unique light.

With Traherne, we move even further from the traditional Augustinianism of the Middle Ages. Traherne's solution to the problems which belabored the theological debates of his day has been difficult to describe succinctly. Critics have long asked about the consistency of Traherne's thought, and it has received no satisfactory explication. Although his work shows an enlightenment tendency to Pelagianism (it is consistent with an interest in the Cambridge Platonists), Traherne also seems to believe in a fall through which man inherits, in the manner of Augustine, the consequences of original sin. Traherne solved the dilemma of reconciling the emergence of secularism and enlightenment with an Augustinian anthropology simply by reviving an alternative and older theory of man at once consistent with the anti-Pelagian edicts of the Thirty-nine Articles and with the optimism of Pico, Hermes Trismegistus, and the Cambridge Platonists. Traherne looked to Saint Irenaeus, and, although he read this early Father from the point of view of his own times and adapted him to his own vision, an Irenaean type of anthropology provides the key to the intellectual unity of Traherne's writing.

Conclusion

In face of the "whirling jumble" of dogmatic stress which this book began by noticing, the contribution of our four Anglican poets has been primarily one of discovery accompanied by a deep concern for preserving the best of what is traditional. But there is, in the poetry, no simple and self-conscious choice of a "middle way." Certainly the celebrated *via media* between Protestantism and Catholicism as a paradigm of Anglican ideology is an oversimplification. In Donne and Herbert and Vaughan and Traherne, new modes of devotion, new and timely apprehensions of human nature, are finding expression, and in each case the innovations are born painfully from the matrices of traditional spirituality. We have examined some of the innovations in terms of medieval and Renaissance views of the fall and original sin, and reverberations from these basic theological issues are felt far and wide: they are recorded in virtually every major institution of seventeenth-century civilization, and each of our four poets was, in fact, involved with the wider issues of politics and the civil contentions of the times. Donne had political aspirations, and his conversion was intimately bound up with his court hopes, even if not determined by them. Herbert's dealings with the court were no less complex, and he, like Donne, was disillusioned by religious wars and frustrated in his courtly aspirations. Vaughan, as a royalist, suffered during the civil war, and Traherne underwent inquisition as the Commonwealth and Restoration made their several demands upon orthodoxy. For each poet, the religious strife was similarly tragic; yet the discovery of means by which traditions could be modified and innovations made acceptable to most men was a slow process. Protestantism, paradoxically, enjoined the return to primitive Christianity, yet assumed a set of doctrines—especially those of the fall and the Trinity—dating from the fifth century. Augustinian anthropology and the traditions of Augustinian devotion thus remained the bastion of traditional Catholic devotion and became also a fundamental emphasis of the Reformation. But as the seventeenth century progressed, there was an increasing modification of the Augustinian and guilt-culture formulas before the pressing needs of the times. In Donne, the enlightenment plea for toleration makes itself heard, and a spiritual ecclesiology and Calvinist individualism (key innovations for the coming secular age) are important elements of Herbert's *The Temple*. Vaughan's cosmological fall is based on

Hermetic sources, and the enlightenment anthropology it implies (latitudinarian, proto-Pelagian) is readily connected also to the enlightenment discovery of man as magus, as empirical scientist. With Traherne, the last poet of our series, who looks to an Irenaean type of anthropology, the Augustinian tradition is no longer dominant, and a subsequent history of Augustinian devotion would record a steadily declining influence. It continued, however, to have spokesmen throughout the seventeenth century, as it has done even to our own times, for it bears witness to an enduring series of truths about human nature. And since all things contain within themselves the seeds of what opposes them, it will no doubt again, in some new formulation, have its say.

Notes

Chapter One

1. Douglas Bush, *English Literature in the Earlier Seventeenth Century, 1600–1660,* 2d ed. (Oxford: Clarendon Press, 1962), p. 1.
2. Marjorie Cox, "The Background to English Literature: 1603–60," in *The Pelican Guide to English Literature,* vol. 3, *From Donne to Marvell,* ed. Boris Ford (Middlesex: Penguin Books, 1960), p. 20.
3. The most thoroughgoing argument for this widespread view is Godfrey Goodman, *The Fall of Man; or, The Corruption of Nature Proved by the Light of Our Natural Reason* (1616). See V. Harris, *All Coherence Gone* (Chicago: University of Chicago Press, 1949), for a full debate on the controversy over the decay of nature.
4. J. B. Bury, *The Idea of Progress* (New York: Dover Publications, 1932), p. 151.
5. *John Donne: The Divine Poems* (Oxford: Clarendon Press, 1964), p. xxi, n. 1.
6. Malcolm Mackenzie Ross, *Poetry and Dogma* (New Brunswick, N.J.: Rutgers University Press, 1954), p. 55.
7. Ruth Benedict, *The Chrysanthemum and the Sword* (Boston: Houghton Mifflin Co., 1946), p. 223.
8. E. R. Dodds, *The Greeks and the Irrational* (Berkeley and Los Angeles: University of California Press, 1968), pp. 17–18.
9. Ibid.
10. Ibid., p. 32.
11. Ibid.
12. Ibid.
13. Ibid., pp. 32–33.
14. Ibid., p. 33.
15. Ibid.
16. Ibid.

17. Ibid.

18. Ibid., pp. 45–46.

19. Gustave Glotz, *La solidarité de la famille dans le droit criminel en Grèce* (Paris: A. Fontemoing, 1904).

20. Dodds, *The Greeks and the Irrational*, p. 34.

21. Ibid., p 47.

22. Ibid., p. 189.

23. Plato *Apology* 24b.

24. Dodds, *The Greeks and the Irrational*, p. 34.

25. *Laws* 878d–e, 929a–c.

26. *Republic* 517b–d (trans. H. D. P. Lee, *Plato: The Republic* [Middlesex: Penguin Books, 1964], pp. 344–45).

27. *Republic* 576e–575 (trans. Lee, p. 348).

28. *Augsburg Confession* 3; *Thirty-nine Articles* 9.

29. Oddone Ortolani, *Pietro Carnesecchi: Con estratti dagli Atti del Processo del Santo Officio* (Florence: Felice le Monnier, 1958), p. 220; trans. José C. Nieto-Sanjuan, "Juan de Valdés, 1509(?)–1541: Background, Origins, and Development of His Theological Thought with Special Reference to Knowledge and Experience" (Th.D. diss., Princeton Theological Seminary, 1967), p. 247.

30. *The Individual and the Cosmos in Renaissance Philosophy*, trans. Mario Domandi (New York and Evanston: Harper Torchbooks, 1963), p. 43.

31. Augustine *City of God* 12.28, 13.3.

32. *City of God* 13.3; *Against Two Letters of the Pelagians* 1.35, 36, 37; *On Nature and Grace* 24, 25; *On the Spirit and the Letter* 9.

33. See *City of God* 13.14. For the importance of the Latin mistranslation of Rom. 15:12, ἐφ᾽ ᾧ πάντες ἥμαρτον, as *in quo omnes peccaverunt*, see G. Bonner, *St. Augustine of Hippo: Life and Controversies* (London: SCM Press, 1963), pp. 371 ff.

34. *On Original Sin* 23.38, 37.42.

35. *On Nature and Grace* 5.5; *Confessions* 8. passim.

36. *On Grace and Free Will* 14.27; *On Nature and Grace* 3.3–4.

37. *Adversus haereses* 3.38.1.

38. *De unitate* 23.

39. *De unitate* 6.

40. *De unitate*, trans. Johannes Quasten, *Patrology* (Utrecht, Antwerp: Spectrum Publishers, 1963), 2:373.

41. *De orat.* 2, trans. Quasten, *Patrology*, 2:330.

42. *De bapt.* 20, trans. Quasten, *Patrology*, 2:330.

43. See Joseph C. Plumpe, *Mater Ecclesia: An Enquiry into the Concept of Church as Mother in Early Christianity* (Washington: Catholic University of America Press, 1943); Clement *Paedagogus* 1.5–6, trans. W. Wilson, Ante-Nicene Christian Library (Edinburgh: T. and T. Clark, 1867); Origen *Exp. in prov. (PG* 17.201).

44. *De symb. ad catech.* 2.13 (*PL* 40.668).

45. *In epist. ad Parthos.* 3.1 (*PL* 34.1998).

46. *Serm.* 216.7 (*PL* 38.1080).

47. *On the Trinity* 12.3, 4, 12.

48. *On the Trinity* 12.12, trans. Arthur West Hadden, *A Select Library of the Nicene and Post Nicene Fathers of the Christian Church,* vol. 3, ed. Philip Schaff (Buffalo: Christian Literature Co., 1887), p. 161.

49. Ibid., p. 162.

50. See R. Klibansky, *The Continuity of the Platonic Tradition during the Middle Ages* (London: Warburg Institute, 1939).

51. See Domenico Comparetti, *Vergil in the Middle Ages,* trans. E. F. M. Benecke (London: Swan Sonnenschein and Co., 1895).

52. See C. de Boer, ed., *Ovide moralisé* (Amsterdam, 1915–54); D. W. Robertson, Jr., *A Preface to Chaucer* (Princeton: Princeton University Press, 1969), pp. 356–57, et passim; D. C. Allen, *Mysteriously Meant: The Rediscovery of Pagan Symbolism and Allegorical Interpretation in the Renaissance* (Baltimore and London: Johns Hopkins University Press, 1970), pp. 163–99.

53. See *Epistolae* (*PL* 33.710). Allen points out that Augustine's letter sets the pattern, and "with spiritual tears in his eyes, Augustine regretfully denies these men [right-living pagans] any prospect of redemption" (*Mysteriously Meant,* p. 43).

54. Jean Daniélou. *Holy Pagans of the Old Testament,* trans. Felix Faber (London: Longmans, 1957), pp. 10, 23.

55. Justin Martyr *Apologia pro Christianis* (*PG* 6.358–82); Clement *Stromateis* 5.14, 89–141. For an account of early Christian theories, see Allen, *Mysteriously Meant,* chap. 1, "Pagan Myth and Christian Apologetics," pp. 1–20. The following references are from Allen's account.

56. Tatian *Oratio adversus Graecos* (*PG* 6.854); Augustine *City of God* 2.4, 2.29.

57. Tertullian *Ad nationes* (*PL* 1.601–3); Arnobius *Adversus gentes* (*PL* 5.1037–38).

58. See the section *De diis gentium* of the *Etymologiae.*

59. *On Christian Doctrine* 2.18.28, trans. D. W. Robertson, Jr. (New York: Bobbs-Merrill Co., 1958), p. 54.

60. *On Christian Doctrine* 2.40.60, trans. Robertson, p. 75.

61. Ibid.

62. *Confessions* 7.14, trans. E. B. Pusey (London: J. M. Dent, 1907), p. 131.

63. *Confessions* 7.15, trans. Pusey, p. 132.

64. *On Christian Doctrine* 2.40.60, trans. Robertson, p. 75.

65. At the beginning of his commentary on the *Aeneid,* Bernardus claims a poem has "a twofold utility: first, a skill at writing . . . second, a prudence concerning right action which is gathered from the teaching of examples"

(trans. in Robertson, *Preface*, p. 343). Theodulf defends his reading of Ovid and Vergil by saying that in their poems, "although there may be many frivolous things, many truths lie hidden beneath the false covering" (trans. in Robertson, *Preface*, p. 345). For Boccaccio, see *The Genealogy of the Gentile Gods* 15.ix; for Herbert, see *The Church Porch*, st. 1.

66. *Epistolario*, ed. F. Novati (Rome: Instituto Storico Italiano, 1905), 4:233–34. Discussed in Robertson, *Preface*, p. 353.

67. *Preface*, pp. 337–65.

68. Ibid., p. 346.

69. *Didascalion* 3, 4. Discussed in Robertson, *Preface*, p. 347.

70. See Robertson, *Preface*, p. 342.

71. See Jean Seznec, *The Survival of the Pagan Gods* (New York: Harper Torchbooks, 1961), pp. 11–37.

72. Allen, *Mysteriously Meant*, p. 51.

73. An interesting account of this aspect of the Renaissance is Rosemary Colie's *Epidemica Paradoxica: The Renaissance Tradition of Paradox* (Princeton: Princeton University Press, 1966).

74. *Opera* (Basel, 1576) 2.1137, trans. in Robertson, *Preface*, p: 360.

75. Allen, *Mysteriously Meant*, p. 23.

76. *The Survival of the Pagan Gods*, p. 146.

77. Ibid., pp. 99, 98.

78. See Allen, *Mysteriously Meant*, pp. 25–26.

79. Ibid., p. 29.

80. At the end of *De veritate* (1624), developed in *De religione laici* (1645) and *De religione gentilium* (1633).

81. *Tractatus theologico-politicus*, ed. C. H. Bruder (Leipzig, 1846), 3:83.

82. Allen, *Mysteriously Meant*, p. 40.

83. *The Court of the Gentiles*, 1:14–17.

84. See Allen, *Mysteriously Meant*, p. 77.

85. *The Antient Religion of the Gentiles, and the Causes of Their Errors*, trans. W. Lewis (London, 1705), p. 269, et passim in chap. 13, pp. 255–70.

86. Ibid., p. 266.

87. Ibid., p. 296.

88. Ibid., pp. 255–70.

89. This opposition, which exactly complements the opposition of guilt culture to enlightenment, is explored by Norman O. Brown in *Love's Body* (New York: Vintage Books, 1968), pp. 3–32.

90. See Frances A. Yates, *Giordano Bruno and the Hermetic Tradition* (London: Routledge and Kegan Paul, 1964), p. 13.

91. See A.-J. Festugière, *La révélation d'Hermes Trismegiste*, 4 vols. (Paris, 1950–54).

92. For a summary of Pletho and his theory of the prisci theologi, see Yates, *Giordano Bruno*, pp. 13–15.

93. Lactantius *Div. inst.* 1.vi, trans. W. Fletcher, *The Works of Lactantius,* Ante-Nicene Christian Library (Edinburgh: T. and T. Clark, 1871), 1:15; Augustine *City of God* 8.23.

94. Marsilio Ficino, *Argumentum* to the *Pimander,* in *Opera omnia,* 2 vols. (Basel, 1576), p. 1836; my translation. For other genealogies see D. P. Walker, *Spiritual and Demonic Magic from Ficino to Campanella* (London: Warburg Institute, 1958), p. 93.

95. Ficino, *Argumentum,* p. 1836.

96. See *Oration on the Dignity of Man,* passim.

97. *Pimander . . . Crater Hermetis A Lazerelo Septempedano . . .* (Paris, 1505), fol. 61 vo. See Walker, *Spiritual and Demonic Magic,* p. 65.

98. Ibid., fol. 52 vo.

99. Ficino, *Argumentum* to *Pimander, Opera,* p. 1836. See Yates, *Giordano Bruno,* p. 40.

100. *Asclepius* 3.24a.

101. Augustine *City of God* 8.23–26.

102. *De vita coelitus comparanda,* esp. 1.34, 11, 20. See Walker, *Spiritual and Demonic Magic,* pp. 1–24.

103. Walker, *Spiritual and Demonic Magic,* pp. 54–55, 75–76, 80, 82.

104. Tommaso Campanella, *Magia e grazia,* ed. R. Amerio (Rome, 1957), p. 180. See Yates, *Giordano Bruno,* pp. 147–48.

105. Yates, *Giordano Bruno,* p. 150.

106. See ibid., p. 151.

107. N. Copernicus, *De revolutionibus orbium caelestium* (Torun, 1873), pp. 16–17. Copernicus quotes Pythagoras, Philolaus, and Hermes Trismegistus. See Yates, *Giordano Bruno,* pp. 153–54.

108. See Yates, *Giordano Bruno,* pp. 150–51 (on Paracelsus), pp. 130–43 (on Agrippa), pp. 140–44 (on Kepler). For Kepler's reliance on Pico della Mirandola, see J. Kepler, *Opera omnia,* ed. C. Frisch (Stuttgart: Francofurtae, 1858–71), 2:570 ff.; 3:29.

109. For a discussion of Bacon's *Historia vitae et mortis* and its derivation from Telesio and Ficino, see Walker, *Spiritual and Demonic Magic,* pp. 199–202.

110. Yates, *Giordano Bruno,* p. 156.

111. Elizabeth Livermore Forbes, trans., *Oration on the Dignity of Man,* in Ernst Cassirer, Paul Oskar Kristeller, John Herman Randall, Jr., eds., *The Renaissance Philosophy of Man* (Chicago: University of Chicago Press, 1948), p. 223. For Hermetic strains in Pico's *Oration,* see Konrad Burdach, *Vom Mittelalter zur Reformation* (Berlin, 1917), vol. 3, pt. 1, pp. 293 ff., 314 ff.

112. *Oration,* trans. Forbes, pp. 224, 230, 234.

113. Ibid., pp. 237, 246, 250.

114. Ibid., p. 252.

115. Nietzsche's term. See Seznec, *The Survival of the Pagan Gods,* p. 237.

116. *Oration,* trans. Forbes, p. 223.

117. Ibid., p. 242.
118. Ibid., p. 244.
119. Ibid., p. 226.
120. Ibid., pp. 246–47.
121. Ibid., p. 249.
122. Ibid., pp. 224–25.
123. See *Heptaplus* 5.7, 7.1.
124. It is not surprising that the church suspected Pico and condemned a number of his theses, among them the remarkable but characteristic suggestion that magic and the cabala help prove the divinity of Christ: "Nulla est scientia que nos magis certificet de divinitate Christi quam magia et cabala." See Yates, *Giordano Bruno*, p. 112.
125. Ernst Cassirer, "Giovanni Pico della Mirandola," pt. 2, *JHI* 3, no. 3 (June 1942): 329–30.
126. Ernst F. Winter, ed. and trans., *Erasmus-Luther: Discourse on Free Will* (New York: Frederic Ungar Publishing Co., 1966), pp. 122, 132, 133. Compare Calvin's similar attack on the Pelagians, *Institutes of the Christian Religion* 2.5.1, et passim.
127. *Erasmus-Luther*, p. 137.
128. Francois Wendel, *Calvin: The Origins and Development of His Religious Thought*, trans. Philip Mairet (New York: Fontana Library, 1965), p. 124.
129. Luchesius Smits, *Saint Augustin dans l'oeuvre de Jean Calvin* (Assen, 1957), 1:97.
130. Wendel, *Calvin*, pp. 124–25.
131. See Thomas Erastus, *De occultis pharmacorum potestatibus* ... (Basel, 1574); Johann Wier, *De praestigiis daemonorum* ... (Basel, 1583); Lefèvre d'Etaples's commentary on Ficino's *Pimander*. These attacks are dealt with in Walker, *Spiritual and Demonic Magic*, pp. 146–70.
132. G. F. Pico, *Examen vanitatis doctrinae gentium*, and *De rerum praenotione*, in *Opera omnia* (Basel, 1573); Martin Del Rio, *Disquisitionum magiacarum libri sex* (Coloniae Agrippinae, 1679). These attacks are dealt with in Walker, *Spiritual and Demonic Magic*, pp. 146 ff., 178 ff.
133. *Examen vanitatis* I.xx, in *Opera omnia*, p. 814.
134. *De praestigiis daemonum*, cols. 146 ff.
135. E. Rodocanachi, *La reforme en Italie* (Paris, 1920), 1:246.
136. See *The Works of George Herbert*, ed. F. E. Hutchinson (Oxford: Clarendon Press, 1967), p. 588.
137. John T. McNeill, ed., *Institutes of the Christian Religion* 4.10.15, trans. and indexed, Ford Lewis Battles (Philadelphia: Westminster Press, 1960) p. 1193.
138. Ibid., 4.17.15, trans. Battles, pp. 1376–77.
139. Ibid., 4.14.14, trans. Battles, p. 1289; 4.17.39, trans. Battles, p. 1416.
140. Ibid., esp. 1.5.5, and 1.13.1.

141. Ibid., 1.15.2, trans. Battles, p. 185: "Now, unless the soul were something essential, separate from the body, Scripture would not teach that we dwell in houses of clay [Job 4:19]."

142. Ibid., 1.5.5, trans. Battles, p. 57.

143. Ibid., 1.5.5, trans. Battles, p. 58.

144. Ibid., 1.5.5, trans. Battles, p. 57.

145. *Oration,* trans. Forbes, p. 249.

146. For Pico's views on the world soul, see *Conclusiones sec. Iamblichum* 9, in *Opera,* p. 75.

147. *Institutes* 1.11.9, trans. Battles, p. 109; 1.11.11, trans. Battles, p. 111.

148. Ibid., 4.18.18, trans. Battles, p. 1446. It is probable that the magic of Ficino and his followers was in fact influenced by the doctrine of transubstantiation in the Mass. See Walker, *Spiritual and Demonic Magic,* pp. 36, 72.

149. *Institutes* 4.17.36, trans. Battles, p. 1413; 4.9.4, trans. Battles, p. 1168.

150. Ibid., 4.16.31, trans. Battles, p. 1358.

151. Yates, *Giordano Bruno,* pp. 166–67. See also Walker, *Spiritual and Demonic Magic,* p. 77, where a chart of the branches of natural magic contains the arts.

152. Walker, *Spiritual and Demonic Magic,* p. 120.

153. Yates, *Giordano Bruno,* p. 167. See J. Gutch, ed., *The History and Antiquities of the Colleges and Halls in . . . Oxford,* vol. 2, pt. 1 (1786), p. 107.

154. John Ferrar, *A Life of Nicholas Ferrar,* in B. Blackstone, ed., *The Ferrar Papers* (Cambridge: At the University Press, 1938), p. 61.

155. J. Tulloch, *Rational Theology and Christian Philosophy in England in the Seventeenth Century* (Edinburgh and London, 1872), 1:5.

156. The question of the church was crucial in this period in a manner unprecedented in the Middle Ages. In the earlier period, problems in ecclesiology were not deeply examined if only because controversy did not force the issue. Aquinas, for instance, has surprisingly little to say on the question, and even Torquemada's *Summa de ecclesia,* written after the conciliarist debate of the fourteenth century, comes up with no clear thesis, although classifying fifteen principal meanings of the word *ecclesia.* Consequently, it is difficult to generalize on "what the Middle Ages thought" about the church as distinct from the Reformation.

157. Geddes MacGregor, *Corpus Christi: The Nature of the Church According to the Reformed Tradition* (Philadelphia: Westminster Press, 1958), p. 33.

158. "Luther favoured the word 'hidden' (*abscondita*), perhaps even preferring it to *invisibilis,* which he is the first to apply to the Church. See *Ad librum Ex. Mag. Nostri Mag. Ambrosii Catharini . . . Responsio* (1521), ed. Weimar, VII, p. 772" (MacGregor, *Corpus Christi,* p. 8, n. 3).

159. MacGregor, *Corpus Christi,* p. 9.

160. These four theologians are dealt with in John T. McNeill, "The Church in Sixteenth-Century Reformed Theology," *The Journal of Religion* 22 (1942):251–69; for a more detailed study, see MacGregor, *Corpus Christi.*

See álso Ray C. Petry, "Calvin's Conception of the *Communio Sanctorum*," *Church History* (1936), pp. 227–28; Henri Reubelt Pearcy, *The Meaning of the Church in the Thought of Calvin* (Chicago: University of Chicago Press, 1941); Wendel, *Calvin*, chap. 5, sec. 1.

161. Cf. Dom Gregory Dix: "The real Eucharistic action is for Calvin individual and internal, not corporate. It is one more example of the intractability of the scriptural sacraments of the Protestant theory, and the impossibility of adapting to a 'religion of the spirit' and pure individualism the institutions of a 'religion of incarnation' which presupposes the organic community of the renewed Israel" (*The Shape of the Liturgy* [London: Dacre Press, 1945], p. 633).

162. Calvin repeats the Cyprianic formula, *Institutes* 4.1.1. "It is the figure of Mother that best pleases Calvin" (MacGregor, *Corpus Christi*, p. 47).

163. William Halewood, *The Poetry of Grace: Reformation Themes and Structures in English Seventeenth-Century Poetry* (New Haven and London: Yale University Press, 1970), is relevant here. My manuscript was virtually complete when Mr. Halewood's study appeared. Happily, I am in agreement with his major premises and interpret his book as a valuable expansion of areas of Augustinian theology which I do not stress. Basically, Halewood argues that seventeenth-century devotional poetry is primarily "a poetry of reconciliation" (pp. 14–15) and that the excitement and disturbance of the poems have a dogmatic basis in the theology of the Reformation which is, in this respect, primarily a revival of Augustine's teachings on human depravity and divine grace. In the course of the present study I will suggest points where Halewood's argument complements and deepens my own. Areas on which we may disagree are more difficult to determine precisely, for Halewood's focus, if bright, is also deliberately narrow. He argues (p. 34) that the Reformation in England was complicated and acknowledges the value of studies like L. L. Martz's *The Paradise Within*, which have a radically different emphasis from his own. Briefly, I argue for a more profound influence of medieval Augustinian tradition than he allows and suggest some means by which a medieval Augustinian spirituality merges, in ways uniquely satisfying to seventeenth-century Anglicans, with the type of Protestantism he outlines. The experience of reconciliation is indeed peculiarly Protestant and certainly heightens the sense of personal strain in much of the devotional poetry of seventeenth-century England. But the experience is of course not "discovered" by these poets—not that Halewood claims otherwise, but his tendency to associate the medieval tradition with Aquinas removes the sense of continuity which I am interested in affirming.

Chapter Two

1. José de Vinck, trans., *The Works of Bonaventure*, vol. 3, Opuscula Second Series (N. J.: St. Anthony Guild Press, 1966), pp. 1–10. For the original

Notes

text, see Clemens Blume and Guido M. Dreves, eds., *Analecta hymnica medii aevi* (Leipzig, 1906), 49–50:571–74.

2. *Holy Sonnet* 11, lines 1–2, ed. Helen Gardner, *John Donne: The Divine Poems* (Oxford: Clarendon Press, 1952), p. 9. All quotations from the *Holy Sonnets* are from this edition; Grierson's numbering is used.

3. Louis L. Martz, *The Poetry of Meditation: A Study in English Religious Literature of the Seventeenth Century* (New Haven: Yale University Press, 1955), pp. 5, 19. The pseudo-Bonaventure is now identified as Friar Joannes a Calibus della San Gimignano.

4. Izaak Walton, *The Lives of John Donne, Sir Henry Wotton, Richard Hooker, George Herbert, and Robert Sanderson* (Oxford: Oxford University Press, 1962), pp. 47–48, 23.

5. "Péché originel," *Dictionnaire de théologie catholique*, vol. 12, pt. 1, col. 432; hereafter referred to as *DT*.

6. Decima L. Douie, *Archbishop Pecham* (Oxford: Clarendon Press, 1952), p. 293.

7. Trans. by José de Vinck, *The Works of Bonaventure* (1963), vol. 2; see the notes to de Vinck's translation, pp. 319–20.

8. "Péché originel," *DT*, vol. 12, pt. 1, col. 468.

9. Fr. Matthaei ab Aquasparta, O.F.M., *Quaestiones disputate selectae*, vol. 2, *Quaestiones de Christo* (Quaracchi, 1914). See *DT*, vol. 12, pt. 1, cols. 492–93.

10. See *DT*, vol. 12, pt. 1, cols. 494 ff.

11. *Summa theologica* 3.2.1. See *DT*, vol. 12, pt. 1, cols. 459–62.

12. See *DT*, vol. 12, pt. 1, cols. 504 ff.

13. *DT*, vol. 12, pt. 1, col. 494.

14. See Jean Fr. Bonnefoy, O.F.M., "La question hypothetique; Utrum si Adam non pecasset . . . au XIII siecle," *Revista Espanola de teologia* 14 (1954): 327–68.

15. See "De Immaculata Conceptione in ordine S. Francisci," *Virgo Immaculata* 7 (Rome, 1957), fascs. 1–3; L. Veuthey, "La pietà mariana nella spiritualità francescana," *Vita Christiana* 23 (1954): 223–37.

16. *Dictiònnaire de spiritualité et mystique, doctrine et histoire* (Paris: G. Beauchesne, 1932–); hereafter referred to as *DS*.

17. David Lyle Jeffrey, "Franciscan Spirituality and Middle English Poetry" (Ph.D. diss., Princeton, 1968). This dissertation is now accepted for publication by the University of Nebraska Press. The author has made few revisions in the sections which contribute to this argument.

18. *Breviloquium* 4.9.4.

19. *Meditations on the Life of Christ: An Illustrated Manuscript of the Fourteenth Century*, trans. Isa Ragusa, completed from the Latin and edited by Isa Ragusa and Rosalie B. Green (Princeton: Princeton University Press, 1961), pp. 317–18.

20. *The Mind's Road to God,* trans. George Boas (New York: Bobbs-Merrill Co., 1953), pp. 43–44, 45.

21. The status of the cross as a special concern of Franciscans is made clear in this hymn by Bonaventure's request: "Sing with *special* praise and honor / This salvation-bringing tree" (my emphasis).

22. *Jacopone da Todi, Poet and Mystic: 1228–1306: A Spiritual Biography,* by Evelyn Underhill, *With a Selection from the Spiritual Songs,* trans. Mrs. Theodore Beck (London: Dent, 1919), pp. 287–88.

23. See M.-J. Picard, "Chemin de Croix," *DS,* vol. 2, cols. 2576–2606.

24. "La spiritualità francescana et l'Immacolata," *Virgo Immaculata,* vol. 7, fasc. 3 (Rome, 1957), p. 228.

25. Jeffrey, "Franciscan Spirituality," p. 114.

26. Ibid., p. 116.

27. "Spiritualité Franciscaine: 1226–1517," *DS,* vol. 5, col. 1325.

28. Jeffrey, "Franciscan Spirituality," p. 268, from *Regula* 9.

29. Ibid., p. 83, from J. S. Brewer, ed., *Fr. Roger Bacon Opera,* Rolls Series, trans. A. G. Little, "The First Hundred Years of the Franciscan School at Oxford," ed. Walter Warren Seaton, *St. Francis of Assisi, 1226–1926: Essays in Commemoration* (London: London University Press, 1926), p. 173.

30. Emma Therese Healy, ed. and trans., *De reductione artium ad theologiam* (New York: St. Bonaventure Press, 1955), p. 38.

31. Jeffrey, "Franciscan Spirituality," p. 79.

32. G. H. Tavard, *Transiency and Permanence: The Nature of Theology According to St. Bonaventure* (New York: St. Bonaventure Press, 1954), p. 252.

33. *Breviloquium* 6.10.1.

34. Alexander of Hales, *Magistri Alexander de Hales, Glossa in Quatuor Libri Sententiarum Petri Lombardi,* Bibliotheca Franciscana Scholastico Medii Aevi, 15 (Quaracchi, 1957), 4.14.210. See Jeffrey, "Franciscan Spirituality," p. 104.

35. Jeffrey, "Franciscan Spirituality," p. 111.

36. Ibid., p. 109, from Thomas Eccleston, *The Coming of the Franciscans,* trans. Leo Sherley-Price (London: A. R. Mowbray, 1964), p. 48.

37. Jeffrey, "Franciscan Spirituality," p. 133. See Ray C. Petry, "Mediaeval Eschatology and St. Francis of Assisi," *Church History* 9 (1940): 54–69; "Mediaeval Eschatology and Social Responsibility in Bernard of Marval's *De Contemptu Mundi,*" *Speculum* 24 (1949): 207–18.

38. Jeffrey, "Franciscan Spirituality," p. 135.

39. See *New Catholic Encyclopaedia,* 7:990–91; Paul E. L. Fournier, *Etudes sur Joachim de Fiore et de ses doctrines* (Paris, 1909).

40. Jeffrey, "Franciscan Spirituality," p. 131.

41. Ibid., p. 186.

42. *Jacopone da Todi, Poet and Mystic,* p. 447.

Notes

43. Ibid., p. 253.

44. *The Mind's Road to God*, p. 45.

45. Jeffrey, "Franciscan Spirituality," p. 89.

46. Franciscan preaching manuals are not well known, existing often only as manuscripts. They contain such titles as the *Speculum sacerdotale, Speculum Christiani, Liber exemplorum, Speculum laicorum*, and the *Fasciculus morum* (Jeffrey, "Franciscan Spirituality," pp. 287–88). The *Speculum laicorum*, for instance, was owned by Sir Thomas Browne (MS University College Oxford, 29).

47. George R. Potter and Evelyn M. Simpson, eds., *The Sermons of John Donne*, 10 vols. (Berkeley and Los Angeles: University of California Press, 1953–62), 6:293; hereafter referred to as *Sermons*.

48. S. T. Coleridge, *Table Talk*, June 4, 1830, ed. Professor Shedd, *The Complete Works of Samuel Taylor Coleridge* (New York: Harper and Brothers, 1868), 6:329.

49. *The Divine Poems*, p. 92.

50. Father Gilbert, O.S.F.C., *B. Agnellus and the English Grey Friars* (London: Burns Oates and Co., 1937), p. 57.

51. Stanza 5. See Gardner's note, *The Divine Poems*, p. 84.

52. Evelyn M. Simpson, *A Study of the Prose Works of John Donne* (Oxford: Clarendon Press, 1948), p. 107.

53. Robert S. Jackson, *John Donne's Christian Vocation* (Evanston: Northwestern University Press, 1970), p. 119.

54. Halewood, *Poetry of Grace*, p. 61.

55. Richard E. Hughes, *The Progress of the Soul: The Interior Career of John Donne* (New York: William Morrow and Co., 1968), pp. 139 ff.

56. Ibid., p. 159.

57. Ibid., pp. 177 ff.

58. "Donne's Christian Eloquence," *ELH* 27 (1960):276–97.

59. D. L. Peterson, "John Donne's *Holy Sonnets* and the Anglican Doctrine of Contrition," *SP* 56 (1959):504–18.

60. *The Poetry of Meditation*, p. 31.

61. See S. Archer, "Meditation and the Structure of Donne's *Holy Sonnets*," *ELH* 28 (1961):137–47.

62. Roy W. Battenhouse, "The Grounds of Religious Toleration in the Thought of John Donne," *Church History* 11, no. 3 (1942):217–48.

63. Letters of 1651, no. 29, ed. Sir Edmund Gosse, *The Life and Letters of John Donne* (London: W. Heinemann, 1899), 1:225 ff.

64. Battenhouse, "The Grounds of Religious Toleration," p. 234.

65. Ibid., pp. 235; 225, n. 31.

66. Evelyn M. Simpson, ed., *Essays in Divinity by John Donne* (Oxford: Clarendon Press, 1952), p. 30.

67. Facsimile Text Society Edition (New York, 1930), p. 21.

68. Letters of 1651, ed. Gosse, 1:226.

69. Simpson, *The Prose Works*, p. 74.

70. *An Hymn, upon the Passion of CHRIST,* ed. A. B. Grosart, *The Complete Poems of Dr. Henry More (1614–1687),* Chertsey Worthies' Library (London: 1878), pp. 185–86.

71. G. Bullough, ed., *Philosophical Poems of Henry More, Comprising Psychozoia and Minor Poems* (Manchester: Publications of the University of Manchester, English Series, no. 20, 1931), pp. 7–8.

72. *The Praeexistency of the Soul,* st. 95, ed. Grosart, p. 128.

73. Plotinus *Enneads* 1.8.7, trans. S. MacKenna, 2d ed. rev. (London: Faber and Faber, 1956), p. 72.

74. *The Mind's Road to God,* p. 45.

75. *Confessions* 10.54, trans. Pusey, p. 238.

76. Thomas Traherne, *Centuries* 4.74, ed. H. M. Margoliouth, *Thomas Traherne, Centuries, Poems, and Thanksgivings,* 2 vols. (Oxford: Clarendon Press, 1968), 1:208.

77. Ibid., 2.33.

78. Simpson, *The Prose Works,* p. 74.

Chapter Three

1. Martz, *The Poetry of Meditation,* p. 143.

2. *Death,* ed. F. E. Hutchinson, *The Works of George Herbert* (Oxford: Clarendon Press, 1967), p. 186. All quotations are from his edition, indicated in the text as *Works.*

3. Martz, *The Poetry of Meditation,* pp. 144 ff. The distinction becomes strained when we consider Donne's hymns, especially *To God the Father,* or one or two of Herbert's more disturbed poems, like *Perseverence* or even the early sonnets to his mother. It is not surprising that poets who shared so many of the same traditions should occasionally write similar poems. The real differences in sensibility that exist between them should not obscure the even greater debt they both owe to similar traditional materials.

4. Walton, *Lives,* p. 273. An account of Herbert's belief in predestination is given in Joseph H. Summers, *George Herbert, His Religion and Art* (London: Chatto and Windus, 1954), pp. 57–58.

5. Summers, *George Herbert,* p. 58. Compare William Halewood's argument that the Reformation sense of reconciliation is felt throughout Herbert's poetry. *Poetry of Grace,* p. 104, and chap. 4, passim.

6. Rosemond Tuve, *A Reading of George Herbert* (Chicago: University of Chicago Press, 1952), p. 47.

7. Carleton Brown, ed., *Religious Lyrics of the XIVth Century,* 2d ed., rev. by G. V. Smithers (Oxford: Clarendon Press, 1957), p. 89. The following quotations are from this edition, indicated in the text as *XIV.*

8. R. H. Robbins, "The Authors of the Middle English Lyrics," *JEGP* 39 (1940):230–38.

9. Jeffrey, "Franciscan Spirituality," pp. 323 ff.

Notes

10. Ibid., p. 268. The following account summarizes Jeffrey's conclusions on Franciscan preaching.

11. Elizabeth Soltész, ed., *Biblia Pauperum, Facsimile Edition of the Forty-Leaf Blockbook in the Library of the Esztergom Cathedral* (Budapest: Corvina Press, 1967).

12. Soltész, *Biblia Pauperum*, intro., p. viii.

13. J. Ph. Berjeau, ed., *Biblia Pauperum. Reproduced in facsimile from one of the copies in the British Museum* (London: J. Russell Smith, 1859); Adam Pilinski, ed., *Bible des Pauvres, reproduite en fac-similé sur l'exemplaire de la Bibliothèque Nationale* (Paris, 1883); Josef Anton-Schönbrunner Einsle, ed., *Biblia pauperum, Facsimile-Reproduction getreu nach dem in der Erzherzoglich Albrecht'schen Kunst-Sammlung "Albertina" befindlichen Exemplar* (Vienna-Pest-Leipzig, 1890); Theodor H. Musper, ed., *Die Urausgaben der holländischen Apokalypse und Biblia pauperum* (Munich, 1961).

14. Soltész, *Biblia Pauperum*, intro., p. vii.

15. Ibid., p. v. See plates 1–5.

16. On the realistic technique of the woodcuts, see ibid., p. xi.

17. Ibid., p. xxiii.

18. Ibid., p. viii.

19. Berjeau, *Biblia Pauperum*, p. 5. The pagination follows Berjeau's *Interpretario typorum*.

20. Ibid.

21. Jeffrey, "Franciscan Spirituality," p. 125. The following account summarizes Jeffrey's argument, pp. 125–27.

22. C. L. Kingswood, A. G. Little, and F. Tocco, eds., *Fratris Johannis Pecham quondam Archiepiscopi Cantuariensis tractatus tres de paupertate*, British Society of Franciscan Studies, 2 (Aberdeen, 1910):24. Erasmus makes a joke about the friars as "wagon wheels" of the church in his colloquy *The Funeral*, trans. Craig R. Thompson, *The Colloquies of Erasmus* (Chicago: University of Chicago Press, 1964), p. 363. R. G. Latham, *Revised Mediaeval Latin Word List, from British and Irish Sources* (London: Oxford University Press, 1965), defines *gyrus* as a "ring" and "hoop" and *gyrovagus* as "stroller," "vagabond," and "strolling monk."

23. *The Mind's Road to God*, p. 4.

24. Berjeau, *Biblia Pauperum*, pp. 12–13.

25. Soltész, *Biblia Pauperum*, intro., pp. ix–x.

26. Ross, *Poetry and Dogma*, p. 155; cf. p. 176.

27. Rosemond Tuve, "George Herbert and *Caritas*," *JWCI* 22 (1959):303–31.

28. Arnold Stein, *George Herbert's Lyrics* (Baltimore, Johns Hopkins Press, 1968).

29. Michael P. Gallagher, S.J., "Rhetoric, Style, and George Herbert," *ELH* 37 (Dec. 1970):495–516.

30. Ross, *Poetry and Dogma*, p. 235.

31. "I would addresse / My vows to thee most gladly, Blessed Maid / And Mother of my God, / But now, alas, I dare not; for our King / . . . / Bids no such thing" (*To All the Angels and Saints* [*Works* p. 78]).

32. Heather Asalas, "George Herbert and Hugh of St. Victor's *Soliloquim de Arrha Animae,*" *N&Q*, n.s.16 (Oct. 1969):368, demonstrates that Herbert's use of contemporary imagery from trade and commerce is not a result of Puritan influence but reflects his reading of (the Augustinian) Hugh of Saint Victor.

33. "Lord teach me to refer / All things I doe to thee," *The Elixir* (*Works* p. 184).

34. Ross, *Poetry and Dogma*, pp. 135–58.

Chapter Four

1. John Valdesso, *Divine Considerations*, trans. Nicholas Ferrar, ed. Frederic Chapman (London: J. Lane, 1905). Ferrar's translation was first published at Oxford, 1638.

2. *Briefe Notes on Valdesso's "Considerations,"* in *Works* pp. 304–20.

3. Summers, *George Herbert*, p. 67.

4. Ibid., p. 66.

5. *Divine Considerations*, p. 185; cf. pp. 3, 48, 114, 132, 135–36, 144, 181, 183, 255, 266, 267, 309, 314, 315, 336. Valdés's view of justification is in the last resort eclectic. Salvation depends on grace, but the degree of perfection depends on the quality of works that emerge from faith.

6. The extremely popular and Valdés-inspired *Beneficio di Cristo* disagrees, much as Herbert does, with Valdés's tendency to exalt the spirit above the Scriptures but remains nonetheless Valdesian. See Ruth Prelowski, trans., *Beneficio di Cristo*, ed. John A. Tedeschi, *Italian Reformation Studies in Honour of Laelius Socinus* (Florence, 1965), p. 31 et passim.

7. *A Dialogue on Christian Doctrine Newly Composed by a Churchman*, ed. and trans. Angel M. Mergal, The Library of Christian Classics, vol. 25 (Philadelphia: Westminster Press, 1957), p. 328.

8. Marcel Bataillon, ed., *Juan de Valdés: Dialogo de doctrina Christiana* (Coimbra, 1925), p. 93.

9. Ibid., p. 26. For accounts of Erasmus's influence in Spain, see: John E. Longhurst, *Erasmus and the Spanish Inquisition: The Case of Juan de Valdés*, University of New Mexico Publications in History, no. 1 (Albuquerque: University of New Mexico Press, 1950); Marcel Bataillon, *Erasme et l'Espagne: Recherches sur l'histoire spirituelle du XVIe siècle* (Paris, 1937).

10. *Dialogue on Christian Doctrine*, trans. Mergal, p. 309.

11. Bataillon, *Erasme et l'Espagne*, 1:2, trans. Nieto-Sanjuan, *Juan de Valdés*, p. 76.

Notes

12. See Bataillon, *Erasme et l'Espagne,* 1:51–60, for a more extended list which includes classical authors and contemplative literature.

13. See Longhurst, *Erasmus and the Spanish Inquisition,* p. 29.

14. Valdés translated the Psalms from Hebrew and Paul's Epistles from Greek.

15. José C. Nieto-Sanjuan, "Juan de Valdés, 1509(?)–1541: Background, Origins, and Development of His Theological Thought with Special Reference to Knowledge and Experience" (Th.D. diss., Princeton Theological Seminary, 1967), p. 77. Alcala was also unusual in having a chair of Scotist theology.

16. Ibid., p. 154.

17. Miguel Asín Palacios argues for the direct influence of Islamic mysticism. See *Huellas del islam: Sto. Tomas de Aquino, Turquemada, Pascal, S. Juan de la Cruz* (Madrid: Espasa-Calpe, 1941), and the unfinished "Sādilīes y Alumbrados," *Al-Andalaus. Revista de la escuela de estudios árabes de Madrid y Granada* 9 (1944):321–45; 10 (1945):1–25, 255–84; 11 (1946):1–67. Americo Castro argues for a social explanation in terms of conflicting *castas* or races coexisting in Spain and equally frustrated in their search for social justice from an increasingly corrupt and worldly church. See *La realidad histórica de España* (Mexico: Editorial Porrua, 1962), pp. 281 ff. There are those who defeat the problem by claiming that mystical spirituality is perennial and therefore not, in this case, an issue about which to be unduly exercised. See Emelio Colunga, "Intelectualistas y místizos en la teología española del siglo XVI," *Ciencia tomista* 9 (1914):209–21, 377–94; 10 (1914):223–42; 11 (1915): 237–53; 12 (1915):5–25. For a summary of critical opinion on this subject, see Nieto-Sanjuan, *Juan de Valdés,* pp. 81 ff.

18. See Nieto-Sanjuan, *Juan de Valdés,* pp. 80–86, and Bataillon, *Erasme et l'Espagne,* 1:72–83, 194–262.

19. The letter is of 22 June, 1524, from "Proceso Alcaraz," MS fols. 6–10, summarized by Nieto-Sanjuan, *Juan de Valdés,* p. 86.

20. The confession extracted from Alcaraz is recorded in "Processo Alcaraz," MS fols. 351–53, dated 19 July, 1527, and summarized by Nieto-Sanjuan, *Juan de Valdés,* p. 88.

21. Nieto-Sanjuan, *Juan de Valdés,* p. 91.

22. Ibid., p. 94.

23. *Divine Considerations,* pp. 220–21 et passim.

24. *Beneficio di Cristo,* p. 34.

25. Frederic C. Church, *The Italian Reformers, 1534–1564* (New York: Columbia University Press, 1932), p. 51.

26. For an account of the sharply changing fortunes of the *Beneficio di Cristo,* see Prelowski, *Beneficio di Cristo,* pp. 23 ff.

27. The break becomes clear with the two Valdesian disciples, Peter Martyr Vermigli and Bernardino Ochino. Valdés himself, says E. Rodocanachi, "était hérétique à la manière des *Fraticelli* ou d'un Jacopone" (*La reforme en Italie,* 1:226).

28. Cardinal Carnesecchi refers to his own introduction by Guilia Gonzaga into the Valdés circle as "introdutto nel regno di Dio." The association of the group with the "Kingdom of God" is of some importance for the tendency of Valdesian theology to equate the church with the body of the spiritual elect. See Nieto-Sanjuan, *Juan de Valdés*, pp. 223–24.

29. See Father Cuthbert, O.S.F.C., *The Capucins: A Contribution to the History of the Reformation* (London: Sheed and Ward, 1928), 1:121.

30. Ibid., p. 126.

31. An account of the closeness between Valdés and Ochino, and of how the *Alfabeto Christiano* came to be written for Guilia Gonzaga, occurs at the beginning of the *Alfabeto Christiano* itself.

32. B. Wiffen, trans., *Alfabeto Christiano* (London: Bosworth and Harrison, 1861), p. 106.

33. Ibid., pp. 26, 53.

34. *City of God* 14.28, trans. M. Dods, *Nicene and Post Nicene Fathers* (Buffalo: Christian Literature Co., 1887), 2:282–83.

35. *Tract upon the Mode of Teaching the Fundamentals of Christian Doctrine*, trans. John T. Betts, *XVII Opuscules* (London: Trübner and Co., 1882), pp. 144–45.

36. Works, however, are not disavowed. A living faith must express itself in works. See *Alfabeto*, pp. 74 ff.

37. Cf. pp. 50–52, where Valdés warns that the external observances of monks and the vows they take are not to be valued in themselves. Note also the insistence that confession is an "inward and spiritual subject" (p. 169).

38. Wiffen, *Alfabeto*, p. xxxvii.

39. It is not surprising that Valdesian theology should soon produce attacks on the doctrine of transubstantiation in the eucharist. Alcaraz, before Valdés, had attacked the doctrine of transubstantiation (see Nieto-Sanjuan, *Juan de Valdés*, p. 101), as Ochino did after him.

40. *Divine Considerations*, p. 262.

41. Ibid., p. xl.

42. Carnesecchi, who was executed for heresy in 1576, feared that the church was returning furtively to Pelagianism. See above, chap. 1, n. 29.

43. John T. Betts, intro. to *One Hundred and Ten Considerations*, in Benjamin B. Wiffen, *Life and Writings of Juan de Valdés* (London, 1865), p. 200.

44. Daniel Rogers's poem was published in Lawrence Humphrey, *Life and Death of John Jewell, Bishop of Salisbury* (London, 1573).

45. A. L. Maycock, *Nicholas Ferrar of Little Gidding* (London: SPCK, 1963), p. 48.

46. Ibid., p. 61.

47. See T. T. Carter, *Nicholas Ferrar: His Household and Friends* (London: Longmans and Co., 1893), pp. 39–41; H. P. K. Skipton, *The Life and Times of Nicholas Ferrar* (London: A. R. Mowbray, 1907), p. 50.

48. See Maycock, *Nicholas Ferrar*, pp. 219–26.

49. Neither Little Gidding nor Valdés's circle was monastic. We recall that although Guilia Gonzaga entered a Franciscan monastery, she did not take vows. Nicholas's community was "essentially a family affair" (Maycock, *Nicholas Ferrar*, p. 197).

50. The Little Gidding community cared for the poor and instructed the young, especially in the Psalms. For an account of Nicholas Ferrar's "Psalm children," see Maycock, *Nicholas Ferrar*, p. 202, and John Ferrar, *A Life of Nicholas Ferrar*, in B. Blackstone, ed., *The Ferrar Papers*, p. 35. For a description of Nicholas's concern for the poor, see J. Ferrar, *Life*, p. 32. Although Valdés is sometimes accused of establishing a merely aristocratic coterie, there is no doubt that he also attempted to reach a popular audience, for instance, through the sermons of Ochino. His desire to instruct on a popular level can be seen from his interest in catechetical matters—from the early *Dialogue on Christian Doctrine* to the *Tract upon the Mode of Teaching the Fundamentals of Christian Doctrine*.

51. J. Ferrar, *Life*, p. 38.

52. Maycock, *Nicholas Ferrar*, pp. 208 ff.

53. See Betts, *XVII Opuscules*, pp. 1–18, 40–60.

54. See Maycock, *Nicholas Ferrar*, pp. 217–18.

55. E. Crwys Sharland, *The Story Books of Little Gidding* (London: Seeley and Co., 1899).

56. Blackstone, *The Ferrar Papers*, pp. 97 ff.

57. Maycock, *Nicholas Ferrar*, pp. 273–75. See Herbert's letters on the subject, *Works* pp. 377–79.

58. *Life*, p. 73.

59. Ibid., p. 51.

60. Ibid., p. 53.

61. Ibid.

62. Ibid., p. 45.

63. Blackstone, *The Ferrar Papers*, p. 266.

64. A record of the Capuchins in the English court was kept by Fr. Cyprien de Gamache, *Memoirs of the Capucin Friars*, ed. R. F. Williams, *The Court and Times of Charles the First* (London, 1848), 2:293 ff. It is interesting that Mary Collet wore a "friar's grey gown." See Maycock, *Nicholas Ferrar*, p. 179. For Sancta Clara, see *Paraphrastica expositio articulorum confessionis Anglicanae* (1646), trans. and ed. F. G. Lee (London, 1865).

65. J. Ferrar, *Life*, p. 71.

66. Ibid., p. 63.

67. Ibid., p. 74.

68. Ibid., p. 71.

69. Ibid., p. 84.

70. See Walton, *Lives*, pp. 314–15.

71. The printer's letter to the reader which prefaces *The Temple* concludes: "We conclude all with his own Motto, with which he used to conclude all things

that might seem to tend any way to his own honour; *Lesse than the least of God's merçies" (Works* pp. 4–5). Cf. *The Winding Sheet*, in Blackstone, *The Ferrar Papers*, p. 178.

72. Blackstone, *The Ferrar Papers*, p. 268.

73. Ibid., p. 303.

74. Maycock, *Nicholas Ferrar*, p. 234.

75. Ross, *Poetry and Dogma*, p. 148.

76. Ibid., p. 147.

77. Ibid., pp. 151–52.

78. *The Winding Sheet*, in Blackstone, *The Ferrar Papers*, pp. 200–1.

79. Blackstone, *The Ferrar Papers*, p. xiii.

80. Cuthbert, *The Capucins*, 1:129.

81. Ross, *Poetry and Dogma*, p. 153.

82. Maycock, *Nicholas Ferrar*, p. 233.

Chapter Five

1. *The Works of Henry Vaughan*, ed. L. C. Martin (Oxford: Clarendon Press, 1968), p. 391. All quotations from Vaughan are from this edition, hereafter cited in the text as *Works of Vaughan*.

2. E. C. Pettet, *Of Paradise and Light: A Study of Vaughan's "Silex Scintillans"* (Cambridge: At the University Press, 1960), pp. 51–70.

3. There are numerous studies of the subject. The following represent the main contributions. R. Garner, *Henry Vaughan: Experience and the Tradition* (Chicago: University of Chicago Press, 1959); Pettet, *Of Paradise and Light;* R. A. Durr, *On the Mystical Poetry of Henry Vaughan* (Cambridge, Mass.: Harvard University Press, 1962); Elizabeth Holmes, *Henry Vaughan and the Hermetic Philosophy* (New York: Russell and Russell Publishers, 1967); M. M. Mahood, *Poetry and Humanism* (London: Jonathan Cape, 1950), chap. 13, "Vaughan: The Symphony of Nature," pp. 252 ff.; A. C. Judson, "Cornelius Agrippa and Henry Vaughan," *MLN* 41 (1926):178–81; "Henry Vaughan as a Nature Poet," *PMLA* 13 (1927):146–56; "The Source of Henry Vaughan's Ideas Concerning God in Nature," *SP* 24 (1927):592–606; W. O. Clough, "Henry Vaughan and the Hermetic Philosophy," *PMLA* 18 (1933):1108–30; R. M. Wardle, "Thomas Vaughan's Influence upon the Poetry of Henry Vaughan," *PMLA* 51 (1936):936–52; L. C. Martin, "Henry Vaughan and Hermes Trismegistus," *RES* 18 (1942):301–7; "Henry Vaughan and the Theme of Infancy," in *Seventeenth Century Studies Presented to Sir Herbert Grierson* (Oxford: Clarendon Press, 1938), pp. 243–55; R. Walters, "Henry Vaughan and the Alchemists," *RES* 23 (1947):107–22; E. L. Marilla, "Henry and Thomas Vaughan," *MLR* 39 (1944): 180–83.

4. Joan Bennett, *Five Metaphysical Poets* (Cambridge: At the University Press, 1964), p. 85.

Notes

5. S. L. Bethell, *The Cultural Revolution of the Seventeenth Century* (London: Dennis Dobson, 1951), p. 134.

6. Helen C. White, *The Metaphysical Poets: A Study in Religious Experience* (New York: Collier Books, 1962), p. 262.

7. I am thinking mainly of Ross Garner, who argues that Vaughan's poetry could not have been radically influenced by the Hermetic philosophy because some of Vaughan's ideas as an orthodox Christian are incompatible with some other central ideas of Hermetism. See *Henry Vaughan*, p. 105.

8. See *Works of Vaughan*, ed. Hutchinson, p. 91.

9. *Henry Vaughan*, p. 126.

10. Augustine's *Confessions* might even have been written for Paulinus. See John J. O'Meara, *The Young Augustine: The Growth of St. Augustine's Mind up to His Conversion* (London: Longmans Green, and Co., 1954), p. 4.

11. *Henry Vaughan*, pp. 23 ff.

12. See Marilla, "Henry and Thomas Vaughan," pp. 180–83.

13. *Anima magica abscondita*, in *The Works of Thomas Vaughan: Eugenius Philalethes*, ed. A. E. Waite (London: Theosophical Publishing House, 1919), p. 81.

14. *Lumen de lumine*, in Waite, pp. 244–45.

15. *Poetry and Humanism*, p. 258.

16. See *Works of Vaughan*, p. 747; and Holmes, *Henry Vaughan and the Hermetic Philosophy*, p. 39.

17. See Pettet, *Of Paradise and Light*, p. 73.

18. See Holmes, *Henry Vaughan and the Hermetic Philosophy*, p. 38.

19. See *Works of Vaughan*, ed. Hutchinson, p. 746.

20. See *Theologia Platonica* 3.2, in *Opera omnia*, p. 119. P. O. Kristeller in *The Philosophy of Marsilio Ficino*, trans. V. Conant (New York: Columbia University Press, 1943), pp. 106–7, contrasts Ficino's fivefold division with the Plotinian scheme.

21. Plato *Symposium* 189c–193, trans. B. Jowett, *The Dialogues of Plato*, 4th ed., 4 vols. (Oxford: Clarendon Press, 1953).

22. *Marsilio Ficino's Commentary on Plato's Symposium*, trans. S. R. Jayne (New York: Columbia University Press, 1944), p. 156.

23. Ibid., p. 161.

24. Plotinus *Enneads* 1.6.5, trans. MacKenna: "We may justly say a soul becomes ugly—by something foisted upon it, by sinking itself into the alien, by a fall, a descent into body, into Matter."

25. *Enneads* 1.8.7.

26. *Enneads* 5.1.1: "The evil that has overtaken them has its source in self-will, in the entry into the sphere of process, and in the primal differentiation with the desire of self-ownership."

27. *Oration on the Dignity of Man*, trans. Forbes, p. 223: "A great miracle, Asclepius, is man."

28. *Anthroposophia theomagica*, ed. Waite, p. 43.

29. *Anima magica abscondita,* ed. Waite, p. 102.

30. *Anthroposophia theomagica,* ed. Waite, p. 48.

31. *Hermetica: The Ancient Greek and Latin Writings Which Contain Religious or Philosophic Teachings Ascribed to Hermes Trismegistus,* ed. and trans. W. Scott, 4 vols. (Oxford: Clarendon Press, 1924), 1:193.

32. *Commentaria* on *Pimander, Opera omnia,* p. 1839.

33. Cited and translated by P. O. Kristeller in *The Philosophy of Marsilio Ficino,* p. 210, from Ficino, *Opera omnia,* p. 749.

34. *Enneads* 1.2.5.

Chapter Six

1. *Thomas Traherne: Centuries, Poems, and Thanksgivings,* ed. H. M. Margoliouth, 2 vols. (Oxford: Clarendon Press, 1958), 1:111. All quotations from the *Centuries* and *Poems* are from this edition; hereafter, *Centuries* will be cited in the text as *C.*

2. See Joan Webber's account of "self" and style in Donne and Traherne, in *The Eloquent "I": Style and Self in Seventeenth Century Prose* (Milwaukee and London: University of Wisconsin Press, 1968), esp. chaps. 2, 8, 9.

3. Stanley Stewart, *The Expanded Voice: The Art of Thomas Traherne* (San Marino, California: Huntington Library, 1970). See esp. chap. 7, "The Expanded Voice: The Dobell *Poems,*" pp. 170–207.

4. *The Expanded Voice,* pp. 139 ff.

5. See ibid., p. 51.

6. See William H. Marshall, "Thomas Traherne and the Doctrine of Original Sin," *MLN* 73 (1958):161–65; J. B. Leishman, *The Metaphysical Poets* (New York: Russell and Russell Publishers, 1963), p. 192; K. W. Salter, *Thomas Traherne: Mystic and Poet* (London: E. Arnold, 1964), esp. chap. 9, "Traherne and a Romantic Heresy," pp. 130 ff.; John Malcolm Wallace, review of Louis L. Martz, *The Paradise Within* (New Haven: Yale University Press, 1964), in *JEGP* 64 (1965):732–38; George Robert Guffey, "Thomas Traherne on Original Sin," *N&Q* 14 (1967):98–100; A. L. Clements, *The Mystical Poetry of Thomas Traherne* (Cambridge, Mass.: Harvard University Press, 1969), p. 31; Stewart, *The Expanded Voice,* p. 60.

7. E. J. Bicknell, *A Theological Introduction to the Thirty-nine Articles of the Church of England,* 3d ed., rev. by H. J. Carpenter (London: Longmans, 1961), p. 171.

8. D. P. Walker, *The Decline of Hell* (London: Routledge and Kegan Paul, 1964), p. 11.

9. See, e.g., More, *The Praeexistency of the Soul,* ed. Grosart, pp. 118–28.

10. See Walker, *Decline of Hell,* p. 9.

11. See *A Discourse on the Freedom of the Will* (London, 1675), passim.

12. *The Free Will,* in *Erasmus-Luther,* ed. Winter, pp. 13–14, 48.

Notes

13. Walker, *Decline of Hell*, p. 13.

14. Ibid., p. 15.

15. Cited in V. de Sola Pinto, *Peter Sterry: Platonist and Puritan, 1613–72* (Cambridge: At the University Press, 1934), p. 87.

16. See Walker, *Decline of Hell*, p. 16.

17. *The Two Treaties of Servetus on the Trinity: On the Errors of the Trinity, Seven Books*, A.D. 1531; *Dialogues on the Trinity, Two Books, On the Righteousness of Christ's Kingdom, Four Chapters*, A.D. 1532, trans. Earl Morse Wilbur, D.D., Harvard Theological Studies, no. 16 (Cambridge, Mass.: Harvard University Press, 1932). Copious quotation from Irenaeus is adequate indication of Servetus's indebtedness. See also Roland H. Bainton, *Hunted Heretic: The Life and Death of Michael Servetus, 1511–1553* (Boston: Beacon Press, 1953), esp. pp. 46 ff.

18. For a concise account of the dispute and summary of Calvin's opinion, see Bainton, *Hunted Heretic*, pp. 68, 194–95.

19. *Opus eruditissium divi Irenaei in quinque libros digestum, in quibus . . . confutat veterum haeresean . . . opiniones . . . Des. Erasmi Roterodami opera emendatum, etc.* (1560).

20. See Walker, *Decline of Hell*, p. 17.

21. John Daillé, *A Treatise on the Right Use of the Fathers in the Decision of Controversies Existing at This Day in Religion*, trans. and rev. T. Smith, 2d ed. (London, 1843), p. 2.

22. Ibid., p. 6.

23. William Whiston, *Historical Memoirs of the Life of Dr. William Clarke* (London, 1730).

24. Ibid., p. 5.

25. Ibid., pp. 22–23.

26. Ibid., p. 310.

27. Carol L. Marks, "Thomas Traherne and Cambridge Platonism," *PMLA* 81 (1966):521–34.

28. Carol Marks, "Thomas Traherne and Hermes Trismegistus," *Renaissance News* 19 (1966):118–31.

29. *Roman Forgeries, by a Faithful Son of the Church of England* (London, 1673).

30. Ibid., "Advertisement to the Reader."

31. Ibid.; see pp. 7, 31, 134.

32. Ibid., p. 6, and "Advertisement to the Reader."

33. Ibid., p. 5.

34. Ibid., "Advertisement to the Reader." The odd selection of the year 420 is not explained, though a provocative suggestion, made to me by Professor Roy Battenhouse, is that Traherne may have wished to avoid Augustine's anti-Pelagian treatises, written mostly after 420.

35. The further similarity of Traherne's teachings to those of Servetus,

though we cannot go into it here, would seem to confirm the indebtedness of Traherne to the same source.

36. *Man in Revolt,* trans. Olive Wyon (London: Lutterworth Press, 1939), pp. 503 ff.

37. *Against Heresies,* trans. Alexander Roberts and W. H. Rambaut, Ante-Nicene Christian Library (Buffalo: Christian Literature Co., 1885), 1:521. All quotations from Irenaeus are from this edition and hereafter will be cited in the text.

38. Patrick J. Corish, "The Fall in Greek Tradition," *Irish Theological Quarterly* 18 (1951):148.

39. Gustaf Wingren, *Man and the Incarnation: A Study in the Biblical Theology of Irenaeus,* trans. Ross MacKenzie (Philadelphia: Muhlenberg Press, 1959), pp. 26–27.

40. Ibid., p. 25.

41. See G. N. Bonwetsch, *Die Theologie des Irenäus* (Gütersloh, 1925), p. 138.

42. See F. Vernet's article, "Irénée," *DT vol.* 7, col. 2460.

43. See John Lawson, *The Biblical Theology of Saint Irenaeus* (London: Epworth Press, 1948), passim, and Wingren, *Man and the Incarnation.* .

44. *Evil and the God of Love* (London: Macmillan and Co., 1966), p. 225.

45. Guffey ("Traherne on Original Sin," pp. 99–100) draws attention to passages from *Christian Ethicks* which talk of man as "perverse and foolish, poor and miserable," having "contracted shame and guilt." Traherne, like Irenaeus, is orthodox though not Augustinian, and both can talk of man as bound to sin and degradation in Adam (cf. *Against Heresies,* p. 456). But a stress on this element is characteristic of neither writer, and their references to guilt and corruption do not necessarily imply a contradiction to the childhood vision, as the "Pelagian" arguments assume.

46. For a summary, see Lawson, *Biblical Theology of Saint Irenaeus,* pp. 200 ff.

47. For Bonaventure, see Martz, *The Paradise Within,* pp. 54 ff.; for Arminius, see Stewart, *The Expanded Voice,* pp. 60, 220.

48. Lawson, *Biblical Theology of Saint Irenaeus,* p. 251.

Plate I

Plate 2

Plate 3

Plate 4

Plate 5

Index

Index

Index

Index